The Only
GRANT-
WRITING
BOOK
You'll Ever Need

The Only
GRANT-
WRITING
BOOK
You'll Ever Need

Third Edition

ELLEN KARSH and ARLEN SUE FOX

A Member of the Perseus Books Group

New York

First edition published in 2003
Second edition published in 2006
Third edition published in 2009

Library of Congress Cataloging-in-Publication Data

Karsh, Ellen.
  The only grant-writing book you'll ever need : top grant writers and grant givers share their secrets / Ellen Karsh and Arlen Sue Fox. — 3rd ed.
    p.   cm.
  Includes index.
  ISBN 978-0-465-01869-7 (alk. paper)
  1. Proposal writing for grants—United States. 2. Grants-in-aid—United States. 3. Fund raising—United States. I. Fox, Arlen Sue. II. Title.
  HG177.5.U6K37 2009
  658.15'224—dc22

                                                                                            2009015901

10 9 8 7 6 5 4 3

To Tess Karsh

and

In Memory of Rubin Karsh and Ruth and Irv Barish

CONTENTS

INTRODUCTION TO
THE THIRD EDITION

As we are preparing this new edition of *The Only Grant Writing Book You'll Ever Need*, the United States and countries around the world are mired in a recession. Although we hope that by the time you are reading the book we are enjoying a strong recovery and a renewed sense of optimism, it is likely that when it hits the shelves your day-to-day life won't reflect a boom or a bust, but something in between. No matter what is going on today, we have learned the hard way that the outlook can change almost overnight for a million different reasons (some of which we probably can't even imagine). We understand from firsthand experience just how fluid the economy can be, and how unpredictable life is. We lived through 9/11 and its fallout. We watched hurricanes—especially Katrina and Rita in 2005, but also Ike and Gustav in 2008—clobber people and their cities and towns. We experienced the catastrophic economic meltdown of 2008, and we hope we will never forget that few—very few—economists, business leaders, and seasoned politicians predicted (let alone planned for) the devastation it would cause.

With all that's going on, has the grants process changed? Yes, in the sense that the worst economic disaster since the Great Depression is taking a terrible toll on grants. Money is scarce. Those of you who write grant proposals in this new climate need to figure out how to convince grantmakers to fund your programs and projects when dollars are scarce . . . and, frankly, when you are desperate. But no, in the sense that the nuts and bolts, the key elements of a solid grant proposal haven't changed.

To better understand the distinction we are making, take a look at our national pastime, baseball. Even if you're not a fan, even if you don't know Babe Ruth from your Aunt Ruth, you may have overheard people lamenting that "baseball has changed." What these folks probably mean is that they liked the supposedly good old days of Joltin' Joe DiMaggio a lot better than they like these bad new days of astronomically high salaries for coddled players and the off-the-charts ticket prices they have to shell out to see a ball game.

But the game of baseball hasn't changed one lick. A pitcher still has to throw a ball 60 feet 6 inches to home plate and prevent the guy in the batter's box with a hunk of lumber on his shoulder from getting a hit. A batter has to hit the pitched ball, just as he had to do 50 years ago, so he can get around the bases to score a run for his team. As in the good old days, today's infielders must acrobatically snare hard ground balls, out-fielders must gracefully shag line drives, and base runners must motor quickly and slide smartly.

No, baseball hasn't changed. But the climate in which baseball is played has changed.

Similarly, preparing a grant proposal hasn't changed but the climate has. What we have tried to do in this new edition of *The Only Grant-Writing Book You'll Ever Need* is to suggest how you can succeed in the new climate. Like baseball players, who may start younger, practice harder, eat better, stay healthier, and use better equipment, today's grant seekers have to be better and more diligent at doing the homework we talk about in this book. You need to push program staff to make your organization's programs even more comprehensive, more carefully thought out, more relevant. And, of course, you must write grant proposals that are clearer than ever, with transparent budgets and rigorous evaluation plans. Some grantmakers have said that in this economy nonprofits must think outside the box. And as much as we hate clichés, sometimes they make sense.

In the first two editions of *The Only Grant-Writing Book You'll Ever Need*, we suggested that "grant writing" is one of those seemingly innocent terms that tap into many of our neuroses. We still think that grant writing triggers quite a bit of angst, probably even more now, but perhaps our neuroses have changed.

- Neurosis 1. It's not just terrorist attacks or hurricanes or tsunamis. Now it's the economy. Isn't it selfish of me to ask perfect strangers for money when others may need it more than I do?
- Neurosis 2. For that matter, what's the point of writing a grant proposal when there's probably no money for anyone these days?
- Neurosis 3. When I look at Craigslist or Idealist and see the demanding qualifications for development specialists, how can I imagine I could write a decent grant proposal when I feel self-conscious writing an email to my mother?

Over the last decade, the events of September 11, followed by hurricanes and other natural disasters and now an economic meltdown have put more pressure on all of us to overcome the panic associated with writing a winning grant proposal. As many newly minted writers approach their task, they often may feel clueless about the grants process and how they fit into it. What is a grant? Who is eligible for one? What are the restrictions on grant funds? How do I even begin to write an effective proposal?

And, of course, even the most experienced development staff can't help worrying about the competition for dollars from new grant seekers.

This new edition of *The Only Grant-Writing Book You'll Ever Need* is for everyone—those who know nothing about grants and those who know a thing or two . . . or much more. Although most grants are awarded to organizations rather than individuals, the strategies we describe here apply equally to funding opportunities available to individuals—writers, artists, scholars, researchers. And although some grant applications (e.g., in the sciences) seem so highly technical and other applications seem totally—and, perhaps, deceptively—simple, you can be certain that the same principles apply, no matter how overwhelmingly complicated or unbelievably simple the application looks.

The *Only Grant-Writing Book You'll Ever Need* organizes the whole grant-seeking experience into three parts (preparation, proposal writing, and follow-up) and 18 lessons, each lesson designed as if it were a workshop, starting with opening remarks, followed by a set of discussion questions, and concluding with a short "pop quiz." These are questions for you, the reader, to mull over or work through before you move on to the next lesson. (The quizzes give you an opportunity to practice what we preach, so we hope you give them a shot.)

There's a lot more to grantsmanship than just the proposal, all of which we'll talk about later. But we were feeling so daunted by the fear that money for grants is drying up that we thought we had to ask grantmakers about their experience with the economic crisis. And we thought what they had to say was so useful that we wanted to give you the benefit of their thoughts before we went any further. So we're starting this edition off with what we're calling an economic summit (how's that for a lofty sounding heading in a little book on grants?). This new section, following the introduction, includes the diverse views of the economy from grantmakers we interviewed for this book.

After the economic summit, Part I starts you off with prerequisite lessons: identifying who you and/or your organization are; what kind of funding you should be looking for; where to look for it; and how to make sense of grant-application packages. Although this part seems to be directed primarily to newer proposal writers, we think that it includes some useful updated information and refreshers for even the most experienced among you.

Part II starts with our philosophy about proposal writing as part of a program planning, development, and evaluation process. We discuss some "intangibles" and assumptions about proposals that you won't find anywhere else. Two writing chapters give you some rules and guidelines for confronting that blank page, and the opportunity to practice writing sections of a grant proposal. Then we take you through the process of developing each element of a typical grant proposal.

In Part III, we walk you through the next steps after you learn whether you have been approved for funding—or not.

At the end of each part, we present a lively funders' roundtable, giving you the responses of a large and diverse group of grantmakers from government funding agencies and foundations to a slew of pertinent questions on the topics and issues covered in that part. Their answers will help even experienced grant writers gain new insight into the grant process and an understanding of what the money people really look for.

Throughout the lessons, we share our own experience in proposal writing. Over the years—and throughout many and varying economic and political climates—each of us has won tens of millions of dollars worth of grants, and we believe now more than ever that our skills are readily transferable.

These lessons and funders' roundtables are followed by our updated appendices. Appendix 1 offers 50 tips to improve your chances of winning a grant (drawn from our own experiences, the comments of our panel of grantmakers, and other successful grant seekers). Appendix 2 is a proposal checklist you can use to make sure you have pushed all the right buttons. (We urge you to create your own checklist for each new proposal that you plan to write.) Appendix 3 is an updated glossary of common terms used in the grants world. Appendix 4 presents sample application forms, including the Washington-area common grant application; Form SF-424, the cover page of most federal applications, and sample letters to grantmakers. Appendix 5 contains a representative list of community foundations across the country; these foundations are a good place to start your search for grants. We think you will appreciate the updated

Appendix 6, a list of useful foundation and government websites. Appendix 7 provides the answers to the pop quizzes (when there *are* any right answers) with brief explanations.

There are some important differences among grant seekers: those from government agencies, those who are applying for funding for not-for-profit organizations of all sizes, and individual artists and scholars seeking money to pay for their projects. There also are enormous differences between smaller and newer nonprofits and the larger, more experienced organizations, some with a great diversity of funding and with their own development departments. Although the overriding principles of grantsmanship are the same for all—develop a high-quality program and use the proposal to convince the grantmaker of your capacity to implement and sustain it, in some lessons we'll examine differences among nonprofits, individual grant seekers, and government agencies, and between larger and smaller nonprofits and grassroots organizations. Generally, however, our focus is on the approaches and strategies that *all* grant seekers will need to use.

" YOUR PROPOSAL WAS SO GOOD
I'M HAVING MY BOOK CLUB
READ IT. "

We've presented two lessons focused on actual writing skills. We think these chapters are important for most readers because they address the continuing concerns of many grantmakers about what they see as a lack of writing skills in the proposals they receive. So in Lesson 6 we've laid out 12 rules of stylish (grant proposal) writing—with examples of how to apply the rules in a proposal. In Lesson 7, we describe in great detail a fictitious organization that is seeking funding for a new program, and we ask you to organize the material as the funder requires and do quite a bit of editing (following our rules for good writing, of course). The writing chapters will be helpful to beginning proposal writers but, maybe surprisingly, to seasoned writers as well.

We hope that by the time you've finished all of the lessons you will have internalized our rules for proposal writing; identified a compelling problem; chosen the partners necessary to help you; decided on a program or activity that you're sure will solve your problem; determined that your program is appropriate for either a government or a foundation grant; figured out the best grant-seeking strategy; and prepared a proposal to a prospective funder. We also hope that you will feel more relaxed about the prospect of writing a grant proposal, more self-confident as you write, and more optimistic about receiving funding for your projects. (That's not expecting too much, is it?)

Throughout the book, we have tried to demystify the process of developing programs, writing proposals, and winning grants so that anyone—even those with the least experience—can succeed. We don't think it's too grandiose (well, maybe just a tiny bit) to say that this really will be the only grant-writing book you'll ever need.

ABOUT THE FUNDERS' ROUNDTABLES...

Before we continue, we want to explain a little about the funders' roundtables, a feature of the book that we continue to find very exciting. As you'll recognize if you're a longtime grant seeker, or as you will understand one of these days, experienced proposal writers can become a little presumptuous at times and, at least where grants are concerned, turn into opinionated know-it-alls about how to do it. Because we had written so many proposals and won millions of dollars in grant funding (we're not mentioning right now how many grants we didn't win); because we'd attended so many bidders' conferences where grant applications were explained in minute detail and participated in so many foundation workshops; because we'd read the newsletters, taken (and given) grant-writing seminars, and spoken with so many grantmakers over the years, we came to feel pretty sure we knew what funders wanted.

But still, we can confide in you: We were secretly a little afraid that maybe we really didn't know exactly what grantmakers think, want, like, hate, or love. So we decided to talk with funders representing foundations of all sizes (giving grants for as little as a $25 savings bond and as much as many millions of dollars) in all parts of the country, as well as with government funders. And we got some insights and surprises that made the effort worthwhile for us and, we hope, for you. Because the first edition was written after the attacks of 9/11, we asked grantmakers about the impact of terrorism on grant funding. Not to suggest we're a jinx, but for the second edition, written just after Hurricanes Katrina and Rita, we asked funders about the effects of natural disasters, disaster planning, and other issues on the grants landscape. And this time we've asked about funding in and for an economic meltdown. Maybe we shouldn't consider any new editions . . .

Although we call our conversations funders' roundtables, in the spirit of complete disclosure we must admit that we didn't hold an actual roundtable. Instead, we interviewed each grantmaker separately, following essentially the same interview format. We wanted to give the interviewees our undivided attention and the opportunity to frame their answers independently and without being distracted by things other panelists said. We also wanted to be able to ask plenty of follow-up questions in response to their remarks.

A word on the roundtable format: Many of the grantmakers were perfectly happy to speak on the record, but others felt that they would have to hold back—limit themselves—if they were going to be quoted directly, or even if they were only acknowledged by name in the book. Because our purpose in interviewing grantmakers was to get frank, uninhibited advice to proposal writers, we decided not to quote anyone directly. The grantmakers whom we interviewed couldn't have been more forthcoming, more giving of their time, more willing to share their expertise and insights, or more clearly committed to the needs of grant seekers and their communities. Whether we name them in the acknowledgments or not, we are deeply grateful to all of them.

FUNDERS' ROUNDTABLE:
ECONOMIC SUMMIT

Is this the worst possible time to be searching for grants? Well, we have to admit that it's not the best. But it's not an overstatement to suggest that grants are more important—and much more competitive—than ever. The good old days when organizations large and small might submit a short $50,000 request for funding to a friendly foundation were (relatively) stress-free times for grant seekers. As we write, even organizations that have been able to support programs through generous individual and corporate donations and sponsorships, gala fundraisers, and endowments. in addition to grants, are finding their resources dwindling as the market affects donors' financial capacity and their own investments.

In preparing this third edition, we have debated whether strategies for developing and writing successful grant proposals have really changed in this economic crisis—or if it is only the climate in which grants are written that has changed. When we wrote the first edition, we had recently lived through the 9/11 terrorist attacks. As we prepared the second edition, we confronted the natural disasters of 2005—the tsunami in Southeast Asia, Hurricane Katrina's devastation in Louisiana and Mississippi, Rita's destruction in Florida, and the earthquake in Pakistan. As we worked on the third edition, we watched the emergence of the worst economic crisis in 80 years. The huge outpouring of financial donations, personal assistance, and other support by individuals, businesses, and foundations after the earlier disasters was as heartening as the disasters were horrifying. We appreciated grantmakers' decisions to set aside funding specifically for disaster recovery, while working to maintain their normal level of giving for ongoing programs. But the times were different then; the economy was stronger. We wondered whether the economic meltdown would have a greater impact on giving than the other disasters; we expected it would but we weren't certain how the impact would be felt. So we asked—and in this initial roundtable we want to share with you what grantmakers and other people involved with the grants process had to say about how the current, challenging economic climate is affecting the world of grants.

It goes without saying that different funding organizations are weathering the changed climate differently. Some foundations' endowments haven't been hit as hard as others'. Some government agencies—those dealing with antiterrorism and emergency management, for instance—may have more money available for grants than agencies that support the arts. And all grant seekers aren't finding the sledding equally tough. Some large not-for-profits may not have been hit as hard as smaller ones; some college endowments have fared better in this economy than others. But we want to give you at least a smattering of viewpoints before you start the grants process.

You should be aware that this Economic Summit covers much more than writing a proposal. Later funders roundtables will go into detail about the proposal itself. Here we address fundraising more broadly, because that's the way funders are talking about it these days.

"So What's the Fallout for Philanthropy?"

The first thing we asked each member of our diverse panel was a question that the *New York Times* raised in November 2008, after the collapse of the housing markets, Wall Street's meltdown, and the worldwide string of bank failures. We were curious to know how grantmakers were reacting to the economy—whether they were as stunned as we were by the suddenness of the crash or whether they (miraculously) saw it coming. And, of course, we wondered how the downturn affected their grantmaking activities.

One funder bluntly acknowledged that the "economic meltdown throws a wet blanket over philanthropy." She said that, to the best of her knowledge, typical foundations lost about 30 percent of the value of their investments as the markets crashed—just as hers did—but some lost 50 percent and more. "Our investment advisors aren't the stupidest guys in the room," she explained. "That's just the way it is." Most of the funders already were thinking hard about philanthropy, and their first responses to our question tended to offer a self-assessment.

What are we grantmakers doing about it? "The economy has forced us to take a pause and look at what we've *been* doing," one said. Most funders agreed that, in a dire economic climate, taking a hard look at their own strategies and practices is a good idea. "We're waiting to see what's happening and what will happen," a panelist explained. "This economy invites us to be self-critical." The self-examination extended beyond grantmaking. One funder wondered whether the foundation "needs all the space we rent—could we work from home instead?"

"Look," said a grantmaker, "when the economy is going badly, it is important for the philanthropic sector to help floundering groups that rely on grant funds so it's not a 'survival of the fittest' contest. In a recession, philanthropists need to analyze their giving strategies so they are more responsive to the needs of the groups that are vying for support." Another funder hoped that foundations would take on other responsibilities—advocacy for instance—and not just write smaller and smaller checks in a poor economy.

On a more positive note, one grantmaker reminded us that, "while many of us took an enormous hit, some foundations and some individuals still have considerable wealth." Another funder reassuringly promised that her foundation was maintaining its level of funding. "We're committed to multiyear grants—they give stability to grantees." And still another told us an anecdote about a foundation actually giving out *more* money in this dire economic climate, because it had never expected to be around this long anyway.

It is probably not an exaggeration to say that, in a time of economic crisis, "the fallout for philanthropy" is pretty much the fallout for everyone else. Philanthropic organizations aren't immune from world events (and most philanthropists didn't see the economic meltdown coming any more than economists, government leaders, or the rest of us did), and it is a good idea always to remember that grantmakers aren't cash cows. As one funder put it, "Foundations need to be modest—in this economy, we should use our money to leverage money. "

Today, it's not just foundations that are tightening their belts. State and municipal government agencies—which receive as well as give grants—not only are slashing their own funding to local providers but also are being asked to find new resources in the wake of huge city and state cutbacks. This is a challenge some city agencies have never faced before. One funder explained, "The Mayor is pushing agencies to seek alternative funding sources—saying, 'If you want your budget to be whole, you'd better find other funding.'" And just in case anyone thinks help is on the way from private philanthropy, a foundation funder warned us that "We [foundations] can't fill government holes, so cities and states had better not expect us to come to the rescue." (This funder did admit that "Once in a while we will come to the rescue if the need is very great and we don't see other options.")

And now (more than ever) we're asking, "Why do you need the money?" A grantmaker from a small foundation explained that since the downturn, "money feels twice as precious and now I want to make very sure that 'best practices' are being utilized by grantees." A funder from a large foundation agreed. "We ask, 'Do you really need that amount of money to do what you say you want to do?' You'd better sell us on why you need the specific amount you're requesting. Grantmakers know how much things cost!" A government grantmaker chimed in with a similar reminder. "We're very experienced about cost. Don't ask for $2 million for something that costs $250,000." Another panelist added, "We're looking hard at what we want to do because—pure and simple—we have to do less. We're raising the bar. Money is worth more."

"If You Are Cutting Back on Funding, Are You Focusing on Fewer Causes (for Example Food and Shelter but not Arts and Education) or Are You Cutting Grants Across the Board?"

With endowments down, portfolios diminished, and government finances in deep trouble, we wondered whether funders who needed to cut back on funding were using a particular strategy to make the cuts.

As we were researching this edition, we read countless articles suggesting—or predicting—that many funders would eliminate all grants that did not have to do with feeding or sheltering people. Surprisingly, most of the funders we spoke to were not changing their priorities, although—we hate to say this—some had to stop giving grants altogether and some saw the downturn as a good time to institute new policies that they were considering anyway.

We'll keep our priorities and honor current grants and grantees— but some things may change. According to one funder, "Most grantmakers aren't going to change their priorities—though some all-over-the-map family foundations might respond to the dire headlines by only giving to organizations with new, compelling needs." This grantmaker went on to explain that in many cases a foundation that wanted to sponsor an initiative around, say, foreclosures, would handle it through a set-aside or a special fund, as had happened after 9/11 and Hurricane Katrina. Another funder agreed. "We will be considering some emergency grants—feeding programs, for instance—but these will not impact the rest of our grant giving." And still another added that in this economy "we are asking other organizations to join us when a problem is identified. We get the best and the brightest together to address ways to tackle the problem as a group—and we get financial contributions—then we create a special fund specifically to deal with the problem we identified. If hunger is an emergency issue in the community, for example, we will create a challenge grant that we make available to local groups working on this problem in ways we believe are likely to make a significant impact."

Some grantmakers told us they were looking at their multiyear commitments first and were trying to work with grantees to renegotiate the terms—for example, to stretch out payments over a longer period so they would not have to lay out so much money at any one time. "We're honoring all existing grantees," one funder explained, "But we're trying to spread out the payments. 'Can you get by with less money?' we ask everyone."

"For us," explained a grantmaker, "There was a decrease in giving right after the meltdown—we reduced some grants, eliminated others. 'I'll give you a smaller grant so I have enough money left over to give someone else a little something too.' But now, we've moved away from that approach and we're giving fewer, but larger, grants because we want to make the kind of impact that only a greater amount of money can ensure." Another funder also looked at the effects of grant funds: "The economic downturn provides a good excuse to stop sprinkling small amounts of money over a large geographic area and start focusing our attention on one community to make more of an impact."

"Are You Supporting Only Current Grantees, or Are You Willing (and Able) to Support Additional Programs That You Think Are Very Important?"

Common sense suggests that new or small organizations may have a much tougher time getting funding when the economic picture is so dire. We asked funders about this.

The good news for current grantees is that most funders will try to continue working with you. The bad news for others is that, in this economy, many funders are only able to support the current grantees. Still, some funders will suggest other sources for funding or will provide technical assistance. And still others admit that if they are blown away by your idea for a project maybe—just maybe—they can round up the funding necessary to support it.

"We're mostly funding renewals and have very little money for new initiatives," said one grantmaker. "But we are always talking with our trustees about what we'd like to do when (notice the word "when," not "if") there is more money—so when things improve we can hit the ground running. We actually collect 'not-at-this-time' ideas from potential grantees." Another explained that her foundation normally invites proposals. "But we'll take in a new group if it's the greatest thing since sliced bread—and it has a track record—and it is proposing something very innovative." If she can't offer funding, though, she might say, "Your work is great—terrific even—but we can't afford to support you now . . . we will put your proposal in a portfolio for next time." (And she assures us that these proposals will be looked at when the economy picks up.)

The funders generally agreed that newer, smaller organizations will have a problem in this economy. "We don't fund teeny start-ups but we do join other grantmakers to fund consortia of small groups," one funder told us. But that doesn't mean new, small groups shouldn't be proactive. One of our panelists said, "Not-for-profits need to communicate—to stay on the radar of a foundation even if they are not receiving funding at the moment. I like to get a personal letter—with so much e-mail, it's difficult to differentiate one group from another."

Another grantmaker added that not-for-profits should make the most of their relationships with funders. "Have conversations with us—even if we can't fund you right now. Ask for candor from us, ask us 'if you *were* able to fund us right now, what would you want and expect from us?'" "Sometimes," a funder said, "You might hear something like 'We can't fund you but we have three other things we CAN do for you. We can incubate your group—give you space and secretarial support for instance. And we can suggest someone who might be able to fund your organization . . . or who is giving away computers.'"

One change we noticed as we spoke to funders about the impact of the economy on grantmaking is that a number of them expressed a greater interest in giving grants to umbrella groups, to collaborative projects, or to organizations that help not-for-profits increase their overall capacity—all in the hopes of maximizing the reach of the funding.

"If a Crisis Really Yields Opportunity, as Some Optimists (like President Barack Obama) Claim, How Would You Suggest That Grant Seekers Seize the Moment?"

As we spoke to funders and read various editorials about the economic downturn, we noticed that some people were trying hard to shine a positive light on the current negative situation. We decided to ask this question, even if some may find it a little too Pollyanna-ish for the times. Believe it or not, we got some enthusiastic replies.

This is a good time to focus on your image. One funder wondered, "How can we take advantage of the economic climate to be more vibrant?" Another suggested that now would be a good time for organizations to "tweak their public image—ask colleagues, friends, and relatives whether they think their organizations are presenting themselves—websites, mailed materials, events—in the best light. People not in the field or not involved in an organization's day-to-day activities often have very perceptive things to say. And they may be more willing to say these things now that there seems to be so much at stake."

Along the same lines, one panelist suggested that everyone who works for an organization should have a 10- to 20-second "elevator speech." "If you meet someone at a party or on the bus—or on an elevator—you have no idea who they are, or who they know. If you can talk about your organization in a clear, concise, heartfelt way—the person you meet may go back to the office and search for more information about your organization because of that very convincing elevator speech of yours. This person may know someone halfway across the world who would be interested in what you are doing." (Thanks to the Internet, interested strangers really *can* find out about your organization in no time at all!) Similarly, another funder suggested, "Get nominated for something. Win awards. Give speeches. Sit on panels. Write blogs. Money is still out there. People are still giving dollars away. Their hearts are still moved." "Develop a public voice," said a panelist. "This is especially true in difficult economic times. Call attention to your work. Write articles."

"Now is a good time to make sure your board is up to speed so they can talk about your organization smartly," one funder pointed out. "You need all the publicity you can get."

Another grantmaker suggested that this climate is a perfect time to encourage volunteers. "Organizations must get much better at handling volunteers especially in a difficult economy when volunteers are really needed."

Diversify your funding sources. Many funders raised an interesting issue that seems especially relevant now. "Groups should expand their resource pool," one funder suggested, "and stop relying only on foundations for funding." Another said that organizations should look for individual gifts. "Push the envelope. Be thoughtful, strategic, relational. Ask for more from the people who have already given." Still another said, "Diversify funding. If you put all your eggs in one basket you're probably already in deep trouble." One person we talked to pointed out that nonprofits can seize the moment by connecting to local religious institutions that care about the same issues—homelessness, after school programs—that they care about. "Religious organizations may have 'special offerings' that can fund local programs. But they have to be asked."

Comb through your budgets for cost savings. Finally, a foundation grantmaker reminded us that "groups tend to be good at the 'fund raising side' rather than the 'cost-saving side'—that not-for-profits are really built for growth." The current economic climate is a good time to address the cost-saving side, with an eye toward streamlining organizations, making them run better, more efficiently in good times and bad.

"Have You Changed Your Expectations for the Organizations You Fund? Are You Looking for . . . Creativity?"

Some not-for-profits, like businesses, are having a very tough time staying afloat in this economy. In fact, as we were preparing this edition, the *New York Times* reported that bankruptcy is touching not-for-profit organizations in ways it never did before. So grant seekers are trying to figure out how to be innovative and entrepreneurial in response to government and potential foundation cutbacks. But what do the funders want to see?

Grantmakers aren't necessarily expecting organizations to do things differently these days, but one defined a successful group this way: "Be flexible, entrepreneurial, willing to take risks. Be willing to fail. Learn from your failures. In this economy, it can no longer be business as usual." Another funder discussed why she opposes the strategy some not-for-profits are considering to address economic woes by charging fees for the services that had always been provided at no cost. She explained, "We're in a recession. But the people we are helping—the poor people—have been in a depression for a long time." One panelist suggested that it would be innovative and entrepreneurial if groups seeking grants would connect with the community, especially with organizations doing complementary work." Another suggested that "creative fundraising is looking at what's hot and what's not. . . . People have been doing the same things over and over again. You should be asking yourselves, 'How can I fit into change without changing my mission?'" Still another added, "Change a program to make it more relevant. Maybe offer a meal; this could open the door to funders who give grants to programs addressing hunger."

The issue is impact. Several funders already had been moving toward assessment of the outcomes of their grants and said this has become more critical now. One explained she takes a "results-based approach to grantmaking": "We're moving from a 'funder' mentality to an 'investor' mentality. We're asking ourselves, 'What do we really want to buy, what are our chances of getting it, how will we know we're getting it, and is this the best use of our money?" A number of others said they were looking harder than they used to at the success—and the likelihood of success—of the programs they funded or were giving consideration to. "For an organization that helps children," a funder explained, "I want to see the deeper impact on the children's lives. Did you actually keep a child out of a gang? A single example can be meaningful."

"We don't just want to know that you conducted workshops," another panelist said, "We want to know how many people got jobs." "Or," she suggested, "You can ask participants what three things they got out of the workshops and whether you can follow up with them later. We like to fund a program not for one year but for three years. We believe that program activities can take place during the first year and follow-up support should occur in the second and third years."

"Because of the economy," another grantmaker added, "we're asking for a mid-year report to make sure things are getting done that have been promised. We want to be impactful."

"Do You Expect High-Quality Grant Proposals to Look Different Now That the Economic Climate Has Changed?"

We wondered if grantmakers expected the elements of a proposal to change, and whether they were adding (or deleting) questions or changing the direction of their questions.

The panelists began by focusing on how nonprofits' proposals are addressing the economic crisis. One made what we thought was a good suggestion, although not everyone may agree with it. "Start your grant proposal by explaining to the funder that your organization is going to be fine. Then be frank about what is happening within your organization right now—for example, 'we just lost 20 percent of our city council funding and 30 percent of this other funding . . . but here is a step-by-step plan for what we intend to do about this loss of money and how we're shaking things up so we can provide services and run programs.'" She referred to this as "scenario planning" and it is one way to acknowledge the elephant in the room: The economy. Funders know you must be hurting; you may as well tell them how much and what you're doing about it. But you have to be thoughtful. Another funder said she doesn't like it when an organization says, "We're cutting 20 percent across the board." She much prefers groups that say, "We're making cuts carefully—using a scalpel and not a buzz saw." She added, "This is not a 'gotcha game'—we only do well if our grantees do well. If they come to us in this economic climate and talk about how they'll grow—we say, 'bull.' We want to hear them say, 'This is how we're approaching our work in light of the recession.'"

But the proposal itself? Most of the people we spoke to didn't say that the proposal should be different now than in flush—or at least less dire—times. But scarce resources mean stiffer competition, which means greater emphasis on a top-notch proposal.

"Answer the questions—especially now!" said one funder, amazed that proposal writers still don't do this. "I won't show a proposal to the board if it's poorly written. Before the economic meltdown, there was more latitude." She was put out by the fact that she still gets very poorly written proposals. She doesn't understand why, "when we ask, 'What is your mission?' their response isn't, 'Our mission is. . . .'"

Pay attention to details. Another grantmaker pointed out that in an economic downturn it is especially important that your proposal shows the funder you're a high-functioning organization worth funding. (How's that for a challenge? But try not to panic; we talk about how to do this throughout the book!) "I'm disappointed how often my name is incorrectly spelled," said a funder with a pretty unusual name. "Can you really afford to be off-putting in these difficult times? Believe it or not, sometimes, instead of writing to me, they write to our founder who is long dead!"

"Evaluation should not be tacked on at the end. Explain how you'll 'course correct' as you go along," suggested a foundation grantmaker.

"And when we ask for demographics—give them! And use spell check."
"Grant writers should show that they bothered to look at research, numbers, data—all of which help frame a problem." "Material too often
doesn't reflect how great an organization is." "It's sad when the written
proposal doesn't represent the power of an organization's work." We fund
proposals, we don't fund ideas. Proposals go out to external review—so
applicants had better get their ideas into decent proposals."

Another funder wondered whether grant seekers' proposals inadvertently downplay some things they do. "If you run a cultural arts program
for children, you should stop trying to 'sell' it as *merely* cultural arts. Look
harder at the problems the program is addressing that may be relevant.
Maybe it's an after-school cultural arts program for very at-risk children."
And, "If I funded you last year—step it up this year. Show me that you're
building capacity—if you've been doing seminars or workshops in one location, for instance, bring them into the community so more people can
attend. We're looking for more bang for the *same* buck in your proposals."

Check out the competition. Here's a suggestion that can help proposal
writers at any time. "I think people who are writing grant proposals
should read great proposals. They should ask foundation program officers
to show them excellent proposals—and they should collect a file of ex-
quisitely written proposals. How are people doing it?" The grantmaker
added, "I've read proposals that brought tears to my eyes. A written grant
proposal should convey that lives are being transformed. Don't say,
'Reading is the bedrock of literacy,' for example, say, 'Reading opens
doors that change a person's life' . . . and your proposal should explain
how reading changes that life."

"Funders should articulate why a certain proposal was so good. They
should, of course, white out the name and address of the group that submitted the proposal. Funders should explain how—by the end of the first
paragraph or first page—they knew exactly what a program would do.
Funders should show how the organization that submitted the proposal

expressed its vitality. How did it manage to be heartfelt? How did it show clarity? How did it manage to tell its story?"

"Are You Focusing More Attention on Things like Collaboration or the Role of Board Members Than You Used to? What Are You Looking at . . . and What Are You Looking for?"

Not surprisingly (if you think back to our baseball analogy), the key elements of a grant proposal don't change much from a good economic climate to a bad one. But we wondered what *does* change, so we asked.

Think collaboration. That word collaboration seems to be everywhere. One funder put it succinctly when she said, "Collaboration should be seen as a survival mechanism." Another added, "In this economy, collaborations look better than ever." (She likes to give a grant of, say, $50,000 to be shared by three neighboring organizations to pay for one development director.) An experienced proposal writer noted that "people usually collaborate best with groups they know but have not necessarily worked with, as opposed to perfect strangers." In her experience, "The best way to approach collaboration is not to have a generic conversation about 'how wonderful it would be to collaborate one of these days,' but to say, 'We have a grant application that we all need to work on together that is due on such-and-such date.'" But a funder disagrees. "We don't want collaborations that spring up just for funding. If groups have been working together in the past, let the funder know it.

Another grantmaker suggested that "In this economy, government must redefine its relationship with not–for-profits. In a downturn like this, they should view themselves as business partners."

Take a new look at your board. As far as boards are concerned, funders didn't say that *they* would be looking any harder at your boards, but they suggested that *you'd* be smart to take full advantage of the members. One grantmaker said, "In this economy look at your board. What are they doing for you?" Another pointed out, "People don't have the human resources skills, the real estate skills necessary to save money by negotiating better leases. This is where the board should come in—to help you." "Instead of looking for big checks from struggling foundations, look toward your community and focus on your board."

"Is There Anything Else You've Been Thinking About, Noticing, Wishing for That You'd Like to Pass on to Grant Seekers?"

We wanted to be sure that we hadn't skipped over anything important so we asked this one last question.

Talk to us. Although we didn't mention the word "communication" to our panelists, the word popped up surprisingly often. Is it a sign of the times that, when the going gets tough, people need to be especially clear and especially straightforward with grantmakers? Or is it always a smart way to work with them? Here are some pretty self-explanatory things funders said. "Don't tell us about your problems at the last minute. Communicate, communicate, communicate." "Foster collegial relationships with funders. It will be easier to admit to foundations that problems are brewing. We don't like surprises (who does?). Tell us. Create a climate where people can talk." "Not-for-profits can approach foundations with their problems and needs—and ask for suggestions about how to go about raising money." "In this economy, it is a time for relationships."

In Closing

It is not surprising that the grantmakers we spoke to feel that money is more precious now than ever—and that they want to make sure that organizations applying for grants really, really need the money. They also want to be certain that the money they give will be spent wisely and make an impact. Funders are looking hard at this concern, and trying to figure out thoughtful ways of measuring impact. You should be doing the same thing! But be careful. If you're trying to make an impact by being entrepreneurial and innovative, don't lose sight of your group's mission and constituency. Remember who you are and whom you serve.

And remember that grantmakers are looking for "more bang for the buck." Why wouldn't they? It is up to those writing a grant proposal to show them that you understand the economic situation, that you aren't living in a state of denial, that you don't expect it to be business as usual.

To conclude the Economic Summit, we have selected two sentiments expressed by grantmakers that can propel you forward in any economic climate:

"You can't wait for a savior. You're a savior."

"Without grantees, we just have money. Grantees are our clients."

PART I:
PREREQUISITES

"I'VE LAID PEOPLE OFF. My office is in complete chaos. I'm desperate for help. Hey, I have an idea. Can I get a grant to hire a secretary or someone to give me a hand?"

No.

"My son is a B student and he really wants to go to college. Can I get a grant to pay his tuition?"

No.

"My book group wants to go on a weekend retreat. Can I get a grant to pay for our trip?"

No.

"My copier is broken."

"I need a job."

"My car has a rattle."

No. No. No.

The word "grant" is tossed into more conversations than "reality TV." Grants are hot. Just attend a grant-writing workshop anywhere and see the room fill with people from every profession. Grants are exciting—money usually is—and completely misunderstood. Mostly, we hear about grants that have been won, not about grants that have been lost. And we rarely hear how time-consuming the grant proposal was to develop and write. Instead, we (think we) hear that someone dashed off a grant proposal, mailed it out, and miraculously got a whopping big check by return mail.

Recent years have seen a huge increase in applications for nonprofit status, apparently because many people believe that all you need to do to get grant money—or get a paid job for something you're doing as a volunteer—is to incorporate as a not-for-profit organization and that there's plenty of money out there for the asking. It seems as if you haven't been listening to the news. We don't want to be discouraging, but if you are one of these new applicants, we urge you to take a step back and look at *who you are*, *when and why you should look for grants*, and *from whom you should look for grants* before you decide to invest the time, energy, and money that it takes to incorporate, get your nonprofit status, and write your first proposal.

Notice that we said write your proposal. We didn't say win a grant. It's true that excellent proposals and programs sometimes do not get funded (and awful ones occasionally do) for a variety of different reasons—politics of all sorts, for instance, or the kinds of natural and man-made disaster we've been experiencing, which force some grantmakers to reallocate their resources, or the impact of stock market movement on the portfolios of foundation grantmakers. But the proposal has to be excellent in order to have half a chance of winning any money. And even if you don't win a grant at first, the proposal lets the reviewers form an impression of you and your organization that could help you (or hurt you) when you apply the next time.

Like the lottery, you have to be in it to win it. But unlike the lottery, in the world of grants it is not enough just to be in it. Of course you have to apply. But your application has to be strong; it should represent you and your organization in the best possible light. If you can't do that—because you don't have enough time or enough help to put the proposal together—then do not apply, at least not now. Waiting until next year—or next month—is sometimes the smartest thing you can do. Submitting a poorly thought out, poorly developed, poorly written proposal is sometimes the most damaging thing you can do to your long-term prospects.

LESSON 1:
Who Am I? (and What in the World Do I Want to Do?)

OPENING REMARKS

More than 15 years ago, the U.S. Department of Education announced that it would fund innovative parent centers to be housed in public school buildings. These centers were supposed to be developed and run by parents, and the types of activities available to parents would be chosen by—you guessed it—parents. To apply for this grant, applicants had to be not-for-profit organizations, not schools. I was a beginning grant writer at the time and I was assigned to write a proposal for a small parent organization whose name I can't remember. As I was completing the grant application and getting ready to mail it to Washington, D.C., I noticed that it asked for proof of not-for-profit status. I knew nothing about this. I figured these parents surely weren't making a profit, so they were obviously not-for-profit. What proof did I need except my word? I was wrong. My proposal was disqualified by the Department of Education. No one even read it. —EK

LEADING QUESTIONS
Who Am I?

It is important to know who and what you are before you start trying to raise money. Organizations come in all shapes and sizes, and they raise money for a wide variety of purposes, from beautifying city blocks or fielding a Little League team to providing services for elderly people with Alzheimer's or creating shelters for victims of domestic violence. Organizations fall roughly into three categories, with a few subcategories, though there's a lot of overlap. Who you are and what you want to do pretty much determine where you need to go for money.

Grassroots organizations usually are small, very local groups like block and tenant associations, neighborhood improvement groups, and merchants' associations. Many do not bother with a formal organization structure or have a minimal structure—a leadership committee or maybe elected officers. Their interests may involve block or building security, neighborhood beautification, activities for local preschoolers, or bringing neighbors together for a holiday party. The kinds of things they want to get funding for might include walkie-talkies for a block-watchers' group; uniforms, equipment, and perhaps rental of a field for sports activities; buses to take kids on trips to a museum, a ball game, or the Statue of Liberty; or money for decorative planters, benches, or other street furniture.

Small grassroots organizations may be able to raise the few hundred or few thousand dollars they need through dues, door-to-door collections, raffles, bake sales, block parties, flea markets, or local business donations. As they grow, they may start looking for foundation or government grants to help support their expansion, and to do this they may need to become officially recognized nonprofit organizations (the parents in our opening remarks were a grassroots group). Sometimes new grassroots organizations make the mistake of seeking grants before they are quite ready. Although certain fundraising activities (such as bake sales) may be appropriate at an early stage in an organization's life, successful foundation and government grants must come later.

We should note that in times of economic turmoil, many of the smallest organizations are likely to find funding scarce. If you are just starting out, you may have to continue relying on volunteers for another few years, or you may want to consider merging with one or more like-minded groups to create an organization with greater capacity to carry out your mission (we'll talk about capacity in Lesson 15).

Social service agencies and other service providers are either *not-for-profit* (also called nonprofit) organizations or local *government agencies* set up to address the needs of groups of people of all ages and types: children (day care, education, after-school programs, literacy, arts, recreation); teenagers (education, violence prevention, pregnancy and substance-use

LITZLER

"NO, I'M NOT TAX EXEMPT. BUT, I CAN MAKE A CLEAR AND COMPELLING CASE FOR THE FUNDS, I'M A FRIEND OF THE BANK AND I KNOW THE P.I.N."

prevention, sports, arts and cultural activities, preparation for high school or college entrance exams, employment readiness and placement); families (immigration counseling, domestic-violence prevention, services to families with children returning home from foster care, employment training and placement, adult education, language training); communities (police, sanitation, health, environmental protection, disaster planning, housing/shelter); or the city or region (transportation, water, sewage). These organizations range in size from a volunteer or paid staff of one or two, serving a very small neighborhood area, to huge, citywide agencies, which may be either governmental or not-for-profit.

Within the social service category, community-based organizations are groups of any size, whether incorporated or not, whose mission is to serve the particular geographic or ethnic community in which they are located, rather than an entire city. Cultural institutions (libraries, museums) are one type of service provider and also may vary dramatically in size. Universities and hospitals may be among the largest nonprofit or government-run service providers in a community.

Some not-for-profit social service organizations may operate one small program (say, caring for a few young children); larger nonprofits and government agencies may run dozens of programs for all ages and needs. Their funding needs may range from a few hundred to many millions of dollars, and they need to raise money from a number of different sources, including individual donors, private foundations, corporations, and government funding agencies.

If service providers are nonprofit groups—as opposed to government agencies—they usually are incorporated under state laws (like any other corporation) and receive tax-exempt status from the Internal Revenue Service. You may hear the term *501(c)(3),** which refers to the section of the Internal Revenue Code that authorizes this type of organization, or the term determination letter, which is the document from the IRS stating that you're tax exempt. You use state incorporation papers or an

---

* 501(c) is the section of the code that authorizes and defines tax-exempt organizations. Subsection 501(c)(3) requires that the organization "be organized and operated exclusively" for defined public purposes "that are beneficial to the public interest," including "relief of the poor . . . advancement of religion, advancement of education or science," and numerous other activities. Private foundations and public charities also come under this section of the code. Organizations that are tax exempt under this section generally are not permitted to lobby, although they are permitted to circulate information that is nonpartisan in nature. There are other kinds of not-for-profit corporations under the code. Section 501(c)(4), for example, governs civic leagues and social welfare organizations like volunteer fire companies and community associations; 501(c)(5) governs labor, agricultural, and horticultural organizations; 501(c)(6) governs business associations like chambers of commerce; and 501(c)(7) addresses social and recreational clubs like college alumni associations, fraternities and sororities, garden clubs, and so on. Churches and other religious organizations, certain schools and colleges, certain hospitals, government units, and certain other entities are established as public charities under another section of the code, Section 501(a)(1).

IRS determination letter to prove you're a nonprofit, because most foundations and government funders only give to such organizations. (By the way, the terms "nonprofit" and "not-for-profit" are used interchangeably in common discussion, but the latter is the technical term in the law and recognizes that the purpose of an organization is "not for profit," although the organization could—in its dreams—show a budget surplus.)

Many kinds of not-for-profit corporations are defined under the Internal Revenue Code (see the footnote). Nevertheless, 501(c)(3) is the section that covers most social service organizations, and the one you most need to be aware of. Contributions to 501(c)(3)s are tax deductible, so individual donors as well as foundations and government entities are more inclined to fund this type of organization. So—if you do not represent a 501(c)(3)—before you think about getting a grant, you need to think about whether you want to spend the money for lawyers and go through the organizing effort and the paperwork required to form a nonprofit corporation. Although it is possible for an organization to do this on its own (start with your state's secretary of state or department of state and the nearest IRS office), we strongly recommend that you use a lawyer. In many communities a private attorney may provide the service at low cost or for free ("pro bono"). There also are organizations like the Legal Services Corporation or Lawyers in the Public Interest that have local offices and can either advise you on the process or refer you to an attorney who can help.

It may take quite a while to prepare the paperwork necessary for a 501(c)(3) application and for incorporation. It can also take a few months for the Internal Revenue Service to begin to review the documentation—so you should allow enough time for the process to be completed.

But we should remind you that, especially in these times, you should think twice about incorporating just to get grants. Because governments and foundations hurt by the economy are being forced to cut back on their giving, they are becoming more strategic in their approach—and a new organization may not be well positioned for this. It will be cheaper and perhaps smarter to focus on working with other organizations that have been around awhile and have a track record. As we said earlier, just because an organization has completed its paperwork and receives its designation as a 501(c)(3) doesn't mean that winning grants will suddenly become easy. Grantmakers look very hard at potential grantees, and the vast majority of them expect to see a significant track record, a committed board of directors, fiscal health, talented leadership, a clear vision, the capacity to implement programs, and the ability to sustain projects, activities, staff, and programs that are grant funded. New 501(c)(3)s have a way to go before they can count on winning grants.

Advocacy groups may be local, regional, citywide, national, or international. They are interested in specific issues, such as trying to convince government agencies to provide more funding for after-school education or charter schools or children with disabilities, or trying protect the environment, or prohibit abortion, support gay marriage, or make marijuana legal for medical purposes. They may be incorporated as not-for-profit organizations but usually are not 501(c)(3)s, because this section of the law specifically prohibits tax-exempt organizations from lobbying the government in most situations. Some foundations will fund their activities, but many will not. Advocacy groups usually need to raise money from individuals and other organizations that care about their causes. They do submit proposals for grants but are more likely to use mailings, the Internet, telephone solicitation, and other individual approaches for their fundraising.

Advocacy groups normally do not receive funding from government agencies either, but there may be exceptions. Each funding agency makes its priorities clear, and you should seek out funders who want and are able to give grants to the type of organization with which you're involved, and the type of project you want to implement. We will talk again and again about how important it is to target appropriate funders based on both what kinds of projects and programs you want to get funded and what kind of organization you are.

Individuals—for example, artists, writers, filmmakers, scholars—are generally interested in getting grants that will fund their projects. They may be associated with a university, research hospital, or cultural institution, which is likely to be the grant recipient although the individual prepares the proposal. Other individuals seek support for independent projects. Research is costly and time-consuming. Shooting a film (and editing it) costs a fortune. We will talk about specific grants for individuals and how some artists form not-for-profit organizations so they can become eligible for a range of grants, and how others connect with existing not-for-profits that can act as the fiscal conduit (we'll talk about this later) for foundation and government grants.

Who Gets the Grant?

Grants generally are directed to specific types of organizations. Some federal grants, for example, may be awarded only to a local or state government agency, local education agency (LEA: a board of education, school district, etc.), or institution of higher education. If these are the only eligible applicants for a specific type of funding, other organizations need not apply.

Most private foundations that require a 501(c)(3) do not fund government agencies, although some government agencies have set up their own not-for-profits or work closely with existing not-for-profits in order to accomplish shared goals. In New York City, for instance, the Police Foundation is a 501(c)(3) that raises money for the police department. The city's Parks Department works closely with the nonprofit Central Park Conservancy to raise supplementary funding for Central Park. Some cities have their own not-for-profits that raise money for special initiatives and for agencies that don't have their own 501(c)(3)s or are not closely associated with local not-for-profit organizations.

There are many legal ramifications for this kind of operation, not the least of which is a real or perceived conflict of interest. For example, a conflict may arise if the 501(c)(3) of a municipality or a government agency receives funds from a corporate source that it is expected to regulate, or if the 501(c)(3) is perceived by the public as a way of getting around the city's own funding rules in order to help political allies. This means that the option must be explored thoroughly with attorneys before it is pursued. If you work for a municipal government agency and want to raise private dollars, check with your budget office or legal department to see how you can proceed.

Pop Quiz

Throughout this book we will be giving you brief quizzes to let you check what you've learned in each lesson. Answers to the pop quizzes are found in Appendix 7.

Multiple Choice

Select the best answer for each of the following questions:

1. Which is the best example of something that a small grassroots organization might be likely to get a grant or donation to pay for?

   a) uniforms for the local Little League team

   b) a neighborhood day care center

   c) a community science and technology museum

   d) a citywide literacy program for immigrants

2. A document known as a 501(c)(3) is:

   a) a license to raise money

   b) proof of not-for-profit status

   c) a description of a certain kind of government grant

   d) a way for individual donors to hide their true identity

3. Most foundations give grants only to:

a) not-for-profit organizations of all kinds

b) cultural and arts institutions

c) municipal and state governments

d) social service agencies and organizations

4. Why is it so important to "know who you are" before writing a proposal?

a) because not every person or organization is eligible for every grant

b) because you may not be eligible for any grant at all

c) because you may need to do a few important things before applying for a grant

d) all of the above are good reasons

Essay Questions

Take 15 to 30 minutes to mull over the following questions. You may want to write out a paragraph or two and save the brief essay to develop in later lessons.

1. Who are you? Briefly describe your organization and place it in the range of organizations described in this lesson.

2. What single project or activity do you think you or your organization may need money for?

LESSON 2:
Wait a Second—What Is a Grant . . . and Where Do I Get One?

OPENING REMARKS

There is a misconception about grants—that just because grants are available, everybody should apply for one. After all, who couldn't use the money? But the truth is that there are times when you really don't need money. You need volunteers or student teachers, student lawyers, student social workers, or donated computers and secondhand books. Or simply a friend to give you a hand in getting a job done. And even if you do need money, there are plenty of fine organizations that have legitimate money needs that are not the least bit appropriate for any kind of grant at all. Sure, you may be able to raise cash through bake sales or raffles, through benefits or scholarships, through donations or gifts. But spend the time and energy to win a grant? No.—ASF

LEADING QUESTIONS
What Is a Grant?

A grant is an award of money that allows you to do very specific things that usually meet very specific guidelines that are spelled out in painstaking detail and to which you must respond very clearly in your grant proposal.

How Do I Know If I Need a Grant?

At first you may not even know if you need a grant. Before you let dollar signs start dancing in your head, you must have a problem that you (and/or your organization) want to solve, decide what you need to do to solve it, and figure out how much that might cost. You may work at the YMCA and feel that there is a serious drug problem in your community that you would like to address through a weekend camping program for

teenagers at the Y. Maybe you're a pediatrician and have noticed a growing number of asthma cases among your preschool patients and want to
find out why, or you're a third grade teacher perplexed by violence that
boys show toward girls during the school day and you want to get expert
help to change this climate. Or you may live on a street where all the trees
died of Dutch elm disease and you want to plant new ones. Or you want to
make a film or compose a symphony or study abroad or write a biography.
The question is, What do you have to do to get the results you want?

Some organizations have learned that chasing grants can take them
away from their core mission or move an excellent program in the wrong
direction. The most successful programs and organizations are not grant
driven, they are mission driven. In other words, they are not created,
massaged, and manipulated to fit the precise guidelines of a grant that
just happens to be available. Rather, they have strong, comprehensive,
well-developed programs or plans that show they have made good use
of all other available resources. If money is needed to implement or supplement a well-designed program, that is where a grant comes in. But
the program is the thing. The better designed the program is to address
the need, and the more other funding you have raised or resources you
have found to support it, the more likely you are to win grants. The same
thing is true for individuals. Some people don't have a commitment to a
topic for a film or book; they just have a commitment to wanting a grant.
But it has to be the other way around, of course.

If the Economy Is Less Than Ideal,
Aren't Grants Even More Important?

We won't lie to you. At the time of this writing, we are facing very uncertain times for grant seekers, to put it mildly. The war in Iraq and the
current economic crisis have generated a shift in government and foundation spending. The huge and growing federal deficit threatens severe
cuts in spending at all government levels because so much federal money

comes through state and local agencies. The global economic meltdown has drastically affected foundations' investments and state and local tax revenues. This means less money for all kinds of projects, from the smallest to the largest. We aren't trying to scare you, we just want you to think strategically. No matter how bad the economy is, there still will be funding opportunities. We want you to understand that when money is scarce you need to be even more active and proactive in finding and obtaining funds to keep your programs going. And remember that it's one thing to do everything in your power to find grants to support your agency's programs; it's something else entirely to pursue grants that distract you from your core mission. If you provide services for senior citizens and then suddenly decide to apply for grants for preschoolers just because there's money available, you may dilute your organization's effectiveness—and raise questions in grantmakers' minds about your strategies.

If community needs are driving you to expand your services, you must do so in a thoughtful, systematic way—never losing sight of your mission. If you are a senior center and know that the community needs children's programs (which no other organization provides), you may think about creating intergenerational activities (bringing together children and seniors) that do not take you so far afield that funders question your ability to do what you say you're going to do. After you have successfully created and operated the intergenerational programs, you may find it easier—and the grantmakers will find it more credible—to branch out into other activities for children.

THE FUNDERS

All kinds of individuals, organizations, and units of government get grants. The federal government gives grants. State and local governments give grant-like funding, usually in the form of contracts for specific services that require paperwork, audits, and accountability. Private foundations and corporations give grants. Individuals give grants, usually through a fund or trust set up for that purpose and administered by a bank or foundation.

In some areas of the country, a regional association of grantmakers (RAG) may publish a standard or common application form that grant seekers can use for all participating foundations in that area (some RAGs also publish a common report form). These forms incorporate headings that structure the way the proposal is written and the information that must be included. The forms differ a bit from area to area but are strikingly similar in content. All require the proposer to state a need, describe the program, present a rational budget, provide supporting materials that indicate the organization's capacity to implement the program, and document the organization's not-for-profit status. All of these issues are discussed in Part II. You can find the common application forms online; a sample appears in Appendix 4.

Government grants are generally announced through requests for proposals (RFPs, also called requests for applications, or RFAs) that specify the nature and cost of the program that must be proposed. They include guidelines, due dates, and so much required information that you will start to wonder why the grantmakers don't just write the proposal themselves. Foundations, on the other hand, tend to be less prescriptive. Most foundations do not issue RFPs, although some large ones, like the Robert Wood Johnson Foundation, may do so. Others, like the Kresge Foundation and the Ford Foundation, may publish requirements that are as specific as the RFP for any government grant.

Foundations

Foundations range in size from tiny family foundations with no staff (grant decisions are made by family members) and budgets under $100,000 to huge organizations that have dozens of professional staff members and give away millions each year. Understanding the differences may save you a good deal of time and energy in preparing proposals.

Family Foundations. Family foundations often have narrowly focused giving patterns based on the intentions of the donor or the interests of current family members who are officers or trustees. Many do not accept unsolicited proposals, some because they are too small to review large numbers of proposals, others because their giving is earmarked for specific organizations.

Independent Private Foundations. This type of foundation usually has at least a small professional staff. It may have begun as a family foundation but is no longer controlled by the original donor or the donor's family. This does not mean that the donor's interests are ignored. Private foundations are ethically and, in most cases, legally bound to follow the donor's intent to the extent possible. If the terms of the original endowment or bequest said the money was to be used solely for organizations that train opera singers, that's what it is used for. The only discretion that the trustees have in making grants is, perhaps, selecting the best organizations to do the training. If the terms of the endowment are a bit broader—say, for health services for children from low-income families—many creative projects may be eligible for a grant.

Federated Funds. Federated funds like the United Way were created to benefit the community by pooling donations from individuals and businesses and using those funds to support nonprofit organizations. Unlike independent and family foundations, which draw primarily on funds from a single donor or an endowment and do not seek funding from the public, federated funds maintain ongoing fundraising operations.

Corporate Foundations. Corporate, or company-sponsored, foundations are independent entities created by large corporations with funds from the businesses themselves or from their founders. Most corporate foundations function like other foundations, receiving proposals and making grants, but their giving may be somewhat tied to the corporations' own goals. For example, a drug company's foundation may be established to fund medical research; a bank's foundation may fund community development.

Community Foundations. In every state in the United States and in Puerto Rico, there are one or more (usually many more; the total tops 600) local foundations called community foundations, community trusts, or community funds. (To give you a taste of their omnipresence, we have included a partial list in Appendix 5.) Community foundations have been set up to administer individual trust funds or pools of funds from individual donors who want to benefit their own city or region but don't want to create a new foundation. To determine whether there is a community foundation in your area, search on "community foundation" and your city, county, or state; check with your local library (or even your local phone book); or go to a listing at the Foundation Center's website (discussed below and listed in Appendix 6).

A community foundation or community trust usually includes funds set up by donors with very specific purposes in mind as well as others with more general purposes. Living donors to such foundations may be able to recommend which organizations should receive grants. Under regulations governing the establishment of donor-directed funds, the final determination must be made by the foundation, but most program officers try to accommodate the donor's wishes.

Financial Institutions. Financial institutions always have administered charitable trusts set up for the donor's purposes; a trend toward this type of trust is growing. Proposals to a trust held at a financial institution often are made in the same way as proposals to foundations.

Most foundations were established to give money to causes that were of interest to their original donors, which means that some give to very narrowly defined programs, like medical research on a particular disease or a visual arts program for senior citizens, while some give money to address a wide range of social, medical, or cultural issues. Some give primarily to support religious purposes; some will not consider giving for religious purposes. A few give to individuals; most do not. Some foundations give only within their own geographic areas; others give globally.

There is a foundation for every purpose, and you have to find the right ones for you.

How Do You Find the Right Foundation? Your first stop is the Foundation Center (www.fdncenter.org), a national organization that provides support to foundations, researchers in the field of philanthropy, and information for grant seekers. It maintains Foundation Center Libraries in five cities across the United States (New York, Atlanta, Cleveland, Washington, D.C., and San Francisco). In many other locations across the country, a public library or nonprofit organization is designated as a Foundation Center Cooperating Collection. The cooperating collections maintain Foundation Center publications, and often provide online research capability. Call 800-424-9836 or go to www.fdncenter.org/collections to find the location nearest you.

The Foundation Center Libraries and cooperating collections offer extensive research materials with which every grant seeker must become familiar. Most important are the Foundation Directory and the Foundation Directory Online, but there are many other directories that describe foundations and corporations by location, program interests, size of grants given, and many other characteristics. The Foundation Center Libraries also maintain foundation annual reports. These references will let you identify grantmakers in your area, find out what kinds of activities they prefer to fund, determine the general dollar amounts of the grants they offer, define eligibility, and locate the addresses, telephone numbers, and names of the appropriate contacts at the foundations. If there is no foundation library in your area, you can go to the Foundation Center's website or subscribe to the Foundation Directory Online (we talk a bit more about this resource in the section on Internet research that begins on page 28). But your local library should be able to get these references for you from the Foundation Center or may have other reference materials that will help you locate foundations in your city or region.

Before you submit a proposal to a foundation, you would be very wise to check its website or call or write for its annual report, grant application form or guidelines (if it has any), descriptions of programs it has funded recently, and any other information you can get. Your proposal is likely to be rejected automatically if it doesn't meet the recipient's guidelines. *Much* more about this later. Oh, and by the way, when you're checking out the foundation's guidelines, you would be wise to make a note of the current contact person's name, address, and phone number, and find out whether the foundation wants you to contact it by mail, phone, or email. As you'll hear from the funders, they get annoyed when you send requests to their predecessors!

Foundations, like all 501(c)(3) organizations, are required to submit tax returns called 990s, which almost always include a list of organizations the foundation has funded during that tax year, and the amounts of money given to each. Some foundations, although not all, include the particular program for which each grant was given. The 990s are available for free on a website called GuideStar (the web addresses for this and other useful sites are listed in Appendix 6).*

It also is helpful to know what kinds of organizations and projects each foundation really funds. For instance, a foundation may say that individuals and all types of not-for-profit organizations are eligible to apply for grants, but when you read its annual report, you notice that this foundation has funded only medical schools for the last five years. Another foundation may indicate in its guidelines that its average grants are between $100,000 and $200,000, so if your project will cost $350,000, you shouldn't expect to get it all from this foundation. If you ask for it anyway, do expect your request to irritate the grantmaker. And if you also notice in the annual report or the 990 that in the last three years this foundation hasn't actually funded anything for more than $50,000, far less than the minimum they specified, you probably should call to find out if they've changed their guidelines.

* Nonprofit organizations also may register on GuideStar to let potential donors know about you and review your 990s. See Lesson 15 for reasons to do this.

Although some foundations are interested in brand-new organizations and may even offer some technical assistance in preparing a proposal, most want to know that you know the ropes. Let the foundation see that you are aware of its work, that you have studied the annual report, that you have looked at the organizations and individuals that it has funded, and that you are making a careful decision to apply based on all your homework. Never be shy about letting the grantmaker see why you chose it and the amount of research you have completed to ensure that there are no holes in your proposal.

Businesses

Corporations and local businesses may fulfill their civic responsibilities through grants and sponsorships to nonprofit organizations. Keep in mind that in a bad economy, many businesses may be forced to cut back on their giving. But when they can help, there is tremendous diversity in the amount and type of support that corporations offer. National corporations may give only or predominantly to national organizations, or they may give only in the cities where they have their business offices or factories. A corner drugstore may sponsor the Little League team from a three-block area—which might mean buying T-shirts with the team's name (and the drugstore's logo). Businesses may give only to major cultural institutions, universities, hospitals, or other large organizations with a strong fundraising track record, or they may be interested in supporting small local groups in a specific region. Their decisions may be made by top management, a marketing department, or their own internal giving offices, corporate philanthropy or corporate responsibility departments, or independent foundations.

Although philanthropy is important for its own sake to many corporations, it is usually tied to business concerns as well. If you can show how a grant to your organization will bring broad recognition or publicity to the donor, even the most public-spirited company will be pleased.

Business donors or sponsors are often a good place for a small organization to begin seeking funding and establishing a track record in using these gifts—and your board members should be involved in this effort. Start with your local bank branch. Ask the manager if the bank provides assistance to a group like yours, and what you have to do to apply for it. Call every major business located in your community to see if the company has a giving program. If you know a business leader well, ask for suggestions about where to go for help. When you are ready to go to a major corporation, you can find lists of companies near you at the Foundation Center website.

Local civic associations, like the Chamber of Commerce, Lions Club, Rotary, and Kiwanis, often have giving programs or provide sponsorships for local organizations. Remember that each civic organization has its own priorities—children, seniors, people with visual impairments—and is more likely to be interested in helping you if the program you operate falls within its guidelines. If managers or board members of your organization join such civic associations, they may make important connections with business leaders in the community and promote the organization's programs.

Don't expect any large gifts from businesses, at least to start, but do be prepared to use the proposal development methods that we describe in Part II.

Federal Grants

Every year the federal government awards billions of dollars worth of grants, but not-for-profit organizations—and even government agencies— often are afraid of the work involved in obtaining (and reporting on) a federal grant. But organizations that go to the trouble of researching and writing a winning federal proposal often find that the federal grant can offer substantial, stable, multiyear funding. Nonprofit organizations also gain credibility when applying for state, local, and foundation funding—

as well as some breathing room to identify additional funding sources. We should note that in recent years the federal government has pushed funding out to state agencies, and sometimes to major cities, that it used to award directly to nonprofit organizations. This is likely to be the case with funding in the so-called stimulus package intended to promote economic recovery. As we write, nonprofit organizations are scrambling to find out exactly what may be available for them in the stimulus package. But, as with other federal funding recently, most of this money will be awarded through government entities. Governments must still apply for such funding, but nonprofits will have to keep track of it and apply through their own states, cities, and school districts. Nevertheless, despite this process and despite our own concerns about the climate for federal funding in the next few years, we urge you to be alert to the possibility of appropriate federal grants in your overall fundraising plan.

Federal grants are made to accomplish some public purpose. The nature of the grant, the eligible recipients, the method of award, and the terms and conditions are specified in the legislation that creates each grant program and in detailed regulations that are either laid out in the statute or added by the funding agency. Some grants have relatively few restrictions, while others are laden with significant limitations and extensive reporting requirements, based on the legislation.

How Can I Find Out What Grants Are Available from All the Different Federal Agencies? This may sound hard, but it is really a piece of cake. The *Federal Register* is a daily publication that reports on all official federal actions—including federal funding opportunities. Once an agency decides to announce a grant program, the announcement, often with the whole application package, appears in the *Federal Register*. (As we discuss below and in Appendix 6, however, most federal agencies are making use of their own and other online sites to announce funding availability.)

Occasionally a federal announcement appears far in advance of the application due date, in a massive projection of all of an agency's or a department's grantmaking for the coming fiscal year. Most of the time, however, notification of an individual grant program occurs within a designated period (after any required public comment, which can alter the final program announcement) and allows 30 to 90 days for a response. It is important to get your hands on the grant information that appears in the *Federal Register* as early as possible, to give you the maximum time needed to develop a proposal. Many libraries have computer access, so you can locate the Federal Register Online, and other federal funding sources as well. For a brief guide to searching the Federal Register Online, see page 30.

Increasingly, federal agencies publish grant information on their own websites, so you'll want to search them in addition to the *Federal Register*. We present some useful sites in Appendix 6, but they change over time, so you may need to update the list at regular intervals. Some cities make grant information available free of charge to residents through a municipal library, government office, or other public information center. School systems may provide grant information to staff, parents, and students. Large not-for-profit organizations are sometimes willing to share funding information with smaller ones, especially if they need to form partnerships to win grants. Not knowing what grants were available used to be a legitimate excuse for an organization or an agency that didn't seek funding. This is no longer true; the information is out there. And it is usually cost-free or close to it. It is developing the grant proposal that is now most challenging—not finding the grant opportunities.

Federal (and state and local) grant proposals are generally complex and time-consuming to prepare; developing and writing a comprehensive, technical grant application in the few short weeks or months that most federal programs allow is difficult. It is a good idea to develop programs well in advance rather than rely on the relatively short turnaround time given in the grant announcement. To do this, you need to know what funding will be available next year. Although funding for each federal program depends on the availability of money in any year's congressional budget, many programs have a multiyear track record that allows you to anticipate that they are likely to be funded again. That's where the *Catalog of Federal Domestic Assistance* (CFDA) comes in.

The CFDA (again, the website is given in Appendix 6), which is published annually, describes every federal grant program: programs available to state and local governments (including the District of Columbia and Indian tribal governments), territories (and possessions) of the United States, public and private for-profit and not-for-profit organizations and institutions, and individuals.

The CFDA's comprehensiveness can be a drawback. It lists every federal program—including those that are no longer being funded. This means you need to do some sorting and cross-referencing to see if the programs you are interested in are still alive; often you must turn again to the *Federal Register* or individual agencies. Nevertheless, the CFDA can be a very good start, and your congressional representative's local office is a good place to find it. Most local offices have staff whose responsibility it is to help constituents with this kind of research. Some offices also have their own grants newsletters, funding workshops, or other funding information. If they don't, they can find out who can help you. (If you are planning a federal proposal, it's a good idea to talk with congressional staff anyway; you may want a letter from the representative in support of your proposal.)

Just one more thing about the CFDA: Programs are classified into many different types of assistance and some of it can be a little confusing. *Formula grants*, for instance, are not the same as *project grants*. Formula grants are allocations of money to states or municipalities "in accordance with a distribution formula prescribed by law for activities of a continuing nature not confined to a specific project," for example, based on the number of residents in the designated area who are living below the poverty level—or just based on the number of residents. Project grants described in the CFDA are the ones most grant seekers are interested in because they include fellowships, scholarships, research grants, training grants, experimental and demonstration grants, evaluation grants, planning grants, technical assistance grants, and many others. All of the federal government grants we mention in this book are project grants.

Elected Officials. Despite the current federal budget climate and the outrage over "bridges to nowhere," virtually all members of Congress still have some ability to include small (or large) pots of money called *earmarks* (sometimes referred to as pork) in the federal budget. Contrary to what you've heard, not all earmarks are wasteful. They are funding that elected officials include in a budget bill specifically for their constituents' projects, and many of these are worthwhile initiatives that benefit the community, like a health center, research lab, or, yes, a bridge to *somewhere*. Some members will work to get earmarks only for organizations they know and respect (so get to know them now; invite them to events, send them newsletters, meet with them and their staff members). Some members have developed an RFP process. They ask eligible groups for proposals early each year, and after a review, they and their staff members work to get any that they feel are worthwhile accepted into an appropriations bill. Keep in mind that even in the best economic times this money is very scarce to begin with. Moreover, funding for earmarks is hotly contested among the members of Congress because they all want to bring money home for their constituents, and your elected official probably has several groups for whom he or she wants to get funding. Ask for what you need, but don't expect to get more than a fraction of your request, if anything at all. And keep trying; with the encouragement of its congressional representative, more than one organization we know continued to submit its request for assistance for several fiscal years, and finally received a grant.

If your representative is successful in getting you an earmark, the agency responsible for administering the earmark will contact you, and you will have to submit a grant application (happily, one that you know will be funded). From this point on, the earmark functions like any other grant.

State and City Government Grants

Some states, and even some cities, have the equivalent of the *Federal Register* or a statewide "e-grants" system in which you sign up via email and automatically receive notices in categories for which you've indicated an interest. (Some of these opportunities are noted in Appendix 6.) However, in many places it may be harder to track down state and local grants information. Check with your library to see what reference sources are available, or begin to identify the state and local agencies that would be likely to fund your programs, and get in touch with the appropriate staff there (often you can be placed on a snail-mailing list for specific funding opportunities). In smaller states and municipalities this usually is fairly easy; it can take just a few phone calls. In larger states and cities you may need to be very persistent in finding the right department.

State and Local Elected Officials. Your local elected officials are an important resource for funding, and it's important that they know and respect your organization because they can help you find and obtain grants, and because they themselves sometimes have small amounts of state or local funding at their discretion. Many localities publish listings of names and addresses of elected officials; again, your library and telephone directories will give you information on how to reach them.

Some state and local officials send out periodic grant listings. For example, New York State Assembly Leader Sheldon Silver publishes *Grant Action News* every month (http://assembly.state.ny.us/gan); this publication describes current and recent New York State agency grants, as well as some federal and foundation opportunities. Virtually all elected officials do mailings, so make sure you are on their mailing and/or email lists and read the mailings to see what committees your officials are on, what causes they are interested in, and sometimes the groups for which they have provided funding.

State and local elected officials' discretionary funding usually takes the form of grants, but the application process often is shorter and less demanding than for other types of proposal. For example, a New York City agency received a $15,000 grant to fund its Community Emergency Response Team (CERT) program after meeting with a state senator whose local district did not have any CERT teams. After the grant was awarded, the agency received the paperwork from the New York Department of State. There was still an application to fill out in order to draw down the money, but it is much more fun to fill out the application when you know you have been awarded the funding!

Funding from state and local elected officials probably will be relatively small (the $15,000 for the CERT team only trains one team, while the agency trains about 30 teams a year), but every bit of funding can help. Also, if you are a new organization or program, this small amount of funding can be vital as seed money to show foundations and other funders that someone has confidence in you. As we will discuss later, funders like to give to programs that show some capacity; they want evidence that their grants will be well spent and that the organization is able to accomplish what the applicant promises.

And even if local elected officials do not have money available themselves, they may be able to help you get funding from other sources. For example, during meetings with state officials, that same New York City agency met with a state assemblyman from one of the city's boroughs and asked for a grant for a CERT team. The assemblyman did not have any funds of his own, but he was impressed by the project and approached a local real-estate company, which agreed to fund a team. In the same way, local elected officials can be helpful in getting donations for after-school programs, fundraisers, and so on.

So call and visit all your elected officials; send them information on your programs, and invite them to events. Often their staff will attend, but they are the ones who will make the funding recommendations so it pays to keep them informed. It may also be easier to get letters of support and/or commitment if they are already familiar with your work. In case you think we're exaggerating when we emphasize the need to call on your local elected officials for help, remember: It's their job. They care about improving the lives of their constituents. And when grant money pours into their communities it can only be a plus for them.

Using the Internet in Grant Searches

By now, we believe, most individuals and organizations are online, but if we haven't said it before, we should: If you do not yet have Internet access, you'd better make this your next priority. The cost is relatively low, and the benefits are significant to any organization and especially to the people who need information to design and seek funding for programs. Moreover, if you can swing it, develop a website for your organization. Having your own website, even if it's rudimentary, puts the agency's name and work into a public space and gives you a certain level of credibility in this information age.

Foundation Center Online (www.foundationcenter.org). In preparing for this edition, we were disappointed to find that much of what the Foundation Center Online once offered free is now available only by subscription or purchase. The website still offers some useful free information and links to individual foundation and corporate websites. For example, if there is a particular foundation you are interested in, you can find out how to reach it (contact person, address, and phone number); learn about its assets and total giving; and link to its latest 990 tax filing (which includes lists of organizations funded). The website also provides plenty of news about foundations and giving trends, links to research materials, reference materials, workshops, and more.

The Foundation Center's major online subscription service, the *Foundation Directory Online,* is found at www.fdncenter.org. The cost of the basic service is $195/year. The advantage to subscribing is that you can search the entire foundation database using a variety of characteristics, including the city in which the foundation is located; the geographic area (state) where its grants are given; the type of grant it makes (program, seed grant, building/renovation, general operating, etc.); its officers or trustees; and programmatic areas of interest (children, aging, health, social services, etc.). The summary for each foundation also includes a link to its 990. This is a site that we use all the time to find new foundation prospects and to brush up on information about foundations we know. Although there are more advanced (and more expensive) versions of the *Directory*, we find that the basic service offers nearly all the information we need.

The most useful of the other Foundation Center sites also are accessible only by subscription. If your library cannot provide access, you may find it worthwhile to explore some of these subscription services. For example, for $59.95 a month, http://foundationcenter.org/findfunders/fundingsources/cgo.html provides information about and links to corporate funders. Or if you're looking for grants for individuals, it may be worth subscribing to http://gtionline.fdncenter.org (at a cost of $9.95 per month), where you can find foundations that make this kind of grant. If you prefer not to subscribe, you can always use the Foundation Center Libraries and Cooperating Collections as you would use any library—visit to get access to all of their free resources and very helpful staff.

The Grantsmanship Center Online. The Grantsmanship Center, a nonprofit organization that provides technical assistance and training to nonprofit organizations, is based in Los Angeles. Its website (www.tgci.com) offers useful information including a chart showing federal government proposals that have been funded by different federal agencies (the full proposals are available for a fee) and tips about how to win grants. For foundation research purposes, the most valuable aspect of this website (www.tgci.com/funding/states.asp) is a map of the United States that connects you to a list of the top 40 or 50 foundations in that state that give grants (for some, web links are provided; for some there's just a name); the names of companies with corporate giving programs; and community foundations (with links and the areas they serve). This is a good place to start your research on grant information in your own state.

The Federal Register Online. If you already use the Federal Register
Online, you can skip the following discussion. Not many years ago, we
pored over bulky, flimsy paper copies of the *Federal Register* each day to
find federal funding opportunities. Application packages could only be
obtained by mail, with a wait of several weeks. But now the *Federal Register* is available electronically at no cost other than that of your Internet
access provider, or for free via Internet access at public libraries. Grant
applications also can be obtained online. (In most cases you'll probably
need Adobe Acrobat Reader, which is free, available by clicking on a
button right at the *Federal Register* site.) Online access means more time
is available to strategize and write the proposal. To access the Federal
Register Online, go to www.gpoaccess.gov. This brings you to the search
page for the *Federal Register*. The process for searching is fairly straightforward, with clear instructions at the site. There are search options including a "simple search," in which you select the year of the funding
you're interested in and enter one or more key words, and an "advanced
search," which lets you select the type of document you're looking for,
the key words, and the specific time period when the announcement was
made. The only tricky aspect of the Federal Register Online is the use of
Boolean operators, which we describe in the following section. The
search instructions may look complicated as you read them, but we assure
you that as you follow these steps right at the site, what you need to do
will be very clear.

SAMPLE FEDERAL REGISTER ONLINE SEARCH

First, highlight (in the simple search) or check the box specifying the
volume you want (normally, the current year). In the advanced search you
also will check the section (type of document) that you want to search
for (usually "Notices"; grant announcements are listed as "notices of
funding availability"). If you know the publication date, or if you just
want to update information since the last time you searched, there is a

box to enter a range of dates or the earliest date from which to begin the search. Then for either the simple or the advanced search, enter some keywords for your search criteria. You may use a phrase in quotation marks ("low-income housing"), keywords separated by capitalized instructions (housing AND grants), or phrases and words separated by instructions ("low-income housing" AND grants). The capitalized instructions are called Boolean operators. Others include ADJ (immediately adjacent, as in youth ADJ employment); OR; AND NOT. The only operator you normally will need is AND, but we recommend that you read the helpful hints provided at the site to learn how to specify your query most effectively.

Once you've specified the search, the system returns a list of documents that match your search criteria (if it does not, you need to refine your search; go to the "helpful hints" section). When the results come back, you have three options for reading each document: HTML, PDF, and Summary. The last is self-explanatory. Use it if you just want to check that the funding is likely to be appropriate for you.

HTML is a text version; it's usually the longest in number of pages, and it doesn't include graphics or tables, but you can save it to a word processing document in your own system to review. PDF is usually much shorter. It's a representation of the actual *Federal Register* document and includes graphics and tables. But it's the one for which you need Adobe Acrobat Reader. You can save or download any of these versions.

Some large nonprofits (generally universities or hospitals), government agencies, and school districts have someone on staff who searches daily by all relevant keywords or phrases. Most organizations can't afford such an intensive time commitment. We recommend that you try to search at least once a week for all announcements published during the period. This will allow you to find funding opportunities in plenty of time to respond; if you search less frequently you may find the perfect grant for you but wind up with only a couple of weeks until the deadline.

Federal Agency Websites. Nearly every federal agency now has its own website, and some sites provide resources that can help you prepare a much more effective proposal. For example, the Department of Education offers information on research and "best practices" in a variety of topic areas. You may find information on a program you want to replicate, or data that are vital to your statement of need. You also will find descriptions of programs that have been funded in the past. Similarly, the National Science Foundation website, which is very user friendly, includes an A to Z Index of Funding Opportunities for researchers, educators, graduate students, and other users. It includes guidelines about how to prepare a proposal, recent articles about current research, and more. See Appendix 6 for a list of some of the most relevant federal agency websites.

Other Sites. Increasing numbers of state and local entities also are providing funding information online. Some of the state and local government sites we've found are included in Appendix 6. You can link to your state's site from the Grantsmanship Center's site at www.tgci.com/funding/states.asp. The amount of information and ease of finding it varies from state to state, but as with most things on the Internet, more and more information is becoming available each day; so if you check your state or its relevant agencies' websites and don't find useful information, bookmark the sites and check back every now and then to see if they have begun to post funding information. Some states have centralized sites that are easy to use. In others, if you dig a little deeper to specific agencies of interest (e.g., education, health, criminal justice), you will find many with a funding section that lists their contacts and grant information. State and local agencies' sites also can be good sources for obtaining statistics and other information that you will need when writing your needs assessment (see Lesson 8).

Many community foundations, regional associations of grantmakers, and individual foundations have an online presence and are often rich with information about grants and topics of interest to grant seekers. For example, the Delaware Community Foundation's website tells you what's available and how to apply. The Chicago Community Trust also has its grant guidelines and application forms online, and carefully describes all of its funding priorities. Its Knowledge Center includes reports on research it has funded on topics of interest to grant seekers (and other residents of Chicago).

In New York City there is an organization called the Nonprofit Coordinating Committee, which regularly searches the *Federal Register* and state and local government agency sites. It then emails its members brief summaries of the announcements in categories that they have chosen from a lengthy checklist. If the summary interests them, members can use the website listed in the announcement to download the request for proposals or other information. Ask at your library and other sources to see if something like this is available in your area.

A Word About Search Engines

Everyone who uses the Internet is familiar with search engines by now, although you may just call them Yahoo (www.yahoo.com), Google (www.google.com), and so on. If you're new to the Internet, you should learn to play with these sites. Like most other people, we look up old movies to find out who the actors were, or search for nurseries that sell African violets, or check out the New York Mets players' batting averages and birthdays. But they also are a great resource for grant seekers. During a recent visit to Google, we typed in "grants" and got 8,890,000 hits. Not so useful, you'll say; overwhelming, you'll say. But the first (unsponsored) item that appeared was Grants.gov, a vital federal site we mentioned earlier and will discuss further in Appendix 6; others were for other federal agencies and sites such as www.schoolgrants.org.

Another search, on "grants in aging," brought up over 3,870 listings. The list included foundations, research grants, training grants, and NIH grants for dissertation research for doctoral candidates. And (note that slightly different searches can bring interestingly different results) the third entry from a search on "aging grants" was to an aging initiative funded by the Environmental Protection Agency (not the first place you might go for funding related to older adults). Your need statements can benefit from the search engines too. For example, a search on "dropout rate" brings you nearly a million entries, including a Child Trends Data Bank report on national trends in high school dropout rates, along with many articles and reports on state and local rates. Search engines can cut some time off your research and lead you to some sources you had not previously consulted.

At the very least, then, if you haven't bookmarked your most important grant sites, you always can get to them from one of the popular search engines—and you may come up with new resources. And of course these sites are the gateway to a wealth of information on topics that may help you formulate and justify the need for new programs. But don't just stick to the major sites; sometimes Lycos, or ask.com, or one of the lesser-known search engines will come up with references that you don't see on Google or Yahoo. One last note about online searching. While you're doing your research, you may as well pick up a few cents for your organization. A search engine called GoodSearch (www.goodsearch.com) allows you (and all of your colleagues, friends, family, and donors) to specify an organization that you are "searching for," and receive a penny for each search. For some reason this site does not turn up the number or variety of appropriate websites as other search engines do, so don't use it as your only source.

Publications and Newsletters

Many for-profit organizations sell newsletters and books providing information about federal grants. Some offer information on foundation and corporate grants as well. We have subscribed to or purchased these publications in the past but have found that our own online research produces results that are just as effective and as timely (or more so). However, some of them do discuss trends in government and foundation funding as well as current grant opportunities, so if you have a particular area of interest (such as youth funding or health care funding), you may want to try a free sample or even a year's subscription to one of these publications to see if it works for you. We prefer not to make any recommendations here, but we will say that some companies appear to do much more exhaustive research and seem to have more "insider information" about future funding prospects than others; we suggest you review them carefully before you subscribe.

You may want to check out a free publication online. The *Philanthropy News Digest* (PND) is a free newsletter at www.fdncenter.org/pnd. It provides updates on trends and news in philanthropy. The Foundation Center Online currently features foundations' response to the economy and allows you to search PND for articles. PND also highlights an "RFP of the day" (and "job of the day"), and it lets you sign up for alerts. It's a good idea to read the trade publications—magazines, newsletters, newspapers—in your field of interest so that your grant proposal reflects current trends and best practices. These publications often include lists of grant opportunities of interest to their readers.

Finding out what government and private grants are available is the easy part of the grant process. It shouldn't cost you a fortune, and it shouldn't take hours of your valuable time.

Pop Quiz

Multiple Choice

Select the best answer for each of the following questions:

1. Most requests for proposals (RFPs) include:

    a) a description of the program you must propose in order to win a grant

    b) guidelines you must follow

    c) a due date for submission of the proposal

    d) all of the above are generally included in an RFP

2. Foundations are:

    a) generally small

    b) always run by an executive director and at least two staff members

    c) unlikely to give grants of more than $15,000

    d) all shapes and sizes, with all different priorities, guidelines, and purposes

3. When applying for foundation grants, you should:

    a) know what kinds of organizations the foundation has funded, but never mention it

    b) apply cold—without knowing anything about the foundation

    c) know what kinds of organizations the foundation has funded, and mention it

    d) ask for at least $10,000 more than the maximum amount of money a foundation says it gives, so you have room to negotiate

4. Federal government grant opportunities are:

    a) not required to be announced anywhere

    b) only announced on federal agency websites

    c) always announced in the *Federal Register*

    d) announced every two months in the *Catalogue of Federal Domestic Assistance* (CFDA)

5. A good way for very small organizations to begin grant seeking is to apply for:

    a) large federal government grants

    b) middle-sized municipal grants

    c) donations from local businesses

    d) foundation grants

Essay Questions

Take 15 to 30 minutes to respond to the following essay questions, based on your answers to the essay questions at the end of Lesson 1 (you may want to write out your responses for future use). Include the following:

1. How much money do I need, realistically, to run my project?
2. What will the budget look like? Will the costs be primarily for staff, or consultants, or equipment and supplies?
3. What kind of funder (foundation, government, other) is most likely to provide the money I need?
4. Who are the three or four most likely funders for this project in this city or state?

LESSON 3:
Making (Dollars and) Sense of Grant-Application Packages: What Grantmakers Want

OPENING REMARKS

When I first started writing grant proposals to the federal government, I paid hardly any attention to the grant application package. It was usually cumbersome and uninviting. The print was small, the pages packed with mysterious words in tiny print, bizarre numbering systems like (iii) and a slew of public laws that meant absolutely nothing to me. I would skim over the thing quickly and not look at the application again until I actually needed to write the proposal—weeks later.

One particular proposal I worked on was for a program for "out-of-school youth." Because I had never heard that term, I figured they were youth who were sometimes in school and sometimes not in school. Children who had chronic asthma, perhaps, or played hooky (do they still say "hooky"?).

I wrote the proposal with my kind of out-of-school youth in mind—students who were absent a lot—and my proposal was disqualified the second it arrived at the U.S. Department of Education headquarters. One intense month—days, nights, weekends—was wasted on a proposal for which my organization wasn't eligible. All because I did not read the dense, critically important application package that defined "out-of-school youth" in no uncertain terms: DROPOUTS. —EK

LEADING QUESTIONS
How Do I Get What I Need from the Grant Application?

No two application packages or proposal guidelines are the same. Let's look at five different packages:

- The U.S. Departments of Justice, Education, and Health and Human Services Safe Schools/Healthy Students Initiative (all three federal agencies collaborated on this one).

- The Kennedy School of Government/Harvard University (Ash Institute for Democratic Governance and Innovation) Innovations in American Government Program application.
- The Independence Community Foundation's application guidelines.
- National Endowment for the Arts Literature Fellowships: Fellowships for Creative Writers.
- The Washington Regional Association of Grantmakers' Common Grant Application Form, a form that needs to be supplemented with individual foundations' guidelines.

The 2008 Safe Schools/Healthy Students Initiative's application package is 119 pages long, with a detailed 2-page table of contents. The Innovations in American Government program guidelines, application, and samples of winning proposals runs about 10 pages online. The National Endowment for the Arts Creative Writing program is 7 pages. The Independence Community Foundation has a slim brochure giving instructions for all applicants except those who are requesting $500 or less. For the latter organizations the brochure includes a 2-page tear-out "coupon" with about 15 short-answer pieces of requested information. And the Washington Regional Association of Grantmakers Common Grant Application Form is a tightly packed document of just over 4 pages. We've even seen application guidelines from a corporate grantmaker that came on a postcard. But don't be fooled by their length. Even the smallest package contains enough information to keep a proposal writer chained to the desk for weeks.

There is a tendency to skim an application package, to speed-read it just as you might scan the eye-strain-inducing pamphlet that comes with your new allergy pills. With the latter, you ignore just about every other paragraph until you get to the part about your new drug causing death if taken with alcohol. That you read carefully (although you may ignore the warning). In a grant application package, most people cut right to the chase—well, actually, three chases: the amount of money being given away; the questions that the applicant must answer in the grant proposal; and the deadline for submission. We'll get to why these items are critically important to understand, but it is a mistake to cut to the chase in a grant application package. There is no chase. The whole package should be read carefully again and again. And again. Each reading will reveal something you missed during an earlier reading.

Don't look at an application package only in terms of preventing disqualification. You want to apply for grants for which you are very, very qualified, and you want to get an edge on other proposal writers who are competing for the same grant by deeply understanding every syllable of the application package. There just may be some concepts, words, hints, which, if taken to heart, will dramatically improve your chances of winning a grant.

Because application packages come in all shapes and sizes, they all can't contain exactly the same information organized in precisely the same way. But each package should answer a slew of important questions; you just have to know what to ask.

A Note on Using Technology

When we said earlier that you must become comfortable using the Internet, we were talking about searching for grant opportunities. But there's another equally important reason. More and more grantmakers, mostly foundations and corporations but some government funders as well, are requiring that you submit your proposal online. Frequently they ask you to email the proposal and all attachments (although some attachments, such as your latest audited financials, can be mailed). Some funders provide a form for you to fill in at their website, and usually there is a limit to the number of words the form accepts. (This can be much more of a challenge than keeping a proposal to a specified number of pages.) Most of these forms can be saved so you can return to finish or correct something you didn't get to when you started the process. But a few require you to finish the entire form at one sitting—or do it over. You will need to know how to download or print the form from the website so you can fill it in by hand, then go back and fill it in online. Get familiar with the process; this kind of application will only get more common in coming years.

Am I Even Eligible to Apply for the Grant?

First and foremost, you must find out whether your organization is (or you are) eligible to apply for the grant described in the package. Somewhere deep in every application is a word or two (or 200) about eligibility. And even these words can be misleading!

Eligible applicants for a recent Safe Schools/Healthy Students grant are: "Local educational agencies or a consortium of LEAs that have not received funds or services under Safe Schools/Healthy Students in FY 1999, 2000, 2001, 2002, 2003, or 2004. Applicants are encouraged to check with the State Educational Agencies to verify their status as an LEA." (Local Educational Agency is not defined until the package's Appendix A: "A public board of education or other public authority legally constituted within a State for either administrative control or direction of, or to perform a service function for public elementary or secondary schools in a city, county, township.") The eligibility explanation goes on in considerably more detail, but it's clear enough: If you are a small, neighborhood-based, grassroots after-school program, this is not the grant for you—unless you work with several much larger partners. We'll discuss how to do this in Lesson 11.

To be eligible to apply for the Innovations in American Government award, a program must, among other things, "be administered under the authority of one or more governmental entities (federal, state, local, tribal, or territorial) and have been implemented 12 months prior to the date of submission and be currently in operation." Again, if you are a not-for-profit organization, you are not an eligible applicant unless there is significant government involvement and oversight.

Until January 1, 2009, the Independence Community Foundation made grants to "nonprofit organizations located within Independence Community Bank's geographic deposit area, defined as New York City, Nassau, Suffolk, and Westchester counties in New York, and Essex, Bergen Union, Hudson, Middlesex, Ocean, and Monmouth counties in New Jersey." In 2009, it shifted its geographic target area to concentrate its grants solely in Brooklyn, a single borough (county) within New York City. If your group is located outside of Brooklyn—say, in Connecticut, or even in Manhattan—you are just not eligible. It's not unusual for foundations and corporations to establish geographic target areas, and extremely rare for them to give grants to organizations outside those boundaries. And note that this foundation "does not fund individuals, make political contributions, or provide funding for religious purposes."

The National Endowment for the Arts Fellowships for Creative Writers are available to published writers of exceptional talent who meet certain very specific publication requirements. You can't apply for a fellowship in Creative Nonfiction Writing (even if you have an exceptional talent) if you have had your work published only in scholarly journals or if you've been published in or written only for student publications. The Fiction Writing Fellowships are for writers who have had at least five different short stories, works of short fiction, or excerpts from novels in two or more literary journals, anthologies, or publications; or a volume or collection of short stories; or a novella or a novel.

Because the Washington RAG's Common Grant Application format is intended for use with every foundation that accepts or requires it, eligibility requirements are not specified. Clearly, however, grant seekers who plan to use this format, or a common application form from another region, must go back to an individual foundation's website, annual report, and guidelines to be sure that they are eligible for grants from that foundation.

As you read the eligibility requirements, you can look back at the exercises you completed earlier. Are you a government agency or a local educational agency? Are you a not-for-profit organization, with proof of your status? Are you located in the specified geographic area? Are you a talented individual who has managed to get 48 or more pages of poetry published in the last seven years?

If you are clear about who you are but can't make heads or tails of who you should be in order to compete for the grant (which sometimes happens with complicated requests for proposals from government agencies at all levels, but much less frequently with foundation guidelines), call the program officer whose name and telephone number, email address, and/or fax number appear in the package and ask about your eligibility. Sometimes you will have to address written questions to a fax number or email address, or leave messages in a voice mailbox. But don't get frustrated. Call again (and again and again) if you don't receive a response in a reasonable amount of time—say, 48 hours. Don't be shy; you have a right to know. But don't be rude either. Remember, the people who develop, write, and oversee application packages and foundation guidelines take their work seriously and are likely to get offended if you call and say something like, "Why in the world would the Independence Community Foundation refuse to give grants in the Bronx? It's still New York City, right?" If this foundation ever does decide to make grants again in other parts of New York City, your organization will find itself very low on its list of priorities!

Does My Idea for a Grant Mesh with the Grantmaker's?

This is where proposal writers can get snagged. Proposals are developed in response to a request for proposals (RFP), request for applications (RFA), or guidelines issued by a grantmaking government agency or foundation. The RFP stipulates in no uncertain terms exactly what the grantmaker has in mind. A foundation's guidelines may be a lot less detailed and a little more flexible, but generally its priorities are equally clear. The grantmaker may not—no, almost certainly does not—care what you have in mind, unless it happens to mesh exactly with the terms of the RFP or guidelines.

You may need funding to start a chorus in a neighborhood day care center. You may feel passionately about the importance of getting children excited about music at a very early age. Unfortunately, the RFP insists that the program this organization wants to fund in day care centers must focus on computer technology and use of the Internet. You feel that the grantmaker is off base and would be wise to give money to the chorus. And you may be right. But don't give this grant any further thought. You may have research suggesting that little children are too young to fool around with computers—and should, instead, be singing. Don't bother. Not only will your grant be rejected, the program officer will think you are unable to read instructions, and this will put you at a serious disadvantage the next time you happen to apply.

If you want to discuss your point of view with the grantmaker, it is reasonable to call and ask whether or not there are plans for issuing RFPs for music anytime soon—and you can explain how excited you and your colleagues are about a children's chorus. For federal and some state and local grants, there is a comment period during which you can express your opinion about their proposed guidelines. Furthermore, throughout the year, you (or, preferably, a coalition to which your organization belongs) are entitled to talk with elected officials and government agency representatives about needs that you see for your community or your target population.

In its application package, the Safe Schools/Healthy Students Initiative explains that successful applicants' comprehensive plan, when implemented, will provide students, schools, and families with a network of effective services, supports, and activities that help students develop the skills and emotional resilience necessary to promote positive mental health, engage in prosocial behavior (a term not defined in the appendix), and prevent violent behavior and drug use, among other things. Does your school district just want to establish a simple drug prevention program, or are you prepared to work collaboratively with a large group of local government agencies and not-for-profit organizations? Don't proceed without asking this important question or you'll end up wasting a lot of time.

The Independence Community Foundation makes it clear that "priority is given to programs or projects that demonstrate a high level of community involvement, have strong, creative leadership, and exhibit thoughtful strategic plans." It "favors organizations that effectively leverage other resources, providing funds to groups that work closely with other nonprofit organizations." The guidelines brochure also describes the kinds of project that would be considered for funding, under several broad program categories: neighborhood renewal; education, culture and the arts; and community quality of life. If your organization is interested in such funding, and if you meet the other priorities, you may go ahead and send a letter of inquiry (we'll get to this in a minute).

What Kinds of Projects Has the Grantmaker Funded Recently?

The *Foundation Directory*, among other references, generally lists the amounts of major grants given by a foundation in a recent year, and the names of organizations that have received them. Government websites often list the winners of recent competitions. Application packages and funding guidelines also may mention past projects that have been funded by the grantmaker, especially if a foundation includes application information in its annual report. The annual report may organize grants into topics and include a brief description of the programs funded and the amount of funding. As discussed earlier, every private foundation and public charity is required to file an annual tax report (Form 990 or Form 990-PF, depending on how the organization is set up). The forms generally are just called 990s. They list the principals of the foundation,

"WE'LL BE ON TIME EVEN IF IT
MEANS WORKING STRAIGHT THROUGH
TWO EXTENSIONS TO THE DEADLINE."

the foundation's resources, and its expenditures. Most foundations list the names of organizations or individuals that received grants, and the amounts awarded; some also describe the project for which the grant was awarded and a contact person. Some include projects for which grants have been approved but not yet paid (such as the second year of a two-year grant).

The Innovations in American Government program package, available on the program's website, not only provides tips but also includes two winning proposals that applicants would be wise to read carefully. It always makes sense to check out a grantmaker's website when you are thinking of applying for a grant, because you never know what useful information you'll find that isn't in the application package.

How Much Money Is the Grant for, and Will It Cover My Expenses?

Proposal writers are often so excited about their projects that they lose sight of the sad truth that grantmakers do not have an unlimited amount of money to hand out, especially when there is a downturn in the economy (because income from investments drops or tax revenues are down). Most grant announcements stipulate the approximate amount of funding that will be awarded. Some announcements just tell you what the total amount will be and approximately how many grants will be given, and let you do the math. Others give a maximum possible award or an estimate of the average award. Some, especially foundations, leave it to you to assess what a reasonable request will be.

Looking back at our sample packages, the Safe Schools/Healthy Students Initiative will provide up to $3 million for urban local education agencies for a 12-month period, up to $2 million for suburban LEAs for a 12-month period, and up to $1 million for rural LEAs and BIA (Bureau of Indian Affairs) schools for a 12-month period. That's a lot of money, so it's worthwhile to read the entire application package to learn how to "determine your urbanicity," among other hints. Somewhere on those pages are explanations of "required partnerships with local law enforcement, local public mental health, and local juvenile justice," "safe school environments," "minor remodeling of school facilities," and so forth.

If you feel that the various descriptions, definitions, warnings, suggestions, and hints are unclear after several readings and discussions with colleagues; if you took advantage of the audio teleconferencing opportunity for this application; and if you visited the Safe Schools/Healthy Students website and still don't get it, call or email the contact person listed in the application package. Don't try to guess what an "allowable activity" is—or, for that matter, what anything else is—because the likelihood is that you'll guess wrong!

The Innovations in American Government program awards five winners $100,000 each after a challenging five-round competition cycle. The National Endowment for the Arts clearly states that fellowships for creative writers are for $20,000.

The Independence Community Foundation doesn't specify the maximum grant it will award, but describes different procedures for proposals requesting $500 and under (groups can use a short form), and for those seeking $50,000 and over (the latter must be approved by the board of directors, and the process may take longer than for smaller grants). This gives you a clue that large grants are possible, but if you've never received a grant from this foundation before, you may want to be fairly modest in your request.

You may be tempted to ignore the amount of money that the grantmaker wants (or can afford) to give. After all, you need $50,000 and you can make a good case for why the project costs that amount. But think about it. If you told your daughter you were going to give her a generous graduation gift of $20,000 for a new car, and instead of kissing your feet she informed you that the pricey convertible that she desperately wanted cost twice that, how would you react?

Do I Have to Answer All Those Questions?

The short answer is yes. Many grant applications include a list of questions or topics that the applicant is expected to address in a specific number of pages—sometimes a specific number of pages for each question. Some requests for proposals even restrict the number of words per question. The first round of the Innovations in American Government application asks this question: "Describe the program. What problem(s) does your program address? What is the innovation? Please emphasize the results your program has achieved." And all this crucial information must be covered in no more than 500 words.

The grant proposal questions can be simple or complex. The Safe Schools/Healthy Students Initiative's first item, Community Assessment, is a four-part question, with each part being worth a certain number of points that add up to 15. In the first part of the first question, the applicant is expected to discuss the extent to which "specific gaps and weaknesses in services, infrastructure, opportunities, and/or resources have been identified and will be addressed by the proposed project and the nature and magnitude of those gaps are based on quantitative and qualitative data for the district, students." Whew! It may seem like a tough question, but with careful reading you should be able to respond easily enough without needing a tranquilizer.

The Independence Community Foundation, like many foundations, requires a preliminary letter of inquiry and accepts proposals only if the letter of inquiry receives a positive response (essentially a personalized request for a proposal). If the proposal is requested, the foundation's website offers very detailed suggestions about what should be included in the seven-page narrative: a proposal summary describing the organization, the project, the grant amount being requested, and the grant period; organizational information, including the organization's history and mission, population served, current programs, recent accomplishments, and details about staff; program and project information, including five specific items that must be described completely and in detail; information on collaborations or partnerships for the project; a description of the evaluation process; and a list of required attachments.

We'll say it one more time: You must answer every question or address every topic that is included in the application. Not only must you answer every question, you would be wise to outline your proposal with subheads that reflect each question to make it clear to the reader that you are very responsive to the funder's interests and concerns and that you have answered all the questions. In Lessons 6 and 7, we address the challenges of writing clear, well-organized responses to funders' questions.

Many government requests for proposals, including the Safe Schools/ Healthy Students application format, contain a description of the criteria the agency will use to score the proposals, and often assign a specific number of points for each section of the proposal. The funding agency obviously considers a section that is assigned a large number of points to be more important than a section with fewer points—but every point counts; in fact, every *fraction* of a point counts. In most government programs, grants are awarded starting with the proposals with the greatest number of points and are awarded to each successive proposal until the money runs out. So you can see that when there are hundreds or thousands of proposals for a particular grant, you want to get every fraction of a point that you can. We suggest allocating the pages in the narrative roughly in proportion to the number of points to be given for that section (unless the application package gives you different instructions). For example, if the question asking you to explain the community's need for the project is worth 10 points, and you're allowed 20 pages for the proposal narrative, consider allocating about two pages—10 percent—to the need section.

When one of us first started writing proposals, she actually thought it was fine to leave out the answer to a question asked by government funders—especially if it was only part of a two-part question or only worth a small number of points—because there were so many convoluted questions. The first request for proposals to which she ever responded asked for a complicated evaluation plan worth five points. She figured that without the five points her excellent proposal would still get 95 percent, which was a good score. Because she didn't really know how to write an evaluation plan for a government grant proposal, she just left it out. Needless to say, she did not win that grant.

Another serious mistake is to change the order of the questions. We actually have seen a proposal with a small box at the top saying: "In order to explain my program in the best possible way, Question 1 will be moved down to become Question 7. Question 7 will now be Question 3." One of the authors of this book is a former teacher—and self-anointed test constructor extraordinaire. She would not have been at all pleased if one of her junior high students had reorganized her examination. She would have tried to like the child, to find the self-confidence and proactive resourcefulness appealing. But she is nearly certain that she would have resented the student and made every effort to give him or her an extremely low mark both on the test and in the class. We all have our pride. The people who write the RFPs and guidelines are proud of their documents. Keep that in mind during every minute you spend on the proposal writing process.

What If There Are No Real Questions in the Application Package or Guidelines?

Some funders describe what they want you to tell them without asking specific questions, or suggest, sometimes in a seemingly casual way, what they would like to see in a proposal. In one foundation's recent annual report, the following paragraph constituted the grant application:

> We are interested in learning as much as possible about the applicant. This includes budget (past, current, projected), audited financial statements, an IRS letter explaining tax status, names and occupations of trustees, and examples of past accomplishments. The individual project proposal should include, in addition to the planned work, a budget, expected outcomes, plans for evaluation, background of those involved and a statement of plans for future support. The main body of the application should not exceed 15 pages. A one-page summary is required.

Take these instructions literally and include everything the funder asks for, in an order that is as close as possible to the order in which the instructions are given.

Sometimes a grantmaker will indicate that a specific application form is not required, but that one (like the Washington, D.C., RAG's common grant application or the New York/New Jersey Area common application form) will be accepted. It's probably a good idea to follow the outline of the "accepted" form, even if you don't have to use the form itself. It will ensure that your response touches on all of the topics that the funder expects to see.

Try a Letter of Inquiry. If a funder does not set forth guidelines, instructions, or specific questions, you may want to initiate contact through a letter of inquiry (LOI). Like the abstract, which we discuss in Lesson 16, this is a brief summary of your organization, its mission, the need in the community that you want to address, the program you want to implement, its total cost, and the amount you are requesting from this funder. In this letter, you should explain why you are writing to this particular funder; talk about the ways in which it appears that your program fits into the funder's overall interests (which should be clear from its annual report or list of grants already awarded). Follow up with a phone call.

Some grantmakers, especially foundations, require you to submit a letter of inquiry before you submit a proposal. If they accept the letter, they will request a full proposal. This process will be spelled out in the foundation's guidelines, and you must respond appropriately.

Keep in mind that the abbreviation LOI refers to both letter of inquiry and *letter of intent.* The latter, a statement that you plan to apply for a grant, is requested by some funders, especially federal agencies, but also some other government agencies and foundations, to determine approximately how many applicants they may hear from and therefore how long the review process will take or how many reviewers they will need to hire.

What Else Is in the Application Package?

Background Information. Some grant applications contain discussions of research on the topic or a historical perspective that explains why the RFP has been developed and why funds have been earmarked for a certain kind of program. The Safe Schools/Healthy Students application, which was first issued around the time of the 1999 deadly attacks on students at Columbine High School in Colorado, explains that significant funding has been provided to "local educational, mental health, social services, law enforcement, and juvenile justice agency partnerships to implement various activities, curriculums, programs and services that constitute community-specific comprehensive plans aimed at youth, violence prevention, early intervention, and healthy childhood development." The Innovations in American Government package points out that the program "strives to identify and celebrate outstanding examples of creative problem solving in the public." And the Department of Education grant described in the opening remarks box at the beginning of this lesson clearly explained what the department meant by "out-of-school youth," as the novice grant writer would have seen if she had done more than speed-read through the application.

Format and Other Instructions. No government grant application package—nor those from a fair number of foundations—would be complete without dire warnings about sticking to a page limit, font and margin size, deadline, number of copies that must be submitted, and instructions about where to send the proposal. These details do matter! When the grantmaker specifies type size and margins, it's for the good of the people who will be reading the proposal. Some reviewers may read dozens of 50-page proposals in just a few days. You do not want to irritate them by giving them eyestrain from type that is too small. Yet one of us has seen a federal proposal in which the writer tried to meet the page limitations by typing all the way to the edges of the pages (no margins at all) and using a tiny typeface that needed a magnifying glass to be read. It wasn't funded.

The Safe Schools/Healthy Students application package includes a full page devoted to format requirements, and instructs applicants to submit one original (signed in black ink) and two unbound copies. All pages should have printing only on one side. All pages must be consecutively numbered—using the style 1 of 40, 2 of 40, and so on. The program narrative section may not exceed 40 pages in length. A "page" is 8.5 inches by 11 inches, on one side only, with 1-inch margins at the top, bottom, and both sides. The text must be presented in 12-point Courier New font. And the requirements go on and on and on, leaving nothing to the proposal writer's imagination. Another RFP we've just seen actually shows examples of spacing that is not double spaced and fonts that are not 12 point to show the applicant what will be rejected.

When you are studying the application package, note especially things like the deadline instruction that the application must be "postmarked by" or "received by" a certain date. If a submission must be received by a certain date, you have less time to prepare the proposal than you do for one that must be postmarked on that date. And if you do not follow the instructions exactly, your proposal will be disqualified from consideration. We hope we've stressed this sufficiently (but we'll say it one more time): Details matter, even if they seem trivial.

Most of the National Endowment for the Arts application package is a dire warning.

- Dire Warning 1: An individual may submit only one application per year. Multiple applications will be rejected.
- Dire Warning 2: You are not eligible to apply if you have received two or more Creative Writing Fellowships.
- Dire Warning 3: Late, ineligible, and incomplete applications will be rejected.
- Dire Warning 4: In the event of a major emergency that affects a large number of applicants for an extended period of time (e.g., multistate power outage or a natural disaster such as a hurricane) the chairman of the National Endowments for the Arts may decide to adjust the application deadlines. If this occurs, it will be announced on the Arts Endowment website.

The instructions go on and on in that scary vein until an applicant gets the picture: Do it right or don't do it at all.

The Independence Community Foundation tells you at the very beginning of its guidelines that a proposal should be no longer than seven pages in length, not including attachments. The Innovations in American Government program not only specifies the number of words the applicant can use to answer the questions but accepts online applications only—no paper applications are accepted.

We cannot emphasize strongly enough the importance of reading the application packages carefully and following every directive, answering every question, sending every attachment, even if you think something is absolutely ridiculous. We sometimes think that grantmakers are testing applicants to see if they know how to read, how to follow instructions— to see if potential grantees can be trusted with vast sums of money. You can't blame the funders for that, can you?

Pop Quiz

True or False?

1. Grant application packages come in various shapes and sizes, but they all contain the same basic information.

2. Don't ever call a program officer to ask a question about the application package. He or she is not permitted to provide any information to grant seekers.

3. Most grant applications will have at least one question that will not pertain to you or your organization. You are not expected to answer every question.

4. When a grant application package lists eligible applicants, it is just a suggestion. This is America: All organizations are eligible to apply for all grants.

5. If you need more money than a foundation or government grantmaker is providing, it makes good sense to try to persuade the program officer

(in your grant proposal) to give you what you need. You'll never know unless you try.

Just for Fun

Just for fun (yes, we call this fun!): Write a three-page proposal to a foundation about the project you identified earlier, using all the elements that we have indicated should be included. You're on your own for this one. There's no right answer.

LESSON 4:
Getting Ready to Write a Grant Proposal

Although grant seeking is a process that is similar in many ways for non-profit organizations, local governments agencies, and individuals, as we worked on this lesson we came to realize that differences can mandate somewhat different kinds of preparation. For example, nonprofits are less likely than government agencies to have unionized employees (though some do). Civil service regulations involve procedural requirements for hiring or transferring staff, whereas nonprofits have greater flexibility. These differences are addressed by dividing this lesson into three sections, one for nonprofit organizations, one for local government agencies, and one for individual grant seekers. Keep in mind that this division is somewhat arbitrary. For example, the complaint about having no time to pull information together for a proposal is heard no less in government agencies than in nonprofits, no less in large organizations than in small ones, and certainly no less from busy individuals who may be faced with application packages several inches thick. Also keep in mind that many proposals from universities for grants to conduct research may reflect the requirements for both foundation and government proposals, so if you are submitting such a proposal, you may want to read both sections.

IF YOU'RE A NOT-FOR-PROFIT ORGANIZATION . . .

OPENING REMARKS

As I did so often when I was a consultant for nonprofit organizations, I told the director of a teen pregnancy prevention program that it would cost her agency a lot less if her secretary pulled together all the documents I would need for the federal grant proposal that I was writing for the organization. But it turned out that the director didn't have a secretary. As in so many nonprofits, it was a small office, and everyone working there did everything. Staff members were getting ready for a board meeting. Nobody had the time to pull together the materials I needed, so I had to charge them for the time I spent going through their files and setting up a separate folder with copies of these materials. They could have saved that money with a little prior planning.—ASF

LEADING QUESTION
There's Always a Crisis to Deal with in This Place.
Who Has Time to Put Together a Proposal?

The answer is that everyone has time to do what it takes to write a proposal, though you may not realize it. Every organization or program has its own rhythm. Every single one has times when staff feel they never get to go home; every single one has times when everyone can sit back and take a deep breath. Some organizations are busiest during the summer, when they run their day camps. Some are busiest in September, when school and after-school programs start. Some are busiest around the holidays, when staff organize special meals for homeless people or when clients are feeling especially lonely or depressed. But for other organizations, holidays can be slow times because clients, or their families, are away.

DISCUSSION

It's a good bet that any slow time your organization may have will not occur during the few weeks before the proposal is due. That's why you feel as if you never have time to deal with a proposal, and that's why we rec-ommend so strongly that you begin now to prepare for that perfect fund-ing opportunity that is bound to come along when you are busiest and most overwhelmed.

In Lesson 15 we talk about demonstrating your organization's capabil-ity to handle a grant if you get one. Many of the same suggestions apply to preparing for a grant proposal—and preparation now will make it eas-ier to demonstrate your capability then. Here's how to start: On one of those slower days, when you're not racing around putting out fires, assem-ble a folder of materials about your organization, its financial status, and its staff. For most of the items you probably will just need to rummage through your files and make a copy for the background folder. For others you may need to do a bit of writing. We're not saying you will need to use all of the documents described here for any particular proposal—almost certainly you won't—but it will save you a lot of time if you have them available to draw from or submit as you need them. If you keep as much of this information as possible in your word processing files, you can just copy or cut and paste when a proposal is due. For example, when you get a résumé by email and hire an applicant, just save the résumé to a folder in word processing. That way it can be updated quickly when you need to submit it. And keep every proposal, every letter, and every budget spread-sheet for possible use in the future.

Different grantmakers require different documentation. Some of the items we mention may have to be submitted with the application; some must be available by the time a grant is awarded; some may not be part of the application itself but will be important in preparing a narrative. Whether you are a not-for-profit, a government entity, or a local educa-tion agency, you should have the relevant and most up-to-date version of these documents on hand before a funding opportunity becomes avail-able. For example, all incorporated not-for-profit organizations have a board of directors or board of trustees. If you haven't updated the list of board members recently, do this during one of those quiet periods. All types of organizations will need updated job descriptions of key staff and the most current résumés. You also will need local, citywide, and school district demographics and other data that are as up-to-date as possible. We'll talk about this in Lesson 8.

Among the documents that may be required or useful for an application are the following:

- **Agency mission statement.** Some foundations will be puzzled if you don't have one, and many application forms usually ask for it. If you don't have one, start writing.
- **Certificate of incorporation** as a not-for-profit organization. Almost every grantmaker requires that you submit this with an application or proposal.
- **Most recent 501(c)(3) letter** or other proof of tax-exempt status. This is another document that usually has to be submitted with a proposal.
- **Employer Identification Number** (EIN).
- **DUNS Number.** Dun & Bradstreet assigns a number (a Data Universal Numbering System number) to every organization that applies for this identification number. This is required for all federal applications and increasingly requested by other government funders. You can apply online (https://eupdate.dnb.com/request options.html). This takes about a month, so if you are preparing a federal grant application and need the number immediately, call 866-705-5711 to get the number within a day or two. You will be asked for several pieces of information, including the organization's legal name, address, web address, name and title of the individual authorized to sign legal documents, purpose of the organization, and so on.
- **List of board members,** including name and home address, place of employment, and position. Many grantmakers ask for this basic board list. For some funding opportunities it is also necessary

to indicate race/ethnicity and gender; for some you may need to show their other organizational affiliations.

- *Organization chart,* showing the overall organization structure, reporting arrangements, etc. Larger organizations may need a chart for each major department.

- *Job descriptions for all positions.* When you plan a new program, create job descriptions, whether you plan to fill these positions with current staff or hire new people.

- *Number of full-time and part-time staff members, and number of regular volunteers.* Sometimes these numbers do not change much from year to year, but be sure there is someone in your organization who updates the information regularly.

- *Current résumés of managers and key staff.* "Key staff" means anyone who has responsibility for a program. For most funders this includes managers and supervisors, but occasionally includes all staff members involved with the program. You receive the résumés anyway when someone applies for a job; you may as well keep them on file. But be sure the résumés reflect experience at your organization as well as what they did before they came; ask all staff to submit new résumés each year or each time they are promoted or change positions.

- *Brief "biographies" of key staff.* In addition to résumés, it is worthwhile to have a document in your files that gives a one-paragraph summary of the background and experience of the executive director and heads of all departments. This is requested instead of résumés by some grantmakers, and should be updated regularly.

- *Most recent (current and previous year) overall organization budget and individual program budgets.* If you don't develop budgets like this each year, you should.

- *Auditor's report* for the most recent and previous fiscal years. Again, if you don't have a yearly audit, you should. We know it costs money and time you don't feel you have. And you may have received minor grants without going to this trouble. But if you want a funder to take your organization seriously, it's absolutely critical.

- *Annual report,* if you publish one.
- **List of all current funding sources, and potential sources of matching funds.** It may help to have a two-year chart showing how much you've received each year from each source. A simple spreadsheet is sufficient.
- *Floor plan* showing access for people with disabilities, or description of plans to accommodate people with disabilities if the facility is not readily accessible. It is rare that you will actually have to submit this document, but you may be asked to describe the facilities available for a program and to show that you have the ability to accommodate people with disabilities. If you cannot do this, you should be able to describe other programs in the community that do. For example, if your school isn't accessible to children with physical disabilities, you may explain that a newer school, designed to be barrier free, accepts all children in the district with this need.
- **Personnel policies and procedures** demonstrating compliance with Equal Employment Opportunity Commission requirements, Americans with Disabilities Act, Drug-Free Workplace, and so on. If you do not have such policies and procedures in place now, you will need them as your organization grows. Borrow and modify examples from similar organizations to make it easier and less time-consuming to put these in place. A board member may be willing to help with this. And have an attorney look over the document to ensure that all current regulations are addressed.

In addition to specific documents, lists, and charts, it is useful to put together some boilerplate materials (paragraphs that can be used repeatedly, with small modifications for a particular grantmaker) in the form of brief narratives. Among these items, include:

- **Your organization's history.** A paragraph or two about when and how the organization started and significant milestones in its history. This "boilerplate" can be used over and over, with modifications to emphasize different elements of your growth (when you started programs for seniors, when you initiated youth programs) for different funders.

- **Current programs.** A paragraph or two about each program you operate, including a description of the population it serves, objectives, and any demonstrated successes.

- **The community.** We'll address a lot of the kinds of information that might go into a description of the community when we get to Lesson 8, describing the need for a program in a proposal. The point here is that a lot of this information can be collected during those few quiet moments and developed as a set of paragraphs on the population, the schools, existing services and institutions like teen centers or hospitals, health issues and data, crime statistics, and other topics that you can pull out as you need them for a proposal. Remember that this information must be updated regularly; it can become obsolete in no time.

- **List of existing formal linkages** with organizations in the community, area, or city, and **letters of agreement** specifying how each organization participates or will participate in collaborative work with the others. In Lesson 11 we discuss funders' interest in giving grants to partnerships rather than to individual organizations, and you need to begin thinking about these things long before a funding opportunity appears. The letters of agreement may need to be updated periodically, but you can establish a basic agreement—for example, that a program for children and parents will refer to a counseling organization when a need is identified; or that a school will provide space and custodial services for an after-school program and that the program will provide snacks as well as activities; or that a church will provide a meeting room for the senior center, and the center will make its programs available to church members. You might keep a chart showing all the existing relationships with other organizations in your community.

- *Any recent needs assessments, program evaluation reports, and examples of forms or procedures* you use. As we explain in Lesson 12, grantmakers want to know that you're using their money effectively and that you are committed to evaluation. Most organizations do not have the resources to hire outside professionals for needs assessments or formal evaluations, but if you've ever been able to do this, be sure the documents are on file. Refer to them in any proposal when it's appropriate (that is, almost every one!). If you don't have any external evaluation documents like this to show, be sure you do have some indicators that you use to inform you about how well your programs are working. You probably should collect data and report at least once a year on every program you operate.

- *Recent publicity* (news clippings) and a *list of awards* to the organization, its programs, and its staff members.

IF YOU'RE A GOVERNMENT AGENCY OR SCHOOL DISTRICT . . .

OPENING REMARKS

When I started working for city government, an agency program manager told me that she wasn't allowed to write grants, except to apply for formula funds or certain entitlements. Her boss felt that if she had time to fool around with "pie in the sky proposals," he wasn't giving her nearly enough to do to keep busy.—EK

LEADING QUESTION

We're Entitled to Plenty of Formula Grants. Why Should We Bother with Proposals That Take So Much Time and Don't Even Bring in That Much Money?

Hey, come on. Every little bit of money helps the residents of every town, city, and state. And wouldn't (and shouldn't) the public be outraged to learn that a city agency didn't bother to pursue a competitive grant that would provide a sweeping rodent abatement program in a neighborhood overrun with rats because no one had the time—or the inclination—to write the proposal? And wouldn't (and shouldn't) the public be outraged if a county decided not to take the trouble to apply for a competitive grant that provided drug abuse prevention programs in schools or housing projects? Such grants provide funding that absolutely would not come to a locality in any other way. Yet unlike not-for-profit organizations, which understand the importance of grants to keep them and their programs afloat, municipalities, school districts, and other government entities too often view competitive grants as optional. Local government managers and staff are supposed to think about these grants only when they have nothing better or more pressing to do with their time.

It's easy to forget that municipalities, counties, and school districts are (or should be) major grant seekers. Many, many interesting and important competitive grants actually require a government agency to be the applicant, specifically excluding not-for-profit organizations or universities, for instance. Everyone knows that the business of government and schools is to provide services to citizens of all ages, dealing with emergencies that rear their heads (such as terrorism, hurricanes, blizzards, epidemics, or floods). And they must defend themselves to the public and the press when children can't read, garbage isn't collected, roads or levees buckle, murder rates soar, traffic is congested. But many local governments are constrained by the difficulty of bringing in enough tax revenues to provide the needed services and constantly raising taxes to meet new demands. This is never popular, if it's even possible. Grants can help.

Income Streams for Local Government

There are essentially four types of income that come to counties, municipalities, and school districts. Everyone knows about *tax levy funds*; these come from income taxes, property taxes, sales taxes, and so on. Money for *capital expenses* like school construction usually is raised by issuing bonds that a government entity has to pay off over many years out of its tax levy income. Other funds come from higher levels of government—state or federal. *Entitlement funding* is written into law, usually at the federal level. It must be spent on behalf of any individual (for instance, a person with the HIV virus) with qualifications specified in the authorizing legislation. The amount of money that the locality gets is based on the number of residents who qualify (thus this kind of funding also is called a *formula grant*). The formula for the grant might include, for example, the number of people with family incomes below a specified amount, the number of children in a school district whose parents' income is below a certain level, the number of elderly people living in poverty, or the number of people with disabilities. Examples are Medicare, Medicaid, and Social Security.

Discretionary grants, the focus of the present section, are available through a competitive process from a higher level of government at its discretion, depending on available funds. At the federal level, discretionary funding covers all government spending other than debt service and entitlements—including the military, the FBI, emergency management, housing, education, transportation, and health.

Discretionary grants of all kinds from higher levels of government can support local entities in providing services. The local agencies may in turn hire—meaning subcontract or issue grants to—not-for-profits to conduct arts programs, provide technology instruction in schools, beautify parks and open spaces, create health centers, develop interesting activities for senior citizens, run after-school programs, and many other services. For successful grant seeking, local governments and schools have to plan ahead—just as not-for-profits do. Competition for grants pits the Los Angeles Police Department against the New York City Police Department and the Indianapolis Police Department; it pits the Des Moines Health Department against the Boston Health Department. At the present writing, the federal deficit is higher than it has ever been, while demands for military expenses and disaster recovery are soaring. This means that federal grants to states and localities will become even more competitive than they have been for all kinds of discretionary funding. And because these grants are competitive—not entitlements, not based on formulas—they require a tremendous amount of the kind of work and homework we are stressing in this book. And sometimes a culture change is required as well. Winning competitive grants—not just relying on formula funding—must become a major priority of school districts, cities, and states.

But Really—We're Not Kidding. When You Work for the Government or the Schools, There Just Isn't Time!

Sure, there are commissioners, superintendents, and other leaders in government and education who claim that if their staff members have time to be thinking about grants, they probably don't have enough to do. This is silly, of course. Every time a worker recognizes a need or gap in services that isn't covered by the budget, that person should be thinking about programs and grants to address the problem; it is, or should be, part of the job description. And the more time staff members spend thinking about and getting ready to write a grant proposal, the more likely they are to win the grant to supplement other local money.

One important way to make sure there is time for a grant proposal is to use slow periods to develop boilerplates (material that can be used again and again) for much of the text and supplementary material that a

proposal will require. In order to be able to spend precious time developing the program for a grant, you should collect and organize the following
information and update it regularly:

- *Overview of your locality,* including the number of residents,
  methods of governance, description of who the local elected officials are, crime and health statistics, immigrant information,
  unemployment rates, number of city workers, unions, and accomplishments. When one of us submitted a grant proposal for
  the City of New York to a large national foundation, she was
  shocked to learn (too late, unfortunately) that although the foundation was located only 90 miles from New York City, the lead reviewer was a consultant from the Northwest who did not know
  that the city is divided into five boroughs and that the mayor and
  the borough presidents don't necessarily see eye-to-eye. All the
  reviewers were so confused about who was in charge of what that
  they couldn't appreciate the enormous effort that had gone into
  building a workable partnership among normally warring parties.
  They kept asking questions such as, "Who's responsible for garbage collection—the mayor or the borough president?" "Where
  does the sanitation commissioner fit into the mix?" As a result,
  we developed a concise two-page description of the political, geographic, and ethnic characteristics of the city that can be used for
  every major proposal.
- *Information about the various neighborhoods or sections of the
  locality,* for example, the number of residents, age and family
  composition, ethnicity, crime and health statistics, and needs.
- *Overview of the school system,* including, for example, form
  of governance, number of schools, number of students, structure
  of the system, number of children eligible for free meals, school
  and district performance, number of children receiving special
  education services, and the types of services they receive.

- *Specific neighborhood/district/school information* (e.g., reading scores, math scores, dropout rates, children with language problems, attendance data, and incident reports).
- *Overview of the particular agency* you work for—and for which you will write proposals (e.g., police, transportation, health). Include the agency structure and mission, overall budget, staffing and "lines," leadership, responsibilities, achievements/existing grants, gaps in services, and awards.
- Gather *résumés of key staff members* and keep them up-to-date.
- It is also a good idea to develop a clear *organization chart* for your agency. Then for each proposal you write, it is easy to plug the proposed program into the existing organization chart showing just where and how it will fit into the organization. Show to whom the grant-funded staff (if there is any) will report and how the program will be an integral part of the agency's business.

Unlike not-for-profit organizations, government agencies and school districts are required to follow very stringent procurement and hiring regulations. While most not-for-profit organizations can hire whoever they feel is the best qualified or the best fit for a grant-funded program (subject, of course, to equal employment laws), governments also must be sensitive to accusations of favoritism, union issues, seniority issues, and other concerns that should be addressed before applying for a grant. If an agency wants to collaborate with a particular not-for-profit on a grant, it may still have to go through some kind of formal bidding or other procurement process. This means that timing and communication are important, and tricky. In order to be ready to write a proposal, the agency will have had to qualify potential partners first; these organizations will have to go through the qualification process knowing that funding may not in fact be forthcoming.

Many cities have been working on streamlining the procurement and hiring processes so they will be able to implement grants quickly and efficiently. New York City, for instance, has developed a negotiated acquisition process that speeds up contracting. There is nothing worse, as we've said before, than winning a whopping competitive grant from the federal government and not being able to spend the money because of bureaucratic roadblocks.

IF YOU'RE AN INDIVIDUAL GRANT SEEKER . . .

OPENING REMARKS

Two friends wanted to make a documentary about a 75-year-old woman—an animation filmmaker who had succeeded against very long odds in a "man's world" after her husband died. Neither friend was a documentary filmmaker, neither had ever written a grant proposal before, and neither was independently wealthy. But they had this dream of making a one-hour documentary. And somehow they did it . . . and had it shown at film festivals . . . and it won prizes! And on the way to making their movie, they found themselves engaged in a smaller project that won them an Emmy. Talk about building a track record!—EK

LEADING QUESTIONS
But I Don't Have All Those Documents That Nonprofits and Government Agencies Have; How Do I Prepare in Advance?

You may not think you have much in the way of documentation to keep in a file, but there are items you can prepare in advance for a proposal.

- **Résumé, curriculum vitae, or professional biography.** You probably have something like this if you've been around for a while; just make sure it's up-to-date. If you don't have one, prepare one immediately, and get help—and samples—from people in your field whom you respect.
- **A portfolio.** If you're an artist in any field, you probably have a lot of samples of your work—whether they're paintings, draw-

ings, poetry, photographs, essays, videos, or any other representative materials. If you haven't done so, select the very best of these to put into a suitable presentation (e.g., slides), and keep them in a portable file. And review and update your selections frequently.

- *Reviews.* You should keep absolutely every scrap of press coverage that you've received—but sort these scraps regularly so you can always show the best ones.

- *List of clients or partners.* If you've worked on projects with or for individuals or organizations, maintain an up-do-date list of the projects and the contact persons. They can serve as references, be considered as possible fiscal conduits for a grant you may receive, or just demonstrate a track record.

You Said Your Friends Got the Film Made?
And It Ended Up in Film Festivals? Please Tell Us How . . .

Basically, they followed the steps we discuss when we talk about nonprofit organizations and government entities. They developed a clear project proposal, describing who and what their film would be about, who the target audience was, what the point of view would be, and why they felt a film like the one they were proposing should be made. In addition, they had to produce a fundraising trailer, and because they had no money even for this, they were lucky to find people who were willing to give them in-kind contributions—of their skills, time, and materials—so the trailer could be made without the two of them going broke. They found that the funders weren't concerned about the quality of the images. They wanted to know if the film was about a compelling subject and whether the filmmakers knew how to put images together to tell a compelling story.

Then they did their homework on funding sources. They paid many visits to the Foundation Center library and searched for potential funders, using the library's reference materials. (Today they might use the center's Internet site; see Lesson 2.) They realized immediately that most foundations do not give grants to individuals, so they found a 501(c)(3) organization called Women Make Movies, which agreed, after seeing the fundraising trailer, to act as their fiscal conduit. The filmmakers refined their search for funders by reading annual reports to see if foundations ever funded documentary films, movies about women, or anything else related to their work. They read industry publications to see if available grants were mentioned. They also found government funding sources like the National Endowment for the Arts and National Endowment for the Humanities (which had a daunting application process), and the New York State Council on the Arts. Then they applied for everything and anything they could. And they got rejected everywhere . . . because they didn't have a track record.

But because of all their efforts and the contacts they made along the way, they got help from an unlikely source. Four filmmakers—including the subject of the film they wanted to make—had received grants to make very short animated films. Our friends proposed incorporating each of these four animated shorts in its entirety into individual half-hour programs in a two-hour series about the process of making animated films and the filmmakers' lives as artists. The result was an Emmy Award–winning series, Animated Women, which featured the four filmmakers and was first shown on PBS in 1997.

Now they had a track record . . . and now they started getting grants for their documentary. They told us that personal contact was extremely important. In each case when they received a grant, they had spoken directly to a program officer at that foundation.

Artists and scholars who need grant funds to write, study, or paint must do the same type of homework that these filmmakers did. Sadly, no one can do it for you. The funding sources and the types of applications you will need to submit depend on the nature of the work you plan to do. Most scholars wonder about applying for a Fulbright or Guggenheim Fellowship, but universities can assist in finding less-well-known sources of funding for study.

Similarly, artists, writers, filmmakers, and teachers can learn about grants, scholarships, fellowships, and awards in professional journals and newspapers—even in labor union publications—that they routinely read (or should be reading). Filmmakers, for example, might want to join AIVF, the Association of Individual Video and Filmmakers. Once again, as much as we wish this weren't so, no one can do it for you. As much as we'd like to tell all painters to contact the So-and-So Foundation to get a grant that will pay for you to work on your canvas, we can't.

What we can tell you is this: Look at our friends the filmmakers. Think creatively. Be resourceful. Hang on to your vision at all costs. Beg friends and relatives to help when necessary. Don't give up without a fight. Link up with a 501(c)(3) if possible. Read everything. Talk to everyone (nicely). And finally, prepare the best-developed and best-written proposal that is humanly possible using all the information we provide in these lessons.

Pop Quiz

True or False?

1. If my organization is a not-for-profit and I apply for a grant that's directed only to not-for-profit organizations, there's nothing special I have to do to prove we're eligible.

2. The process of applying for a grant for individuals is completely different from the process of applying for a grant for a nonprofit or a government agency.

3. Not-for-profit organizations only get foundation grants, never government grants.

4. Individual artists only get foundation grants, never government grants.

5. School districts should stick to the three Rs and leave grants to the not-for-profits.

6. In order to get a grant, an individual must have a 501(c)(3).

Essay Question

1. Whether you are a not-for-profit, a government entity, or an individual grant seeker, describe the three best ways to prepare yourself for a proposal in advance of a funding announcement.

FUNDERS' ROUNDTABLE I

In the preceding lessons, we looked hard at how to get ready to write a grant proposal—Okay, maybe that's an understatement. We looked more than hard at the preliminary work successful grant seekers need to do. Next, we wanted to see what our panel of grantmakers had to say about all this . . . preparation. Before we started talking about the basics of proposal writing and the components of a grant application, we asked the people who give grants to suggest ways that organizations could increase their chances of getting funded. We should warn you that funders' responses are as diverse as their organizations. There are certain things that every funder cares about and certain things that are unique to an individual. Do your homework!

Let's start with the groundwork.
Where do grantmakers think we should begin?
The funders' roundtable for Part I includes suggestions from our panelists about why and how grant seekers should do some homework (mainly, finding the funders who are the right fit for your organization and your project) before even thinking about writing grant proposals. It probably should be called the Guidelines Roundtable because we learned that grantmakers too often find that applicants haven't read a word about the foundation that receives their grant proposals—not the guidelines, the biography of the original donor that often appears on the foundation's website, the annual report, the names and projects of current and former grantees, or the composition of the board of directors. Some applicants don't even know the name of the current program officer (let alone how it is spelled). So most of the funders suggested a few ways not to get ready:

"Less than 10 percent of the proposals my foundation receives fit our guidelines—and the ones that don't fit are rejected," said one funder.

"Believe it or not," said another, "some proposals that come my way have cover letters addressed to the program officer who was here 10 years ago!" She tried not to let this fact affect her perception of the applicant but acknowledged that it did call into question the competence of the writer. "I've been in this job for more than two years and still get letters addressed to my predecessor," yet another funder said. "Doesn't it make sense to check the website or call the foundation and ask for the name—and correct spelling—of the foundation staff? It sure would save me a lot of aggravation and save the applicants from a subconscious blot against them."

"There's nothing worse a grant applicant can do than come out of left field, which means not being strategic," explained one of our panelists. "The way to make sure that our foundation is one that you can create a partnership with is by reading the guidelines."

"Less than 10 percent of the proposals my foundation receives fit our guidelines—and the ones that don't fit are rejected."

Can we talk? Are grantmakers willing (and able) to talk to grant seekers?

Not surprisingly, every foundation grantmaker we spoke to emphasized the importance of knowing the foundation's guidelines before applying for a grant, which used to be a much more difficult task before the Internet came into wide use. Some are willing to discuss those guidelines (and other matters) on the telephone or in email correspondence with prospective grantees, and some emphatically are not. Government grantmakers, on the other hand, have procedures established for contact with applicants who request it; they almost always will talk with you but what they can say is carefully circumscribed. They are required to operate in such a way that no group gets a leg up on any other group because of personal contact. We'll talk a little later about how they handle this.

We asked our panel of funders where they stand when it comes to chatting on the telephone. Here's what the foundation representatives had to say.

Some said, "Sure . . . give us a call." "Since we only fund projects that fit our guidelines," explained one program officer, "grant writers should do their homework, know the intricacies of the foundation, and give us a call—with a short verbal pitch. Ask, 'Can I take 5 or10 minutes of your time to find out if your foundation might be able to fund my project?'"

Another funder agreed. She takes calls from prospective grantees who have read the guidelines. "When someone calls and asks for five minutes of my time, I give it. I personally believe that program officers should be like guidance counselors."

"The telephone rings incessantly," another grantmaker explained, "but frankly, I'd rather that a group call to get clarification than waste its time—and my time—later on." But keep this in mind: "If prospective applicants call first to make sure we are the right foundation for their projects (which is fine), their letters of intent should reflect what we talked about beforehand."

"I personally believe that program officers should be like guidance counselors."

If you call and find out that a foundation is unlikely to fund your project or organization, don't send in a proposal anyway—mentioning the conversation in your cover letter—on the off chance the program officer or board or executive director will have a change of heart. The funder will surely wonder what part of "no" confused you. And that's not a good thing for your reputation in the funding community.

Be considerate of the person you're calling. "Speaking on the telephone is a bit of a 'workload issue.' I get about five calls a day from people who want to pitch projects—and each call lasts at least five minutes. Sometimes I wonder if my time could be put to better use reading the proposals. But we are responsive to callers," said a member of the panel. "With all those calls, though, I don't usually retain much information about the caller."

And others said, "Write . . . don't call." Most funders are not amenable to—well, that's not fair: simply don't have time for—phone contact. One panelist said, "We don't encourage personal contact. We just don't have time. We suggest that if you have something that looks like it will fit, send either a letter of inquiry or, better yet, a proposal."

Going back to one of our favorite themes, the panelists all agreed that grant seekers must do their homework (the word that nearly every funder used) before any contact and learn as much as possible about the foundation. "I don't take calls," said one of our panelists, "unless I have a piece of paper—a proposal or a letter of inquiry—in front of me that tells me there's room for additional discussion."

With government funders, when it comes to human contact, it's a (bit of a) different story. Government grantmakers generally have a great deal of contact with potential applicants, although much of it is systematic. One government funder explained that his agency has five or six bidders' conferences in all sections of the country. "These sessions give the public a chance to get to a senior staff member. And as a follow-up to bidders' conferences, questions and answers from all the sessions are compiled and made available on the Internet." But he added, "You can still call a program officer, and we are inclined to add new questions and answers online as they arise."

"We want people to call
if they have questions."

"When in doubt, ask.
You have nothing to lose."

Another government grantmaker said, "We want people to call if they have questions. We prefer that they talk with us and not waste their time giving us something that we won't fund or that won't work. We won't help them write, but we're always happy to talk." This funder explained that her agency has a process that differs from most government agencies. Instead of a single deadline each year, her agency uses a less common "rolling" deadline two or three times a year for the same grant program. This gives applicants time to develop a proposal, send a draft, and get feedback before the next deadline. But, the panelist said, "it has to be understood that just because you receive feedback, there's still no guarantee of success. The program staff are separate from the review process for a purpose: to ensure fairness."

One government panelist admitted that he doesn't have much time to talk to prospective grant seekers. "But I list my bartenders just in case someone is desperate to get in touch with me." (We *think* he was kidding—so we decided not to list the names of the bars he frequents after work and on weekends! But we know for a fact that he answers emails from home.)

"I list my bartenders just in case someone
is desperate to get in touch with me."

Yet another government funder suggests, "When in doubt, ask. You have absolutely nothing to lose." She reiterates that for government funders, "What you tell one [applicant] you must tell all. We'll give generic information freely—questions like, 'Is there a cash match or can we use xyz to make a match?' But more elaborate questions are harder to generalize about." She added an important bit of advice: "Check the agency website constantly. Agencies may create subwebsites for certain grants—and they can be a wealth of useful information."

But don't bother calling after the closing deadline for proposals. The review is considered confidential, and no information is given. This is to protect the review process, and to protect the reviewers from harassment. There's no point in calling because nobody will tell you anything. Of course you may call "if, after several weeks you haven't received a postcard or email saying that your proposal was received."

And still another government grantmaker offered a hint that applies to any funding phone call, whether to a foundation or government program officer: "Get your questions together, don't keep repeating yourself, and try to find a friendly person when you call. The truth is, though, there is a trend toward putting questions in writing these days. It seems like a more consistent way to get the information out to everyone."

Final thoughts on calling . . . Before we leave the question of whether or not to call, it might be useful to look at the reason for your call. Clearly the only telephone calls that are appreciated are intelligent, carefully thought-out questions that reflect a good knowledge of the foundation's or government agency's guidelines and mission. Calling just to say, "Hi, would you give us a grant?" is not a smart strategy.

If you have methodically done all your homework and still have a question about your eligibility, or about something that you didn't understand in the guidelines or request for proposals that may affect whether you submit an application, then by all means call. But if you are calling to chat up the funder to make an impression, it's probably not a smart move. Better to let your proposal or letter of inquiry or whatever else the funder wants to see do the talking for you. Sure, many funders will take your calls (and many won't), but they're busy people, just as you are.

And finally, a foundation grantmaker has this reminder: "We all talk to each other. So don't tell something to one funder and something different to another."

So just how important are the grant guidelines? (Don't mince words.)

In Lesson 2 we talked about the constraints grantmakers are under because of the way in which the donor set up a foundation, or because of the language of the law establishing a government grant. The grantmakers recognize those constraints and find it difficult to understand why applicants don't. We kind of understand the applicants' problem: In some locations, grant seekers are familiar with one or two foundations. They may be aware that their projects don't fill the bill for these foundations, but they don't know of any others. They may have an impulse to try to fit a round peg into a square hole because they can't think what else to do. But as you'll see in the panelists' comments, the better impulse is to do the research. Take the time. Don't send a proposal to a foundation just because you know it's there, or because you know that its director is a nice person. Our panelists were very clear about this.

"I don't want to reward people
who don't read the guidelines."

"I don't want to reward people who don't read the guidelines," explained one foundation funder. Another added, "So many applicants are so damned sure that they're the perfect partners for us . . . but they have no idea because they haven't read the guidelines. They're out in left field."

"I like to see evidence that grant seekers read the guidelines versus getting a very bad sense that they sent shotgun applications to everyone in the world. Show some thinking! It shouldn't just be about asking everyone for money," warned a panelist. "And another thing: Check out our application format on the web instead of using any format you can get your hands on." Another grantmaker had this advice: "Do homework. Get annual reports. See which groups have gotten funded. Look at the board members; you may find that the board chair is your uncle's best friend." In fact, "learn about our board," suggested another panelist. "We send the whole proposal to the board, so it makes sense for an applicant to know something about the members."

"Show some thinking! It shouldn't just
be about asking everyone for money."

"There's nothing that bothers me more than a proposal that has no business being sent to us," added a panel member. "We say that we fund in two counties—so why would someone send us a proposal from another part of the state?" Also he suggested, "Do research to see who we've funded. Don't just look at the guidelines, which could be broad—saying we support 'education,' for example. We do support education, but only middle schools these days."

"I'm a believer in relationship building. Get to know what my foundation does and work with the people we work with," one funder said. "I like to see evidence that applicants have a grasp of the focus of the foundation—and even looked at who our grantees are and paid them a visit."

Finally, one grantmaker managed to give us a bit of a shock. "Grant seekers should read the guidelines and if they don't see anything in the material that is similar to their project, don't send a proposal," she said. "Believe it or not," she added, "one applicant actually called and scolded us, 'You've made an oversight. You're not funding what our organization does!'"

Do you ever . . . well . . . not follow the guidelines?

"We've funded groups that don't fit our guidelines," said a foundation grantmaker, "if their work is addressing a clear, poignant, immediate need." A foundation funder pointed out that "there are exceptions to eligibility—where the applicant has a relationship with a board member, perhaps; but, in general, eligibility is about empowering certain groups—which is why we have an eligibility requirement in the first place."

"It is possible," said a member of our panel, "for the program officer to send a quirky idea to the foundation's board, as long as it is in the guidelines' ballpark." She described a grant to an individual, which normally is not within foundation guidelines. This individual's project, however, was connected to an interest of one of the board members and did relate directly to the foundation's interest in historic preservation, so she brought it to the board—and it was approved.

"It is possible—once in a blue moon—that you meet a person who is so smart that you make the program fit the guidelines," explained another funder. But one foundation grantmaker offered this wise reminder: "There is great diversity in the foundation world—so find the right fit."

"There is great diversity in the foundation world—so find the right fit."

While talking with the grantmakers about the importance of reading—and studying—guidelines, it became clear that there is no such thing as going overboard. Grantmakers mentioned everything from simply reading the guidelines, to visiting groups that already received grants from the foundation, to talking to people who know about and are known to the foundation. One moral of this story is that when it comes to doing guidelines homework, less is not more. A second moral is: Don't ever—not even if you think the program officer is kind and compassionate—suggest that the foundation change its guidelines in order to give your organization a grant.

What about government and large foundation grants . . . aren't your guidelines a little different?

As we said in Lesson 3, most government agencies and large foundations announce funding opportunities through a request for proposals (RFP) process that includes a detailed description of who is eligible to apply and what is required in the proposal. RFPs also include a detailed description of the scoring criteria for each section of the application. Reading, understanding, and adhering to the eligibility requirements and the scoring criteria are exactly the same as understanding and following the guidelines for a foundation—only more so. One federal funder explained, "We may see an incredible, creative proposal that we can't even review. We evaluate on the criteria in the application . . . The message is, develop the proposal in response to the requirements of the announcement. If you don't, it could well earn you a very poor score or even get the application tossed out before it's even read."

Furthermore, "Eligibility is nonnegotiable once the RFP is out."

"We may see an incredible, creative proposal that we can't even review. We evaluate on the criteria in the application."

"In a 'call for comments' (which can be found in the *Federal Register*) prior to the issuance of the RFP, you can put anything on the table."

Another government funder explained, "People applying for grants from the government have to be aware of authorizing language [the language given in the legislation creating the grant]. It's not our call who is or isn't eligible."

If you forget "the required certifications and licensures, the signature of the CEO—it seems minor—but it's required," noted one program officer, "then we have to exclude the proposal before it's reviewed."

Are big cities and small towns equally eligible for a grant?

"Although all cities and states may be eligible for a government or national foundation grant," one federal funder said, "large cities and states sometimes score higher because they know how things get done. Small places are often a little unsophisticated. One grant proposal I saw, for example, suggested that a clergyman and a secretary could run a million-dollar program alone." She offered a suggestion for smaller groups or smaller cities: "When applying for grants, don't be afraid of things that seem out of your realm—like doing an evaluation plan. Someone can help you, even if there is only a small junior college not too far away that has a graduate instructor who will work on your evaluation plan with you. There are always resources out there."

Another federal program officer explained that review committees are established specifically to reduce bias against any particular area, offset the lack of sophistication smaller locations may demonstrate, or overcome a lack of awareness by reviewers in some parts of the country about conditions elsewhere: "We pull together review committees from the types of area the proposals come from. For example, reviewers from Chicago would review applications from New York City."

How do the really little guys—grassroots organizations—get on the grant funding map?

Many small grassroots organizations are anxious to break into the grants process to start raising more money than they can get from membership dues and bake sales. We asked panelists to suggest how the grassroots groups can begin the process of successful grant seeking.

All the funders we spoke to acknowledged that small organizations are generally at a disadvantage when it comes to grant seeking. But one funder commented, "Certain foundations are willing to fund grassroots organizations—but the organizations need at least some fundraising track record." She suggested some strategies: "Figure out a way to show community support, recruit volunteers, document in-kind contributions to your organization [things other than money that are donated, such as meeting space and supplies], even develop a relationship with your local bank branch."

"Figure out a way to show
community support."

Another funder also looks for a track record: "I ask, 'What are they thinking, what is their leadership like, what kind of groundwork have these brand-new groups done? How well do they know their community? Are they open to talking to existing, established groups that are doing a really good job?' I check to see whether a new group actually follows up by contacting existing groups that I recommended. But, with all that, we don't fund a lot of start-ups."

Yet another grantmaking colleague agreed. "We suggest that grassroots organizations—especially small immigrant groups—talk to other groups to see what they are doing. We will give start-up grants (but the applicants should ask for a small amount of funding at the beginning) to do concrete projects, for instance, instead of for operating expenses."

A government grantmaker agreed that "small and new programs are disadvantaged. They often have a lack of sophistication about how to get things done. Occasionally there are start-ups funded, though," she added. "You just have to keep your eyes open for the announcements."

"We've given authentic grassroots organizations their first grants," said a foundation grantmaker. "But we give in a modest way to new and grassroots groups. For new groups we try to find and talk to contacts who know about them. It's risky. I wouldn't take a big financial risk but I would take a small one."

"If it's a start-up," said another funder, "it's hard to get in the door. But if we decide the organization is pretty good, we'll try to market it to other foundations. Then we'll suggest that they work with an organization that helps small groups get their 501(c)(3)s and do board development with them. If they show effort, we'll provide funding for these types of technical assistance activities."

"We love to help small groups.
They deserve a push."

Another grantmaker added, "We love to help small groups. They deserve a push. We're sympathetic about their size. Their proposals don't have to be glossy—they just have to tell a compelling story."

A member of our panel offered a good hint: "Foundations may not say directly that they fund grassroots organizations, but they may indicate that they fund 'seed grants' [grants, usually small, intended to get a project started], which may be a subtle message that grassroots organizations should apply."

The guidelines say that this grantmaker doesn't accept unsolicited proposals. Is there anything I can do?

Lots of small foundations (and a few large ones) say they do not accept proposals; their trustees usually allocate money to preselected organizations working in the donor's areas of interest. Funders were asked to give some advice about whether (and how) a frustrated proposal writer who has read the guidelines carefully and thinks that her program would be a perfect match might approach such a foundation. First, keep in mind that there seems to be a lot of effort by foundations to find the organizations from which to solicit proposals. One funder noted that, even though her foundation does accept proposals, and has clear guidelines for them, "90 percent of the proposals we fund are solicited by asking around. Who's doing good work in the area we're looking to support?" Another said, "Part of our job is to go out looking for people doing the kind of work we like to support."

Although in most cases there's not much you can do to persuade a foundation to fund you if it has its own pet causes, another panelist told us, "People fund people. Get the attention of a staff member or a board member. Send newsletters and other information about your work. Savvy individuals can make connections with people who can swing the door open for them."

"Part of our job is to go out looking for people
doing the kind of work we like to support."

"If foundations don't accept unsolicited proposals," said another grant-maker, "then a board member of your organization can call a board member of the foundation. If your board members don't know people on the foundation's board, you can send a letter just to say that we'd like to tell you what kind of work we're doing (acknowledging that you know the foundation doesn't accept proposals, of course, because you always want to show your deep understanding of those guidelines!)."

And when I do submit an application, do I need to know someone?

Many grant seekers worry that they'll be shut out of grant funding if they aren't lucky enough to know a board member, a program officer—or someone—at the foundation. We asked funders whether grant seekers need to know someone to have a shot at getting their proposals funded. The answer is, absolutely not.

Both government and foundation funders are clear that when there is an application process it's completely open. "No, you don't have to know anyone to get funded," promised one of our panel members. Even more encouraging, "One hundred percent of the grants we give are to groups we don't know," said another. "We accept unsolicited applications. That's where I live. I want to hear the idea I haven't heard before—like, 'I'm going to climb Mt. McKinley on my hands.' Every great organization or idea starts small . . . everyone starts with less capacity and less visibility."

"People think you have to know someone,
but you don't."

Another foundation grantmaker said, "We get a lot of proposals sent in cold. People think you have to know someone, but you don't." She does talk to other funders who know an applicant organization. "Or we'll talk to our grantees to ask them about an organization that has applied to us for funding. We actually rely on grantees to help us keep up with what is going on in the field."

And in case your uncle knows a board member and you think this will help you get a grant, one of our panelists had this observation: "At staffed foundations, it's not a good idea to make an end run around the program officer directly to the trustees. If you happen to know someone, 'cc' him or her. Strategic philanthropy is not supposed to be about who you know."

For government grants, do we need a letter from our elected officials to give us a chance?

We asked government funders whether a letter of support from an elected official would help or hurt. (We asked about the "hurt" part because we wondered if reviewers saw input from local political officials as pressure, rather than simply as support.) A panelist from the federal government said, "Every unit of government has protections of the procurement process, but we're all human and it can't hurt you. There are several levels of review. But the secretary has complete discretion on what grants are made. We have to maintain objectivity, but we have to maintain [geographic] balance as well. We had 160 applications [for a particular grant opportunity]. Even if all the best proposals had come from one state, we couldn't make all the grants there."

> ### "A letter wouldn't hurt—but it wouldn't
> ### help much, either."

Another government funder agreed that such a letter wouldn't hurt but said it wouldn't help much, either: "It's nice but doesn't do a lot of good." He offered this very technical analysis of the grants process for his program to show how objective it is and why support from a politician may not be particularly helpful: "The applications are read by a panel of three peers. The average panelist reads 15 applications over a four-day period. Eight sites, 2,780 applications received. Scores are fed into a computer, standardized to account for reader bias (the national standard deviation is 16)—too lenient, too severe—then rank-ordered, 1 to 2,780. We fund down the slate until the money runs out. There were 308 grants last year."

Whether you win or lose, a grant is not about "who you know." Although other factors (such as the resources available to a foundation or government agency) affect grantmaking decisions, the quality and substance of your proposal make the difference. Our panelists told us that if you do good work and manage to develop a good reputation in your field, among your clients, and in your community, local grantmakers will know and respond. They said over and over again that they want to fund organizations and individuals doing excellent and important work.

One other thing to keep in mind: Grantmakers may not want you to throw names at them, but they are interested in which other funders support you. Tell them. And encourage them to speak with those other funders about you. They will anyway!

Any other suggestions for preparing to write a proposal?

"Thoroughly understand what you are writing," suggested a government grantmaker. "Have a clear idea about what you want to do. Don't start thinking about it as you write . . . think things through before you write." Another government panelist said, "Don't assume anything. Reviewers don't know about your programs, and even if they did have knowledge they couldn't consider it. Like a jury. They can't consider anything but what's in the application, the words printed on the page." She also commented, "There is a skill, an art, to writing a proposal. Put yourself in the reviewer's chair."

"I like an application that's tight and clear and has a logic I can follow, from exactly what the need is to how they're going to respond to it, what they'll do, who'll be included," said a government panelist. "That clarity tells me they've really thought it through and that they're able to pull off what they say they're going to do."

"Our job is to look for good ideas, good things. We are actually looking for things to fund," said one panelist. Another added, encouragingly, "To make a credible 'ask' shouldn't be hard."

"I like an application that's tight and clear and has a logic I can follow."

"We are actually looking for things to fund."

Several funders offered these final thoughts and suggestions: "It's like dating—you're not going to meet your wife at the first party you go to" (so don't worry if you don't get a particular grant). "Try to write your proposal imagining yourself as the reader." "Find a way to make yourself known and appreciated through the written word. There are so many flat proposals—like white bread."

Part II will help you to write proposals that are nothing like white bread and more like 12-grain home-baked straight-out-of-the-oven loaves. But before we go on, we need to make a small digression to try to look at the big picture, as we've advised you to do.

What impact do disasters such as September 11 and Hurricane Katrina have on grantmakers and grant seekers?

In our first edition, as we were thinking about preparing to write a proposal and the need to put programs into a broader context, we wondered to what extent the attacks of September 11 had affected grantmakers' ability to sustain their regular priorities, and whether there was a lasting impact on nonprofit organizations and government agencies. For that edition we asked our panel of funders how—or if—the combination of the attacks on the World Trade Center and the downturn in the economy had affected their ability to give grants. For the second edition, we were concerned about the impact of 2005's natural disasters, such as the tsunami in Southeast Asia, hurricanes Katrina and Rita, and the earthquake in Pakistan, so we spoke with selected members of our funders roundtable about this and reached out to grantmakers on the Gulf Coast. We believe that the responses for the earlier editions are still relevant here. For the current edition, of course, we wanted to know whether the economic downturn has affected grantmaking, and in what ways. For those responses we refer you back to the Economic Summit on page xx. Regarding the other disasters, funders had this to say:

"We're finding new needs now, rather than noticing them right after September 11," said a funder. "And the weakened economy caused a 20 percent hit in corporate giving. In fact, the huge national funders aren't able to fund the large national policy groups that had always counted on their financial support."

"After 9/11 we set aside $10 million to help those with needs related to the attacks," said a national-foundation funder. "We haven't changed our grantmaking yet, but we are thinking about the issue of international peace and security more than we did before." Another foundation also set aside a special fund to address immediate issues after September 11. "We haven't received more proposals but we are hearing more tales of woe—especially from arts organizations. I'm shocked at the number of small arts groups there are. In the aftermath of 9/11, many of them postponed or cancelled their fundraisers. Now the groups are searching for new sources of funding. They are digging deeper to find what I call 'non-household-name' foundations." And one funder found that "since 9/11, requests for money are up two or three times over the number of requests we had in the previous year."

In response to Katrina, one funder in the New Orleans area said, "We didn't wait for proposals, because the local groups were so overwhelmed. We went out to the shelters, assessed the need ourselves, and made grants immediately, without proposals. Now we're back to our normal process, reviewing proposals and making grants bimonthly."

One important thing for grant seekers to keep in mind is the relationship you establish with the grantmakers. After Katrina we heard from funders, "We know who the great groups are—the ones who can handle the money in this situation."

PART II: IT'S FINALLY TIME TO WRITE THE PROPOSAL

IT'S ALWAYS A GOOD idea to view grant money as exceedingly scarce, even in flush economic times. In lousy economic times, it's critical to view grant money as almost nonexistent. The best advice we can give is that proposal writers need to understand at *all* times how the process of developing and writing a winning proposal really works. Preparing a grant proposal is a process; it is not just a simple matter of responding to a series of detailed questions and attaching a batch of forms and adding columns of dollar amounts. The grants process starts long before a funding opportunity appears. To be a successful proposal writer, you have to put your grant in perspective. You have to understand the mood of the country at the time you are submitting your proposal, because this affects how a reader will respond to your proposal. You have to understand the issues facing your city or town, and the concerns of philanthropy. You have to know the particular grantmaker you're approaching, whether it is a government or private funding source. And, of course, you have to know yourself and/or your organization, and be able to place your program in the context not only of your organization's mission but also in the context of what the community—and the grantmaker—needs and wants.

Each and every concept we discuss in this book is part of the "foundations of proposal writing." How should you view the grants process? What should you expect from the application process? What are the reasons for doing and not doing certain things? All these learnings, these intangibles, affect your chances to persuade grantmakers to entrust your organization with their precious dollars. Getting the funder to believe in your organization, to trust it, to feel sure that its leaders know what they're

doing . . . all go into the foundations of proposal writing. Getting a funder to recognize that you've thought things out, that you're not greedy,
that you're honest . . . all go into the foundations of proposal writing too.
That's why we begin this part with Lesson 5, highlighting some intangibles that are rarely talked about but are important to keep in mind as you
develop your program and frame your argument for funding it.

Lessons 6 and 7 focus on the actual writing of the proposal. Because
bad writing can undo all your hard work in preparing for a proposal, in
Lesson 6 we lay out some of our own admittedly idiosyncratic dos and
don'ts to ensure that the words you put on the page will communicate
what you want to communicate to grantmakers and not offend them. In
Lesson 7 we show you how to organize your proposal—while you deal
with the dreaded "blank page"—by creating an outline before you write a
word. In the succeeding chapters we go into more detail about the separate sections of the typical grant proposal.

Lesson 8 begins our discussion of the components of the proposal itself.
This lesson focuses on identifying and describing the need for your proposed program. Lesson 9 helps you figure out something that often stumps
all of us: how to describe the goals and objectives of your project. And
Lesson 10 continues with a discussion of how you can develop and describe the program in light of the objectives—and communicate all of
this to the grantmaker. Lesson 11 addresses a topic of interest to many
of our funders' roundtable panelists: collaboration as a way to strengthen
the program. Lesson 12 focuses on evaluation, another concept that is
hard for many organizations to master, and provides a few alternative
ways of dealing with this issue. Lesson 13 explains what it takes to convince a funder that your budget makes sense, and Lesson 14 addresses an
increasing concern of grantmakers: how you will sustain a program once a
grant runs out. Lesson 15 tells you how to persuade the funder that your
organization is amply capable of managing a grant if you get it. Lesson 16,
the last lesson in this part, pulls together all the bits and pieces of a pro-

posal that should accompany it—or not: the cover letter, the abstract, the table of contents, and the appendixes (attachments).

Closing this part, we present our third funders' roundtable, giving you a chance to hear the panelists discuss the importance and value of each part of the proposal.

LESSON 5:
Foundations of Proposal Writing

OPENING REMARKS

A few years ago, I was contacted by the State Department about the possibility of conducting a 90-minute workshop (from the U.S.) for AIDS educators in Botswana—they were desperate for grant funding. As I listened, though, I realized that I was being asked to spend 80 minutes of the workshop discussing where the educators could find grant funding and only 10 minutes on how they should develop and write a successful grant proposal. This is backward! For some reason, the workshop planners saw writing a grant proposal as simple as filling out an application for a credit card.

What they didn't realize is that there is actually a whole way of thinking, a body of information, that makes up the foundations of proposal writing. To be successful at proposal writing, you have to have certain "understandings" that illuminate and clarify the grants process, and you have to think of each proposal as part of an overall process of program development, planning, and evaluation.

If you don't really "get it," finding funding sources won't be nearly enough.

—EK

LEADING QUESTION
What Are the "Intangibles" That Don't Appear in the Application Package . . . and Why Are They Left Out?

First and foremost, as we've said often and will say again, before designing a program or writing a word, it is important to know as much about the grantmaker as possible. It is just common sense. You are rarely asked to show explicitly how the proposal will serve both your organization's mission and that of the grantmaker, but this is one of those intangibles that underlies everything else you say in your proposal.

If the U.S. Department of Education (or the local board of education) is the funder, for instance, grant seekers should know about the current administration's policies on reading instruction, preschool education, technology in the classroom, or anything else you're interested in providing in your school or after-school program. Find out what the agency is responsible for, what issues are controversial within the funding agency and externally, how many grants are given out, and what kinds of programs are funded. If the grantmaker is a foundation, don't just send away for the annual report and read the list of recent grantees. Read the whole report and the foundation's 990 form online. Look at descriptions of the founders. What was the foundation created for, and what does it stand for? Once you know about the grantmaker, you can reread the application package with a deeper understanding of how to respond.

Then there are the intangibles that "everybody knows," but that you will never see written anywhere. Sure, the application may explain the program guidelines, legislation, other relevant information and research, selection criteria, eligibility requirements, deadline, page limit, font and margin size, and many other important and helpful facts. But it does not explain underlying assumptions about the entire grant process. Somehow, you are supposed to understand certain truths about the grantmakers and the process of winning a grant. These truths are different from tips and helpful hints. These truths are the base on which the world of a successful grant seeker is built.

For example, nowhere does any application package or set of guidelines remind the applicant not to be greedy. You will never see any indication that $200,000 a year is too much to pay a grant-funded project director of a community youth program, or that the executive director's entire salary won't be paid out of a grant to treat substance abusers at a community clinic. And if you ask a funder how much is appropriate, he or she'll probably tell you it depends on the program, or the organization, or the skills of the executive director; you need to exercise some judgment.

The package also won't tell you to treat your employees fairly and pay a reasonable salary for the responsibilities they are entrusted with—again, judgment.

Nowhere does the application warn you not to fib, embellish, or lay out unrealistic plans—which you can be sure the reader of your proposal will recognize immediately. Nowhere does it tell you to confer with the head of your organization or agency to make sure he or she not only supports the project but has offered input into its design and development; or to look at the grant in the context of your organization's mission to be sure the program, if funded, would fit; or to consult with program staff to be sure they can absorb the additional work the grant will pay for.

The application package or guidelines won't tell you how to design your program or formulate your budget or your evaluation plan. Nowhere does it indicate what type or caliber of staff should be hired for a particular program, or how much they should be paid. Rarely will it tell you what proportion of a grant—if any—can be allocated for project supervision or for support services like bookkeeping or a security guard. As we discuss in Lesson 13, you always have to decide what's reasonable, and make the case for each item in your proposal. And unless legislation or regulations require it, you will rarely see any suggestion about showing commitment to the project by contributing "in-kind" personnel and resources to supplement the grant funds. But you may be providing such resources (space for the project, volunteers, management oversight, bookkeeping) anyway. Doing this, and saying so in the proposal, demonstrates your commitment to the project.

Nowhere does any guideline say that an organization's reputation can help or hurt your chances to get a grant. If your programs are known, if your staff members are recognized experts in their field, if you generate model programs that others replicate . . . all of these things speak to your organization's capability to manage a grant. So publicize the good things you're doing and awards you receive, and talk about them (and the publicity) in your proposals. Send out cheerful newsletters describing your organization and programs, and include them in a proposal package if it's appropriate. Speak at conferences, host conferences, become known as an expert on your most cherished issue. (And, no, you are not too busy. This is an important part of your work. It should be a top priority.)

Nowhere does any application tell you to write in a clear, reader-friendly manner. Nowhere in any instructions does it state that you should not include drawings or cartoons to make the case (though the funder may tell you not to send videos, or to limit illustrative materials like news articles to a certain number). Nowhere does a grant application say that one abbreviation after another strewn throughout the pages of a proposal only confuses bleary-eyed reviewers. As we discuss in the next lesson, it is very important to be aware of the way you describe your target population, partners, and everyone and everything else. Sometimes you may think that avoiding certain terms is just too "politically correct." But you never know. One of us was planning a capital campaign and developed an "adopt-a-room" initiative, only to learn that some parents of adopted children hate to see the term applied to anything else because they feel it cheapens the adoption process. If we had used the term in a proposal, we might have offended the very program officer we were trying to impress.

Grants aren't lottery tickets. You don't win them (for the most part) because it just happens to be your lucky day. There are no right answers on a grant application, but there are plenty of wrong ones. Put yourself in the shoes of the person reading your proposal—the person representing the interests of the grantmaker—and think about what would make sense to her or him. And remember that the person who reads your proposal is usually someone you do not know and who does not know you.

As you read the following chapters and as you develop your own proposals, keep these important (but unmentioned) intangibles in mind.

"I'M REALLY NOT MUCH OF A
PROOF READER BUT I DID CATCH
MOST OF YOUR B.S."

Pop Quiz

True or False?

1. In most ways writing a grant proposal is as straightforward as filling out an application for a credit card.

2. Let's be honest about it—winning a grant takes luck, just like winning the lottery.

3. People who give grants expect grant seekers to be a little greedy—it's part of the process.

4. If a grant application doesn't say, "No abbreviations," use them as often as you want; they save space.

5. Rarely does a grant application tell you the specific qualifications of staff you must hire with grant funds.

LESSON 6:
Writing (Proposals) with Style:
Twelve Basic Rules

OPENING REMARKS

A friend of mine who's an experienced proposal writer recently told me that when she starts writing a proposal she sometimes finds herself cutting and pasting words, phrases, paragraphs, and pages from old proposals she has written, even when they have no relation to the current proposal and make absolutely no sense because she panics when she sees that dreaded blank page.—EK

LEADING QUESTIONS
Shouldn't It Be Pretty Easy Just to Tell a Reader About My Great Program in My Own Words?

If you believe that, we have a swell bridge to sell you. Many important elements separate winning grant proposals from those that are turned down. One element that often is neglected is the actual writing style. Some proposal writers don't think enough about stylish writing because they are too busy trying to make sense of the application and attempting to flesh out the program . . . with an immovable deadline that is just around the corner. They cross their fingers, hoping that their responses to all the questions the grantmaker asks will glide—error-free and in appropriate language—onto the blank sheets of paper (in 12-point type, with adequate margins, and in the required number of words and pages).

No such luck. Although grantmakers don't usually comment about the quality of the writing unless it's so bad that they can't make heads or tails of the proposal, they notice it, so you've got some work ahead.

DISCUSSION

There has been a lot of hand-wringing about writing lately, with people lamenting that "no one can write anymore" (and those who write grant proposals aren't immune from this charge). Teachers, employers, grantmakers, and just plain folks like us attribute this variously to all that TV watching, computer game playing, or iPod listening—activities that keep people from reading. And if you're not reading, you're probably not writing very well either. Or maybe email and text messaging are the culprits, pushing people to a telegraphic writing style. For whatever reason, good writing is seen less and less often by people who care about it.

Yet those who write grant proposals have to be effective writers no matter how sound their programs are or how highly regarded their organizations happen to be. It's just common sense. If a proposal is a mess, grantmakers will tend to think the organization may be equally sloppy.

THE BASICS

Good proposal writing follows the principles of good writing in general, but there are some rules that we urge you to observe that would not necessarily apply to essayists, fiction writers, journalists, biographers, or poets. Sure, proposals can—and should be—enjoyable to read. But the reason for writing them is not to entertain. Grant proposals are written to convince grantmakers to hand over money to you; that's their unique and specific objective. In this chapter, we lay out 12 "rules" describing our strong preferences and pet peeves about proposal writing. Although there are exceptions to each of these rules (and we sometimes break them ourselves), we have found that you can't go wrong by following them most of the time. If you break any of these rules, you should have a very good reason to do it.

Rule 1. Before you write a word, create an outline that exactly follows the funder's guidelines, questions, or selection criteria for the proposal.

Not only will an outline demonstrate to the grantmakers that you have read and understood what they are looking for (and in what order), it also will break the paralysis that sets in when you look at the blank page by letting you get something down on paper.

We've said this before and will say it again: Follow the funder's outline to a T. If the first question on the application asks how you plan to evaluate the program (even if you haven't been asked yet to describe the program) then, as strange as that may be, it will be the first item on your outline. As we said in Lesson 3, don't omit questions or portions of questions on the outline, even if you think they're irrelevant to your program, and don't change the order of the topics because you think the funder asked them in an illogical sequence.

Use subheads for each topic in the outline to make sure you don't lose your way. This sounds obvious, but it's important because a poorly organized proposal will make even good writing seem incomprehensible. You may not use all the outline's subheads in the final proposal; often there is just too much information to include in some shorter grant proposals. But subheads—the more the merrier—are useful when you're trying to get started, and they keep you focused as you write. They also ensure that you don't inadvertently omit important information. In the next chapter we'll show you how each question on a typical grant application might look in subhead form.

Before you start filling in the outline, organize the material you have available. As we said in Lesson 4, you should have on hand all sorts of information about your organization, programs, and target population, including census data, historical facts, program descriptions and performance statistics, demographic material and other statistics on participants, staff résumés, articles, newsletters, and much more. All of this material should be organized—all résumés together, all crime statistics and other research together, all budget and funding source data together—before you even think about starting to write. If you haven't done this already, do it *now*. (We'll remind you to do this again and again.)

Remember, though, that some of the information you have on hand will be left out of some proposals and featured prominently in others. For example, programmatic details about your senior center may have no relevance in a proposal for a new youth program; details about the qualifications and job descriptions of your organization's staff members may be inserted in an appendix (if appendices are permitted), or left out completely if the grantmaker doesn't want them. Often you will struggle with what to include and what to leave out. The funder's guidelines and the way each question in the grant application is framed will tell you what to cover in the narrative, what to add to the appendix, and what to save for another proposal.

Rule 2. Write as you speak (or as you should speak), not as a Shakespearean actor speaks . . . or as your awesome 14-year-old nephew speaks.

You should not be overly formal, pretentious, or ponderous in a proposal. Nor should you be so casual that the grantmakers are left scratching their heads in confusion. Compare the three statements below:

- The executive director of the Meridian Mews Center, the delightful Ms. Jane Manning, is erudite, learned, and has never been known to bloviate when she addresses her comrades at worldwide conferences.
- The executive director of the Meridian Mews Center, Jane Manning, is way cool and all the kids at the center think she's hot. (Okay, maybe no self-respecting proposal writer would ever sink this low, but you get the idea.)
- In April 2008, the executive director of the Meridian Mews Center, Jane Manning, was voted Most Popular Executive Director and one of the 50 Most Respected Leaders of Nonprofit Organizations by the 3,000-member National Association of Children's

Programming at their annual conference—and more than one teen participant has called her "way cool."

The first two statements obviously break this rule; the third one is direct, to the point, and actually sounds as though an adult wrote it!

Don't grantmakers have 14-year-old nephews also? Don't they know exactly what the proposal writer means by "people enjoy chillin' at the Meridian Mews Center"? They may know what it means to "chill" and to be a "hottie," but that kind of lazy writing by adults suggests lazily, casually run programs. Some grantmakers feel it is disrespectful for the proposal writer to assume that they are comfortable with that level of casualness. Many grantmakers feel that adults should not talk the way teenagers do but act as well-spoken role models. So, dudes, stick to conventional words and phrases. Besides, isn't it more meaningful to the reader to learn that the executive director of the Meridian Mews Center has won recognition from respected professional organizations rather than to hear that she is "way cool"? The best strategy for writing about your executive director is to let the facts about her speak for themselves. Even if she is gorgeous, it is not appropriate to mention that tidbit in the proposal.

Rule 3. Double- (and triple-) think your choice of words . . . and never, accidentally or on purpose, fall back on slang, or on imprecise or insensitive terminology.

We aren't going to get into a discussion here about good slang and bad slang or the merits of political correctness—we may be opinionated, but we aren't lexicographers! We recognize that some slang expressions are used by people of all ages, while others usually are restricted to the vocabularies of preteens and teenagers—and yes, we realize that many slang words even make it into the dictionary. But we don't think they belong in a grant proposal. We also believe you must take great care in describing, precisely, the traits and attributes of the people who participate in your program or who live in your community or city. Compare the statements below:

- The cops think the Meridian Mews Center has helped the kids in the 'hood stay out of the slammer.
- The girl who runs the youth program has a master's degree in psychology and has worked with the retarded at the Meridian Mews Center for ages.
- Kids in the program are really messed up.
- The Meridian Mews Center provides programs for homosexuals.
- Children between the ages of 7 and 10 who have learning disabilities will be recruited by staff members to participate in all the activities at the Meridian Mews Center.

The first four are loaded with slang as well as imprecise and insensitive terminology. The fifth statement uses appropriate terms and sticks to the facts.

What's the big deal about saying cops instead of policemen? And everyone knows what the 'hood and the slammer are. No big deal. But why not play it safe and use the correct words? The reader's father may be a policeman who complains about the disrespect he encounters on the street. You have to admit that there are some people who are really adamant about referring to young ones as *children* and not *kids*. And many groups prefer or resent being referred to in certain ways. It's up to proposal writers to keep on top of changing trends in language. It used to be perfectly acceptable to say "retarded children" or "the retarded." Now it is much more sensitive to say "children with mental retardation." If you think this is petty, just check with a parent of a child with special needs and you may very well get an earful.

Rule 4. Don't exaggerate.

No, your organization is probably *not* doing the most cutting-edge, innovative, earth-shattering computer instruction on the planet—and grantmakers often just laugh and shake their heads when they see this kind of
grandiose claim.

Is there a proposal writer around who isn't constantly searching for
words that convey the extraordinary attributes of the program? (Hint:
Terms like "cutting edge" have become clichés.) Let the organization, the
neighborhood, the program, the staff—and the facts—speak for themselves. (Who likes to eat in a restaurant just because it advertises fine dining? After you finish your meal, you'll decide whether the dining was
fine.) Do use a few appropriate facts, statistics, or examples of program
outcomes. Compare the following pairs of statements and decide which
of each pair is strongest:

- The Meridian Mews Center offers cutting-edge basketball instruction to the children who participate in the program.
- The Meridian Mews Center offers basketball instruction to the
  children who participate in the program. The instructor is a basketball coach at Meridian University who received a grant from the
  Basketball Institute to teach the art and science of basketball to
  children. (Now that is an innovative, cutting-edge program—but
  you don't have to use the words!)

- The executive director of the Meridian Mews Center, Jane Manning, is a most brilliant scholar.
- The executive director of the Meridian Mews Center, Jane Manning, received her master's degree in psychology with high honors from Metropolis City University. Her articles about children
  have appeared in *Family and Youth,* among many other journals.

- The extraordinarily innovative basketball program at the Meridian Mews Center helps teenagers succeed in life.
- One of the teenagers who participated in the Meridian Mews Center's basketball program during the 2007–2008 session received a full scholarship to Metropolis City University and will be a student coach for the college's intramural basketball teams.

- The Meridian Mews Center is located in the poorest section of America.
- The Meridian Mews Center is located in a Metropolis neighborhood where 80 percent of the residents are on public assistance and 60 percent of the children under 16 live in single-parent families.

In each of the pairs of statements, the second one in the pair doesn't exaggerate to make a point. The proposal writer takes the trouble to explain why the program is extraordinary, a staff member is brilliant, and a neighborhood is considered disadvantaged.

Rule 5. Buy a grammar book . . . and use it when in doubt (or when you should be in doubt).

Nothing is more disheartening to a grantmaker than poor grammar. Right or wrong, it suggests either that you are poorly educated or don't care enough about the proposal to proofread and rewrite. What funder wants to give money to an organization that allows a proposal to be sent out with grammatical errors? We aren't going to give you grammar instructions . . . you know the rules . . . or you know where to find them.

Rule 6. . . . and a dictionary and thesaurus while you're at it.

Your computer has a spelling checker and many other tools that can help you. No excuses for misspellings and no reason to discuss this any further.

But we realize that spelling software isn't foolproof (the computer doesn't distinguish among two, too, and to, for example), so you should also proofread carefully, ask friends and colleagues to read and edit your proposals, and use a dictionary to double-check when you are the least bit unsure.

Rule 7. Stick to the active voice. It is a more straightforward way to write, and it is the only way to keep from getting tripped up— or tripping up your reader—in a grant proposal.

All sorts of people (not just proposal writers) rely on the passive voice— saying things like "you are loved," rather than the active but often terrifying, "I love you." And how often have we heard politicians say, "Mistakes have been made," rather than the more earth-shattering, "I blew it!" In grant proposals, the active voice keeps you honest and clear. In the following paired statements, decide which is more straightforward, giving the reader the most detailed information:

- Students will be recruited to participate in the Meridian Mews Center's activities.
- The Meridian Mews Center's outreach workers will recruit children to participate in the center's activities.

- Parenting workshops will be conducted for parents of the children who participate in the Meridian Mews Center's programs.
- Nurse-practitioners will conduct parenting workshops for parents of the children who participate in the Meridian Mews Center's programs.

- A project director for the grant-funded program will be hired.
- Jane Manning, executive director of the Meridian Mews Center, will hire a project director for the grant-funded program.

After reading the first item of each pair, the funder is left wondering exactly who will do what to whom. The second statement of the pair uses the active voice and leaves nothing to the imagination.

What if we don't know who will recruit students, conduct workshops, hire staff, evaluate the staff, and so on, at the time that we are writing our grant proposal? Wouldn't it be misleading to give the funder inaccurate information? Aren't we better off using the passive voice? No! Funders want to be sure that you understand how these tasks will get done; they don't necessarily expect to know the names of the individuals who will be doing them. And in any case, you don't need to use the passive voice. You can say, "The program director (or executive director, or whoever is responsible) will hire the appropriate workers." "The manager will develop a contract with a professional evaluator."

Rule 8. Keep your value judgments, controversial ideas, political views, and sense of humor out, out, OUT of the grant proposal.

Proposal writers often mistakenly think that everyone reading their proposals agrees with them about the state of the world, politics, educational philosophy . . . and that their idea of a good joke will make the people reading the proposal fall over laughing. Compare the statements below (we'll help you along on these):

- The Meridian Mews Center was created to counter the federal government's shocking lack of interest in children. (This is a political point of view and a value judgment.)
- The Meridian Mews Center staff thinks "children should be seen and not heard" and often punishes them for talking if they haven't been spoken to. (There may be people who agree with this, but it is a controversial idea.)
- The Meridian Mews Center is only for good little lads and lassies in the neighborhood, not for little ones with problems of any

kind. Just kidding. (This is the kind of joke that beginning proposal writers think livens things up.)

- The Meridian Mews Center's entire staff voted Republican in the
last election. (Political point of view—and who cares?)
- The Meridian Mews Center posts rules that explain to children
how they are expected to behave when they participate in the
program. (Whew! No controversy and no humor.)

*What if I believe that a nontraditional program is better suited to my
participants than the same-old same-old?* Can't I request grant funding
for projects that are a little different? It depends. Do you have any solid
research and/or anecdotal information that back up your ideas? If you do,
you may present the program as innovative and a potential model for
others. (For example, you might have research supporting your proposal
to include children with severe disabilities in general education classrooms rather than assigning them to segregated special education classes
where all the children have the same level of disability.) If you don't have
this sort of background information, you may want to seek funding from
sources other than grants—asking for donations from parents of the children you want to serve in a nontraditional way or running benefits, for
instance—for programs that may be too controversial, too hot to handle
for either government or foundation funders. Of course, programs that involve spanking children wouldn't and shouldn't receive funding. (Some
may say that the preceding statement is expressing a value judgment,
which is a no-no, but we don't think so; actually, in most places these
days it's the law.) The topic of program development is discussed in Lesson 10.

**Rule 9. Limit the (yawn) adjectives . . . readers stop believing
them very quickly when you keep tossing more into the
sentence.**

When too many modifiers are tacked on to a noun, verb, or phrase, the reader is likely to see them as just the opinion of the proposal writer rather than documented facts. Overusing adjectives can seem to be a shortcut for the proposal writer—saving the time and trouble of explaining what is meant by the adjectives. Excessive use of adjectives smacks of desperation. Look at the following statements:

- The Meridian Mews Center runs high-quality, exhilarating, well-regarded programs for poor, disadvantaged, disabled children.
- The Meridian Mews Center runs four programs that have been cited for excellence by the National After-School and Weekend Program Society. Attendance at all four programs is over 90 percent. During the last year, parents have written more than 50 letters to the executive director praising the programs.

The first statement is just . . . words. It doesn't really say anything that has meaning. The second statement is meaty and informative.

Won't the grant proposal be dry and drab—okay, boring—without some juicy adjectives perking it up? Adjectives *can* be effective if you don't scrimp on fleshing them out and explaining exactly why you have selected them. For example, "This innovative program is one of the first in the city of Metropolis to pair college students and preschool children for basketball lessons." Otherwise, adjectives like innovative are meaningless—and annoying.

Rule 10. A grant proposal is neither a personal essay nor an autobiography. Save "I," "we," and "our" for your memoirs.
If you are writing on behalf of a not-for-profit organization, a school or school district, a college, a consortium of groups, a faith-based organization, or a government agency, it is not a good idea to get personal in grant proposals when talking about the organization and the project that you

hope to get funded. Compare the pairs of responses below and decide which is perfectly clear, leaving nothing to the imagination:

- We are located at 12 North Meridian Street in downtown Metropolis, Indiana.
- The Meridian Mews Center is located at 12 North Meridian Street in downtown Metropolis, Indiana.

- We will conduct workshops for members of our community.
- Staff psychologists will conduct workshops for parents who live in the North Meridian Mews community.

- Our executive director is Jane Manning.
- Jane Manning is the executive director of the Meridian Mews Center.

- Our partners include local schools, churches, and businesses.
- The Meridian Mews Center's partners include local schools, churches, and businesses.

In each pair, the example that specifically mentions the Meridian Mews Center, the staff, or the executive director is crisper and less confusing.

Don't you think you're being a little rigid with this rule? Yes, it's rigid, because so many people either overuse the first person or use it inappropriately. It's much easier to tell you to avoid it altogether than to tell you when to use it and when not to. One of the authors agrees with this rule in principle, but in practice she finds that there are times when the less formal use of the first person plural is more effective. This choice depends on her familiarity with the prospective reader or the feeling she is trying to convey about a proposed program or the organization. The point is that it should be done consciously and for a reason.

Moreover, if you're not careful about using the first person, you may confuse the grantmaker. If you say, for example, "We will run workshops for our parents," the reader may have to stop to figure out if you're talking about your own parents, the parents of the children in your program, or any parents in the community. Every time the grantmaker has to stop to think about what you mean, you lose a little momentum in what may otherwise be an excellent proposal.

Rule 11. Unless you are trying to confuse the grantmaker, abbreviations and ACRONYMS have no place in a grant proposal.

Believe it or not, even the most commonly used acronyms are bound to confuse someone—and that someone may be a potential funder. PTA, NFL, NYC, and probably a few others shouldn't stymie even the most in-sulated grantmaker, but as a general rule, the term represented by an acronym should be spelled out over and over again—or not used at all—unless you've just explained it in the same paragraph (or at least on the same page). Even talking about acronyms gets confusing. Compare the following:

- The Department of Health (DOH) has a staff of 450 physicians, nurses, and nonmedical personnel. Starting on January 4, 2010, DOH will begin offering free tuberculosis screening for children at the Meridian Mews Center.
- The Meridian Mews Center has collaborated for the last eight years with professors from the PE Department at MU. DOH has a branch at MU and also works closely with the IT Department and the local Y.

In the first example, the Department of Health is spelled out first—then the acronym is used again quickly. The second statement is filled with enough acronyms to make your hair hurt.

Rule 12. Very little of what you write is common knowledge, even if it seems obvious to you. Grantmakers want to see backup information, proof that what you say is true.

Certain statements express universally agreed on knowledge that you don't have to prove: The sky is blue (at least once or twice a year), grass is green (if there is any), winter is cold. But the unproved, unexplained statements that are thrown into grant proposals drive reviewers crazy! Compare the following pairs of statements:

- Everyone in the community thinks the Meridian Mews Center runs educational and enjoyable programs.
- According to surveys that were conducted in two community churches and two schools, 60 percent of residents of Meridian Hills Mews think the programs offered at the Meridian Mews Center are educational and enjoyable.

- The police are excited about the Meridian Mews Center's activities.
- According to interviews with police officers in the Meridian Mews precinct conducted by program staff, 20 of the 25 officers questioned feel that the center's programs encourage children to stay out of trouble.

In both cases, the second statement of the pair takes nothing for granted and offers proof for every proclamation.

IN CLOSING

Following the rules that we've highlighted in this chapter will not guarantee that your grant proposal will receive funding, but you can be certain the grantmaker won't be too confused, too frustrated, too offended, too angry, or too shocked to fund your project.

Pop Quiz

True or False?

1. Don't be a stickler for political correctness. The PC police went out of style years ago.

2. Being too organized in your grant proposal writing puts you at risk of seeming stiff or stilted.

3. It is a good idea to show funders that you relate to your clients and program participants by using the words and phrases they use as much as possible throughout your proposal.

4. If you are a published poet, it is perfectly acceptable to include some poetry in your grant proposal as long as it answers the question.

5. It is not enough to say that you are running a "reading program." Make sure that you let the funder know it is a cutting-edge reading program.

6. Make sure your grant proposal contains every statistic you have available or you will be disqualified.

Short Answer

Which rules are broken in the statements below? (Hint: Some of these statements have more than one broken rule, and some may have grammatical or spelling errors.)

1. The Meridian Mews Center is known all over the world.

2. Everyone in the neighborhood respect the executive director of the Meridian Mews Center, Ms. Jane Manning.

3. Volunteers will be recruited for the Meridian Mews Centers programs.

4. The Meridian Mews Center has the smartest, best-educated, most experienced staff in the city of Metropolis.

5. The Meridian Mews Center uses neighborhood schools and churches for it's activities.

6. After-school and weekend programs, such as the ones offered at the Meridian Mews Center, help children improve there grades in school and there behavior at home.

7. The Meridian Mews Center receives grants from HHS, DOJ, and DOE.

8. The mural that was recently painted on the wall of the Meridian Mews Center's activity room is awesome.

9. The Meridian Mews Center's Geezer program is an intergenerational program for old folks and young kids.

10. We are requesting funding for the Meridian Mews Center's cutting-edge basketball program and its innovative intergenerational program.

LESSON 7:
Writing (Proposals) with Style: Tackling the Blank Page

OPENING REMARKS

Vigorous writing is concise. A sentence should contain no unnecessary words, a paragraph no unnecessary sentences, for the same reason that a drawing should have no unnecessary lines and a machine no unnecessary parts. This requires not that the writer make all sentences short or avoid all detail and treat subjects only in outline, but that every word tell.—William Strunk Jr. and E. B. White, The Elements of Style, 4th ed. (New York: Allyn & Bacon, 1999).

LEADING QUESTION
How Can I Remember to Use All These Proposal-Writing Rules When I'm Working Under Pressure with a Deadline—and Confronted with a Blank Page?

We think the rules will become second nature. And once you understand them, the blank page shouldn't throw you for a loop if you have a good program to describe—unless writing in general terrifies you. But we'll assume you have a well-designed program and if you're terrified of writing (believe it or not), proposal writing will help you become less frightened.

Here's why: As we discussed in Rule 1 in Lesson 6, the best grant proposals follow a rigid—yes, rigid—outline that originates with the grantmaker. Once you've created the outline, you'll find it much easier to decide what to say in each section. And as you methodically follow that outline, and the clearer and more straightforward your writing is, the more likely the funder is to understand what you are proposing and why you are asking for money. Short, crisp sentences are very much appreciated by reviewers, who often have many proposals to read in a short time. Bullets, charts, and tables (if they are used thoughtfully, of course) can help a tentative proposal writer get important information across and are often welcomed by the grantmaker because clearly labeled charts and tables help concretize and clarify complex material.

OUTLINING THE GRANT APPLICATION
Let's Start by Describing Your Organization

One of the early items in most grant applications is the seemingly (and deceptively) simple description of your organization. Because many grantmakers ask for something like a four-hundred-word statement about the organization, we'll focus on brevity. An overview of the organization normally will be presented as part of a summary statement at the beginning of any proposal; in many proposals it will be expanded further in a section on organizational capacity or organizational capability. We will talk more about what goes into this section in Lesson 15, but here we just want to show you how to get started. This lesson will apply to almost every section of a proposal.

A clear, concise introduction to your organization is especially important. It introduces the funder to the organization, and introduces the funder to your writing. Just how clear is this grant applicant? How well does the proposal describe the organization? So, congratulations! You are, for the rest of this chapter, the proposal writer for the Meridian Mews Center.

As the proposal writer, you have many facts and figures about the Meridian Mews Center. Here is what you know and have on hand (in no particular order):

- *Address:* The Meridian Mews Center is located at 12 North Meridian Street in downtown Metropolis, Indiana.
- *Facility:* The center occupies five rooms on the barrier-free ground floor of Mewshaven Middle School. The center has access to the school's gym and playground. It also has a satellite program at the North Meridian Elementary School. Exercise

equipment, swimming lessons, and pool time are made available to participants by the local YMCA.

- **Demographics of the target population:** More than 1,000 residents of Metropolis live in the downtown area called North Meridian Mews. Of these, about 45 percent are age 18 and under. More than half of the families are African American, over 25 percent are Hispanic (largely Mexican immigrants), and just under 25 percent are white. Ninety percent of the children who participate in center activities live below the poverty line, and at least 20 percent of them have physical, emotional, or learning disabilities, and health problems such as cancer and asthma. About 60 percent of their parents receive public assistance, and some of the parents are incarcerated.

- **Community statistics:** North Meridian Mews has a higher youth crime rate than the city as a whole. For the last few years, gang activity has been minimal, but there is still a gang presence. The community also has higher rates of substance use among teenagers than the rest of the city, and higher rates of certain health problems such as childhood asthma.

- **Demographics of the city:** Of the 873,000 residents of Metropolis, about 35 percent are age 18 and under, fewer than 20 percent live below the poverty level, and fewer than 20 percent of families with children receive public assistance. Metropolis is home to large corporations, including Jones Pharmaceuticals and Smith Life Insurance, a university, and professional sports teams.

- **Staff:** Jane Manning has been executive director of the Meridian Mews Center since 1995, when the center was founded. A former teacher, principal, and school superintendent, she is a leader in the field of education and has been featured in news articles. For example, in 2008, the *Metropolis Tribune* described her "generosity to the children and her enthusiasm for her work." The center's staff includes three full-time licensed social workers and one part-time clinical psychologist who provides counseling to children and parents twice a week. It also has on staff a recreation director and up to four part-time recreation specialists (depending on funding).

- **Board:** The Meridian Mews Center's 12-member board of directors includes local business executives, school teachers and university faculty, representatives of churches and hospitals, and two parents of children who use the center's facilities. The chairman is William Martinez, the chief operating officer of the Smith Life Insurance Company of Indiana. Half of the board members are women; 25 percent are white, 25 percent Hispanic, and 50 percent African American, reflecting the ethnic composition of the community.

- **History:** The center was founded in 1995 by concerned parents living in the North Meridian Mews neighborhood to address the growing crime rate among youth that local residents and law enforcement officials suspected was attributable to a lack of after-school and weekend programs for children of all ages living in the community.

- **Number served:** Since it was founded, the Meridian Mews Center has provided services for approximately 3,000 children, teenagers, and their families, with more than 500 people participating in program activities each year.

- **Partners:** The center's partners include the Mewshaven Public School District, which provides the center's main facility and makes school computer labs available to the center; the Meridian Mews Baptist Church, which provides meeting space for parents; and the YMCA in the North Meridian Mews community.

- **Finances:** The center has an operating budget of $1 million per year. It receives funding from the City of Metropolis Departments of Child Welfare and Education; the Indiana State Department of Child Welfare; and from local foundations, including the Pacer & Colt Foundation and the Better Hoosier Fund. Copies of the budgets for fiscal years 2007 and 2008 are available. The audit report for FY 2007 is available.

- **Programs:** Current programs at the Meridian Mews Center include computer instruction, reading instruction, sports, English as a second language, leadership development (in a peer-led substance abuse prevention program), mental health counseling, and parenting counseling.
- **Awards:** Executive director Jane Manning has won numerous awards, most recently the 2008 One of the Hoosiers of the Year citation.
- **Miscellaneous information:** You can "find" this information in your files as you need it.

We know we've told you this before, but now is a good time to put this book down (unless you have a grant proposal due in 24 hours—in which case you'd better put the book down anyway) and gather, organize, and update the important information about your organization just as we did for the Meridian Mews Center. If you do this, you'll thank us one day.

Outlining the Organization Description

Because you have so much information available, it is necessary to develop an outline that covers everything you think it is important for the funder to know before you start writing. Following is an outline that we think introduces material in an orderly manner.

Description Outline

a) History/location
b) Programs

c) Community/city demographics

d) Participants

e) Partners

f) Facilities/resources

g) Staffing

h) Board of directors

i) Budget

j) Additional information

Filling in the Outline

Because we want to make the actual proposal-writing process as easy as possible, we've included two brief descriptions of the Meridian Mews Center for you to analyze. Each is approximately 400 words long and covers identical information. The first one was written by an experienced proposal writer (who used ordinary subheads instead of a numbered, lettered outline). The second one . . . wasn't.

Description of the Meridian Mews Center (1)

History and Overview: The Meridian Mews Center, located at 12 North Meridian Street, was founded in 1995 by concerned parents living in the North Meridian Mews neighborhood of downtown Metropolis, Indiana. The center was created to address the growing crime rate among youth that local residents and law enforcement officials suspected was a result of the lack of after-school and weekend programs for children of all ages living in North Meridian Mews. Since it was created, the center has provided services for approximately 3,000 children and their families, with 500 people participating in program activities each year.

Programs: Current programs at the Meridian Mews Center include computer instruction, reading instruction, sports, English as a second language, leadership development (in a peer-led substance abuse prevention program), mental health counseling, and parent counseling.

Characteristics of the Community and Participants: Of the 873,000 residents of Metropolis, 1,000 live in North Meridian Mews. Ninety percent of the children who participate in center activities live below the poverty line and a majority of them have a full range of physical, emotional, and learning disabilities, and health problems (such as cancer and asthma); their parents often receive public assistance, and some of the parents are incarcerated.

Partners/Facilities: The center's partners include the Mewshaven Public School District, which provides space for the center in the North Meridian Street Elementary School and makes its computer labs available; the Meridian Mews Baptist Church, which provides meeting space for parents; and the local YMCA.

Key Staff: The executive director, Jane Manning, has held that position since the Meridian Mews Center was founded. A former teacher, principal, and school superintendent, she is a leader in the field of education and has been featured in news articles (for instance, in 2007, the *Metropolis Star* described her "generosity to the children and her enthusiasm for her work") and has won numerous awards, most recently the 2008 One of the Hoosiers of the Year citation. The center's staff includes three full-time licensed social workers and one part-time clinical psychologist who provides counseling to children and parents twice a week. Currently it also includes a recreation director and two part-time recreation specialists.

Board of Directors: The Meridian Mews Center's 12-member board of directors is made up of executives of local businesses, faculty of universities and schools, representatives of churches and hospitals, and two parent representatives. The board chair is William Martinez, the chief operating officer of the Smith Life Insurance Company of Indiana.

Budget: The center has an operating budget of $1 million per year and receives grant funding from the City of Metropolis Departments of Child Welfare and Education, the Indiana State Department of Child Welfare, and local foundations, including the Pacer & Colt Foundation and the Better Hoosier Fund.

Notice how religiously the writer followed the rules that we spelled out in the preceding chapter. Of course in the final draft, some subheads can be deleted to make the response seem less choppy.

Compare the well-crafted description to the following one produced by a beginning writer. Keep an eye on the underlined items; you'll be asked to correct them.

Description of the Meridian Mews Center (2)

My organization, the Meridian Mews Center, provides cutting-edge programs for young kids who are no older than 16 years old, in downtown Metropolis, Indiana. Our address is 12 North Meridian Street and our neighborhood, the North Meridian Mews, is a diverse community located smack in the heart of Metropolis.

Unfortunately, the children who come to our center are very poor and many of them have handicaps and other tragic health problems of all types like asthma and cancer. Many of their parents are on welfare and some are even in prison or on probation. Our center was founded in 1995 by a bunch of concerned neighborhood parents because there was many kids who had nothing to do on weekends and after school and often got into hot water with local cops.

Metropolis has about 800,000 people living there and the North Meridian Mews neighborhood has about 1,000 residents, many of them being kids of all ages. Our program has served about 3,000 kids and parents and brothers and sisters since the beginning and we handle about 500 kids a year. We teach computer, reading, sports like basketball (Metropolis is very into basketball), and English as a second language.

Our board of directors is made up of people from the local businesses, churches, and hospitals.

We receive grants from the City of Metropolis DCW and the ED, the relevant state government agencies, as well as from a few foundations like the Pacer & Colt Foundation and the Better Hoosier Fund.

The executive director, Jane Manning, has been around since the Meridian Mews Center was founded. She is a leader in the field and has an MA in psychology from Metropolis City College. She has been written about a lot—the *Metropolis Tribune* wrote a story about her a couple of years ago that talked about her generosity to the kids and her enthusiasm. A few years back, she received an award as One of the Hoosiers of the Year which made us all very proud. We have three full-time social workers on board and one part-time psychologist who comes in on Mondays and Thursdays. The center's activities take place all over Metropolis—we use school computer rooms in Mewshaven and basketball courts at a YMCA nearby. The Meridian Mews Baptist Church allows us to hold meetings in their basement for parents when their isn't anything going on in the church.

Before you throw up your hands in frustration after reading this disorganized description of the Meridian Mews Center, we're going to take a slightly different approach, and give you an exercise in the middle of the chapter to give you a chance to practice what we've preached.

Editing Exercise

Although both of the preceding descriptions cover important information, the one written by the inexperienced proposal writer breaks many (okay, most) of the rules we suggested for writing with style. Fill in the table below, explaining why we identified the items in the left-hand column as needing correcting. Which rule from Lesson 6 was broken, and how would you change the sentence in which the item appears? We've answered the first few to get you started.

Item	Broken Rule No.	Correction
Paragraph 1 My	#10 (It's not an auto-biography, it's a grant)	The Meridian Mews Center
cutting-edge	#4 Exaggeration	(Be specific!)
kids	#3 Slang	Children!
our		
smack in the heart		
Paragraph 2 Unfortunately		
handicaps		
tragic health problems		
bunch		
was		
kids		
hot water		
cops		
Paragraph 3 kids		
Our		
kids		
We		
Metropolis is very		
into basketball		

(continues)

Paragraph 4 Our		
Paragraph 5 We		
DCW; ED		
a few foundations		
Paragraph 6 has been around		
a couple of years ago		
kids		
us		
We		
on board		
We		
their		

Outlining the Rest of the Grant Proposal . . .

Now that you've gotten a little experience in outlining and critiquing the description of your organization, we can talk about the rest of the proposal. The remaining lessons in Part II will go into great detail about each section of a proposal; here we just want you to focus on the outline and the types of information that should go into each section.

For our purposes, here is the short version of the program at the Meridian Mews Center we're hoping will receive grant funding. (You, as the proposal writer, would have much more information about the program you're proposing than we can include in this chapter.)

Program: You want to request $10,000 in funding from the Meridian Mews Community Foundation for a basketball project, in partnership with Meridian University and the local YMCA, that will promote the physical and emotional well-being of 25 teenage boys who have been identified with behavioral problems.

Selection Criteria: The Meridian Mews Community Foundation grant application guidelines request that you explain the following: need for the project, goals and objectives, a program description, partnerships, an evaluation plan, budget information, and capacity of the applicant to implement the program. The foundation requests that your proposal be no more than five double-spaced pages.

As we explained in Rule 1 in Lesson 6, before you begin responding to the questions, you should outline the proposal, using the application guidelines as the topic headings. To be sure that your outline helps you as well as the funder, use as many subheads as you need to keep you organized.

Based on everything that you will study in greater detail in Lessons 8 to 15, which discuss the sections of a typical grant proposal, here is how your outline might look for the Meridian Mews Community Foundation proposal:

A. Need for the Project
1. Documented problem the proposed program addresses
2. Research/statistics to demonstrate that the need is compelling
3. Absence of other programs in the community to tackle this problem, or the existence of such programs and reasons why this program is still needed

B. Goals and Objectives
1. Overall goal of the proposed project
2. Objective 1: (Outline for each expected outcome)
3. Expected outcome
4. Date you hope the outcome will be achieved
5. How you will know if the outcome has been achieved

C. *Program Description*
1. Target population
2. Proposed activities
3. Staff for the program (duties and responsibilities of program staff)

D. *Partnerships*
1. Name of each partnering organization
2. Specific involvement of each in project

E. *Evaluation*
1. Ongoing evaluation: How you will determine you're implementing the program as intended
2. Final evaluation: How you will determine if you have met the objectives

F. *Budget Narrative*
1. Personnel costs
2. Other costs
3. Other funding sources
4. In-kind contributions
   a. Meridian Mews Center
   b. Others
5. Sustainability; plans for future funding

G. *Capacity of the Organization to Implement the Program*
1. Description of facilities and resources
2. Honors and awards
3. Results of past evaluations (by funders or external evaluators)

With a well-organized, detailed outline like this, aren't you practically chomping at the bit to start writing your proposal?

AND FINALLY, THE PROJECT SUMMARY: YOU BE THE FUNDER!

We can't leave this lesson without talking briefly about a writing challenge for every proposal writer. Many grantmakers admit that a short project summary, or abstract, is far more important than proposal writers realize. Often grantmakers will use it to present information about your project to their boards. If you don't prepare a solid summary, they have to. Wouldn't you rather be the one who writes the summary and designs it to sell the project?

In Lesson 16 we discuss what goes into preparing an abstract or summary; in this lesson we just want to mention that summaries must include a very brief sentence or two touching on each of the major heads of your outline. They should be clear and well written according to our 12 rules of proposal writing. The following two versions of a project summary give you an opportunity to compare writing styles. You tell us which was prepared by the novice, and which by the experienced writer.

Project Summary 1. The Basketball Project at the Meridian Mews Center

We are really excited about the basketball project for 25 boys ages 13 to 16 who live in North Meridian Mews. The program will be sponsored by our organization, the Meridian Mews Center. This center's neighborhood is downtown Metropolis, Indiana. The kids who will take part in the project are badly behaved and have acted out in school. Well-qualified instructors will teach the kids basketball skills and also how to dress for success. They will receive different types of counseling also and gift certificates from Ace Sport Supplies will be given out to the kids on the winning team in the basketball competition.

The basketball project will take place after school and on weekends and the boys will behave better as a result of being in the program. The basketball project will run from September 1, 2009, to June 30, 2010, and activities will be held at the Meridian Mews Center, Meridian University, and the YMCA. We are asking for $10,000 to help cover the expenses for this excellent program that we're running with the help of Meridian University and the YMCA.

There are many staff members who will make sure the kids get solid instruction. We are hoping that the kids who join our project will stay in school longer and behave much better. They will probably enjoy the trips we'll take to basketball games and we're looking forward to having guest speakers.

Project Summary 2. The Basketball Project at the Meridian Mews Center

The Meridian Mews Center is requesting $10,000 for a basketball and mentoring project designed to engage troubled youth and lead to improved behavior in and out of school. Center staff will recruit 25 boys between the ages of 13 and 16 who live in the North Meridian Mews neighborhood of downtown Metropolis, Indiana. Participants, identified by families, teachers, counselors, and others, will have demonstrated acting-out and behavioral problems.

The overall goal is to increase the likelihood that the teenagers who participate in the activities will stay in school longer and become productive members of the North Meridian Mews community. Specific objectives include improved basketball skills and teamwork, and knowledge of how to create a positive appearance through dress; these skills in turn will improve self-esteem and reduce acting-out behavior.

Activities will include basketball instruction, team competition (with gift certificates from Ace Sport Supplies as prizes for members of the winning team), dress-for-success lessons by the coaching staff, one-on-one and group counseling, trips to professional and college basketball games, and visits with professional and college athletes. The program will operate twice a week after school and on Saturdays from September 1, 2009, to June 30, 2010. Activities will be held at the Meridian Mews Center, Meridian University, and the YMCA. Staff will include basketball coaches, a physical education professor, and a psychologist from Meridian University, as well as a social worker and recreation specialists from the Meridian Mews Center.

In this chapter, we've tried to concretize the proposal writing process— to make it real and accessible. Some people believe that writing can't be taught; you either have it or you don't. But, as you must realize by now, we disagree! We hope that in this lesson we've taken some of the anxiety out of the process. In the pop quiz that follows, you can apply what you've learned.

Pop Quiz

Proposal-Organizing (Short-Answer) Exercise

This exercise has two purposes. One is to give you practice in organizing the information needed in a grant application. The second is to give you a chance to look hard at the way proposals are actually written—the writing style that most effectively makes your case for why your project should receive funding.

The following exercise includes a proposal outline and a series of statements for you to organize. We believe the statements represent models of the style you should use in your proposals. For each section of the outline, write in the number or numbers of the statements that should be placed in the section. We understand that some of your choices will be guesswork because you haven't yet studied all the parts of the proposal. That's okay; it's your reasoning that counts here. You may want to come back to this exercise after you've read the rest of Part II, to see if you'd do anything differently.

Outline Sections Statement Number(s)

A. Need for the project:_____

B. Goals and objectives of the proposed project:_____

C. Project description and activities:_____

D. Target population:_____

E. Project staffing:_____

F. Partnerships:_____

G. Evaluation plan:_____

H. Budget information:_____

I. Sustainability of the project:_____

J. Organization's capacity to implement the proposed
   project:_____

Statements

1. Although there are tutoring and recreational programs for very young children, and sports and job training activities for older teenagers, boys between 13 and 16 have few structured activities after school and on weekends.

2. The center's 12-member board of directors includes executives of local businesses, faculty of universities and schools, representatives of churches and hospitals as well as two parent members. The chairman is William Jones, the chief operating officer of the Municipal Life Insurance Company of Indiana.

3. Basketball coaches from Meridian University will teach basketball skills, teamwork, and rules of good sportsmanship to 25 boys ages 13 to 16.

4. The basketball project will improve the boys' physical and social skills, enhance their self-esteem, improve their awareness of options for themselves, and help them control their behavior.

5. Throughout the program, staff will work to communicate the positive impact on sports achievement of good nutrition and other healthy habits and the negative impact of substance use.

6. By the end of the first year of the program, 80 percent of the 25 boys in the basketball project will demonstrate a significant decrease in acting-out behavior in school.

7. The boys who will be recruited for the project live in the North Meridian Mews neighborhood of downtown Metropolis, Indiana, which has a disproportionately low income and a population that is approximately 50 percent African American, 30 percent Hispanic, and 20 percent white.

8. Since it was founded, the center has provided services for approximately 3,000 children, teenagers, and their families, with more than 500 people participating in program activities each year.

9. Project participants will receive lessons on "dressing for success" and will participate in individual and group counseling.

10. Jane Manning has been executive director since the center was founded. A former teacher, principal, and school superintendent, she is a leader in the field of education and has been featured in news articles. For instance, in 2008, the *Metropolis Star* described her "generosity to the children and her enthusiasm for her work."

11. By the end of the first month of the project, the staff of the Meridian Mews Center will recruit and hire a project director and staff for the basketball project.

12. There are swimming programs at the YMCA, but they attract children who are younger than the ones who will participate in the basketball project.

13. The center's all-purpose room is large enough that all 25 boys who are in the program can participate in group activities.

14. No other local youth programs in this community have attempted to tackle the problems confronting 13- to 16-year-old boys with a history of behavior problems.

15. Facilities and resources will be donated by organizations and businesses in the community at no cost to the project.

16. John Jones, in a study conducted in the summer of 2005, found that teenagers from North Meridian Mews were terrorizing the malls and shopping centers of the north side of Metropolis. Almost all of the 15 teenagers he interviewed complained that they "didn't have anything else to do."

17. Basketball coaches, a physical education professor, and a psychologist will participate in the basketball project activities.

18. Team competition will culminate in an award ceremony at which members of the winning team will receive gift certificates from a local business, Ace Sports Supplies.

19. The overall goal of the basketball project is to increase the likelihood that the teenagers who participate in the activities will stay in school longer and become productive members of the North Meridian Mews community.

20. The Meridian Mews Center will contribute the time of the executive director, social worker, bookkeeper, and secretary to the basketball project at no cost to the project.

21. School guidance reports and teacher evaluations will be used to measure this outcome.

22. The proposed basketball project targets 25 teenage boys between 13 and 16 with severe behavior problems and a history of acting out in school.

23. The project director will be a licensed social worker with a minimum of three years' experience directing programs.

24. The Meridian Mews Center is committed to supporting the basketball project in the second year, through additional foundation grants, support from local businesses, and other approaches (see letter of commitment from the board chairman in the Appendix).

25. To measure whether acting-out behavior in school has been reduced in the participants of the basketball project, project staff will develop a short questionnaire that can easily be completed

by the coaches, recreation specialists, teachers, and guidance counselors who work with the boys.

Project Summary (Short-Answer) Exercise

Project summaries should be short and sweet. Looking at each of the program summaries presented just before the pop quiz, answer the following questions:

1. Do they break any of the 12 rules of writing given in Lesson 6?
2. Do they explain the program concisely and clearly?
3. Do they make you want to fund the project?

LESSON 8:
Identifying and Documenting the Need: What Problem Will a Grant Fix?

OPENING REMARKS

A group of three well-dressed women, looking perplexed, asked if they could speak with me after a meeting. They explained that they had to give up their health club memberships because they could no longer afford them. Their companies had downsized, their salaries had been slashed, and their positions were in jeopardy. "I know this might sound far-fetched, but would it be possible for us to convince our local YMCA to get a state-of-the-art gym so we can work out just like we used to?" one of them asked. "The facilities at the Y now are decrepit and the equipment is ancient."

"Well," I pointed out, "you're identifying a compelling problem that affects you, but you aren't framing the problem in a manner that would be likely to entice a foundation that is dealing with one major problem or need after another.

"But maybe you could . . . with a little thought . . . and by thinking of others as well as yourselves."—EK

LEADING QUESTION
Why Would a Grantmaker Give Money to My Organization?

Most foundations and government funders prefer to give grants to address problems where the need is greatest. So how could a YMCA make the case that it needed funding for a state-of-the-art gym in what is presumably a middle-class neighborhood? In this example, the organization would have to think about a broader issue than a few women who want to keep fit. Some questions you might want to raise and answer in a proposal could involve the relationship of exercise to health, and the lack of exercise facilities in the community—not just for adults, but for children, teenagers, and older people as well. Information could be presented showing how many children are sedentary and overweight, or how many older people in a cold or rainy climate fail to get regular exercise. Data that support a need for exercise could be just as relevant to a senior center that wants to get funding for an exercise program for its participants or to an evening teen program that currently offers only boys basketball and wants to engage young women (and young men who may not be great basketball players but do want to be in shape!).

Although the Y may be located in a community that appears to be affluent, that can be deceptive. Forest Hills, a community in New York City once famed for its annual tennis tournament, is perceived as a wealthy suburban area and has its share of affluent residents. But it also has a significant number of lower-income residents with needs that can be documented. Whatever the community's demographics, you must know them in detail, and you must use facts to demonstrate the need or problem you have identified.

DISCUSSION

It should be clear yet again that before you start writing a proposal, you have a lot of ground to cover. You know that a grant is given for specific programs and services that are directed, first, by the grantmaker and then by you, the grant seeker. Even if the grantmaker doesn't appear to require anything specific—there's no rigid application form to fill out, no due date to adhere to, no seemingly limitless program requirements—don't believe it for one second. Read the guidelines and the latest annual report to see what recent grants were approved by the foundation, go to the website, and talk to people who have received funding from the grantmaker. Be sure that the needs you have identified (like health and fitness) are important to the funder and relevant in the current climate.

Because grants generally are earmarked for specific purposes, almost anything (notice we said *almost* anything) a grant will fund is a *solution to a problem* or a *strategy for addressing a need* that you've identified. In the example in the last chapter, the Meridian Mews Center was created by concerned parents to address a growing crime rate among youth. If you're a fifth grade teacher and you want to start an intergenerational program with a neighborhood senior center, it's probably because you've identified a problem that you are anxious to solve. Something is bothering you. Maybe you're concerned that your students aren't getting enough nurturing because their parents are working long hours, or they're from single-parent households. Maybe you've seen some of the school's elderly neighbors sitting on their porches or in front of the senior center looking very bored. Maybe you feel your students are too self-involved and uninterested in the community. Whatever the problem is that you've noticed and that concerns you, the idea for developing a program with the senior center is your way of addressing it. It's your idea for solving a demonstrable, compelling problem.

Even if you're not always sure where in the world your ideas come from, you can be certain that, most of the time, ideas for grant programs don't come out of the blue. You can bet that they're creative, thoughtful responses to identified and compelling problems that are worrying you. But the funder is going to want something concrete to go on, and here's where research—a little or a lot—comes in.

How Do I Prove There's a Compelling Problem That Deserves a Grant?

First of all, don't think that submitting a fabulous program idea to the grantmaker will be enough to win the money. Think about all the fabulous ideas there are. Soothing programs for rambunctious children. Helpful services for harried parents. Technology centers for the whole family in inner-city neighborhoods. Drug prevention programs for middle school girls. Or how about a cutting-edge program for children, including middle school girls and their harried parents, that addresses both technology and drug prevention? So what will persuade a grantmaker that your comprehensive intergenerational program—or the Y's gym mentioned in the opening remarks or the basketball project at the Meridian Mews Center—fills a critical need or addresses a compelling problem?

Too many proposal writers assume that the existence of the problem (and, for that matter, the wisdom of the solution) is obvious. Who could dispute that parents of rambunctious children are harried? Who would argue that drug abuse prevention programs are not needed for middle school girls? Who could imagine that an intergenerational program for fifth graders and nearby seniors is not a great idea? But common sense doesn't always persuade. You can be certain that, no matter how much or how little money you are requesting from a grantmaker, you'll be competing with organizations that have carefully documented their need by using (formally or informally) one or more of the following:

- A variety of economic and demographic statistics about the community, including the latest census data
- Relevant and up-to-date research, trends, and literature
- Anecdotal information from participants, staff, and community residents
- Waiting lists for their programs (or for those of other community organizations)
- Focus group results
- Assessments of needs and evaluations of past programs
- Newspaper reports
- Police precinct data
- Health department data
- School report cards, test scores, attendance figures, demographic data, and incident reports

A few websites listed in Appendix 6 tell you where you can get statistical information that can help in formulating your statement of need.

Examples include the Clearinghouse for Federal Information and the U.S. Bureau of the Census.

Does Every Grant Application Include a Question About Need?

Certain funders, such as the National Endowment for the Arts, do not require an applicant to demonstrate need. Instead, the funder assesses the artist's portfolio and track record. Some fellowships are awarded because of educational achievement. Certain award programs (MacArthur Foundation; Innovations in American Government) do not judge the applicant's need, although Innovations in American Government winners have usually solved enormous problems in creative ways.

Many foundations' grant applications and guidelines don't say a word about a need or problem. They simply ask you to describe your program or your innovation in no more than five pages. But it doesn't matter. Whether or not the funder uses the word "need" or the application package stipulates that a problem must be solved, it is smart to address the need, even if you have to condense it into a couple of paragraphs. In fact, if the foundation grantmakers are local, they may already know the demographics and problems but want to hear, briefly, which issues have a specific impact on your community or program—and to be sure that you know about them.

What Are the Components of a Strong Needs Section or Problem Statement?

If you're like many other proposal writers—especially if you work for a small grassroots or even a medium-size organization—you wear many hats. You have a lot of duties besides looking for grants. The idea of developing a high-quality proposal that everyone is counting on to receive funding is difficult enough; finding data for the need or problem section may send you into panic mode. But it doesn't have to.

First of all, for more reasons than we've yet described, it is important to put yourself in the grantmaker's place. Instead of seeing the program officer of a foundation or government agency as a nasty professor assigning a research paper to an overworked student, look at her or him as someone who has to make an informed decision and persuade others to come to the same conclusion. Foundation program officers must justify grants to a board of directors or trustees. Government agencies are responsible to legislators, who in turn must account to the taxpayers who are footing the bills. So if you were the grantmaker, how important would need be to you?

With a finite amount of money to spend and two delightful arts programs requesting that money, would you give it to the applicant who writes, "All children need exposure to artists and the opportunity to paint on weekends to keep them out of trouble" or the one that says,

> Children in the Wishbone Housing Projects have the highest school dropout rate in the city of Rosemont. Their family income is the lowest of any Rosemont housing project. According to their parents and teachers, as well as police officers, clergy, and local business owners, children who will participate in this weekend arts project have no other activities to occupy them. The proposed arts program has been shown in other cities (e.g., Memphis and Sacramento) to provide children with an outlet that increases reading scores, reduces their participation in vandalism, and encourages them to stay in school.

If you have space, you might insert a chart here, documenting the facts you are presenting. No contest, right?

Target Population. As the example above indicates, you need to describe a target population, the group that has the need and to whom your program will be directed. In this case, the population is low-income children living in public housing in Rosemont, but it could be elderly immigrants in Milwaukee. You need to show that those living in the target area are needier than those in other areas, using key indicators such as income, age, education, employment status, crime, and many other statistics that we will describe later in this lesson. You would collect data for the target area, for the city as a whole, and perhaps for the state as well. The table below (with invented numbers for an invented housing project, city, and state) shows how you might analyze this information. You may decide not to include a chart like this in the proposal, but organizing the data will help you explain clearly how your target population differs from the rest of your city, town, or state.

Sample Population Statistics

Indicator	Wishbone	Rosemont	Statewide
Average family income	$16,000	$32,000	$36,000
Percentage of single-parent households	67%	25%	22%
School dropout rates	44%	22%	18%

Context. The best way to approach the need section is to put your particular problem in a context. If it's relevant, you may want to start with a national context. The teacher who is concerned that her students don't get enough nurturing would probably find a great deal written on the topic, and the information should not necessarily be disregarded because it reflects a research study that was done in California when her school is in Maine. What are the national trends? What kinds of research have been done and with what findings? Once a national perspective has been addressed, move in closer to your own city, town, or neighborhood. Often a simple search online, or at the local public or college library, will bring you a wealth of relevant information.

Are Proposals Different for the Federal Government and National Foundations?

The need or problem statement for a proposal to a federal agency or a national foundation usually requires some extra work. Just like other grantmakers, these funders look for a detailed description of the population to be served and strong justification of the need for the proposed project (the funding agency may call this a needs assessment, a problem statement, or something similar). Unlike private funders in your state, however, who probably are fully aware of conditions in your community, the people who read and score federal applications may be from anywhere in the country, and those who read for national foundations may be consultants hired to develop and judge specific grant programs. Although they are experts in their own fields, they are likely to be unfamiliar with the physical, political, and social conditions in your area. They know nothing about your experience and qualifications in the field (although a separate section of the proposal will document this), and usually they are giving very substantial grants for which they expect clear results. So for these proposals it is doubly important to include:

- Proof that the target population in the community is in fact eligible to receive services under the federal or foundation guidelines
- Data that demonstrate the existence and extent of the problem in the community, including specific gaps in service that the proposal will address
- Full understanding of the theories and practices that have been put forward to attempt to solve the problem in your community and elsewhere
- Knowledge of relevant solutions that have worked in your community and elsewhere, especially when some elements of these efforts are incorporated into the proposed program plan
- Explanation of why there is still a need for a new program if successful solutions already exist

Example. Here's one way of moving from a sweeping national perspective to a local one. (It's pure fiction, by the way.)

Many researchers have identified a lack of parental nurturing as a problem for children in today's economic and social environment. The absence of nurturing is, according to Ames (2008),* Reese (2008), Bolger (2003), Uncles (2005), and others, the primary cause of student alienation and disenfranchisement, which can lead to violence, suicide, and other dangerous behaviors.

In studies in Texas (Jones, 2007) and California (Smith, 2006) researchers have found that 75 percent of teachers report that their students "practically seem to be raising themselves." Piazza (2005) indicates that 56 percent of fourth graders in his Pennsylvania research study don't see their parents until after dinner, and Wilson (2008), in Wisconsin, suggests that more than half of the state's seven-year-olds go to day care centers for at least three hours after school.

The lack of nurturing is both a national and a local problem in Indiana. For example, in Metropolis, Richardson (2009) found that more than 60 percent of elementary school children studied in a citywide project were "latchkey children" at least three days a week. In North Metropolis, the problem is even greater. A citywide study of what children do after school and on weekends (Johnson, 2008) indicated that more than 80 percent either go to crowded day care centers or sit in front of their television sets watching programs in an unsupervised manner. And in the target neighborhood of Meridian Mews, Johnson found the situation even worse. Ninety percent of the children under 16 who live in the neighborhood served by

* This form of documenting sources is from the American Psychological Association, and we use it because it doesn't clutter the text or take up room for footnotes at the bottom of the page. We would put an alphabetized reference list at the end of the grant proposal, giving the authors' names, date of publication, city of publication, publisher's name, and page of a quotation, if any. But any other reference system can be used (e.g., putting all of the reference information into a footnote), as long as it is consistent throughout the proposal.

the Meridian Mews Elementary School do not see their parents until after 9:00 P.M.

Warning. There is a temptation to throw research data, statistics, and other documentation of need into the grant proposal haphazardly. Proposal writers can be so ecstatic over finding usable information that they may neglect organizing the material to make their case for the need. But this portion of the proposal is not too different from a research paper. The variable is how much research—and what kinds—makes the most sense for a specific grant proposal. You almost certainly wouldn't do the kind of work involved in the example above for a $5,000 grant. But even if you are requesting only $5,000 and the proposal is only three pages long, it is a good policy to show you are informed about the problem and include some documentation, even if only in a footnote or parentheses. Again, put yourself in the program officer's shoes. Wouldn't a presentation of pertinent information encourage you to think highly of an applicant's seriousness—and appreciate her respect for you as a grantmaker?

But I'm a Nonprofit Staffer, Not a Doctoral Candidate at Harvard . . .

Stay calm. A closer look at the components will reassure you that the grant proposal is not the equivalent of a doctoral dissertation—well, not exactly. The information you need should be readily available if you've done the prep work we described in Lesson 4. Much of this information can be pulled from your files and just updated. Let's talk about other kinds of information, and then go back to "the literature."

Community Demographics. Most government grants (and many foundation grants) are targeted to communities with predominantly low-income populations. Many are targeted to specific members of a low-income community, like children, AIDS patients, unemployed or underemployed individuals, a particular immigrant group, and so on. Your first stop for this kind of information is the municipal or county agency that deals with the population of interest to you—a child welfare agency, a housing agency, a board of education or school district office (the LEA), a department of employment, and so on. Localities maintain a gold mine of statistics on issues like homelessness, poverty, income, race/ethnicity, public assistance, foster care, substance use, schools, recreational facilities, hospital admissions, vital statistics, vandalism—you name it.

Another excellent place to start is the local census office, if there is one, or your city or county planning department. You also may try your main library (most have terminals you can use to access census data), or nearby college and university libraries. You often will find important data in city or county management reports, and at municipal, state, and federal government websites. Local United Ways and other large not-for-profit organizations collect all sorts of statistical information and may publish it online or make it available at their offices. Get on every mailing list and send for free newsletters and other documents that may be useful. The school district or central board of education will have information on students and should be delighted to talk about educational and other school needs as you prepare your proposals for grants that will help youngsters. Similarly, the department of health will help you identify needs for health-related proposals.

(Of course, if you are developing a grant proposal that includes schoolchildren, you should be working closely with the schools and school district on program planning. If you just walk into a school and announce, "I'm applying for a grant to provide after-school services to your students," the school personnel will likely feel excluded from a process to which they could and should add important insights. The same principle holds true for proposals that affect all local government agencies.)

Remember that your own records also provide important data. Whenever possible, the program should have an entry form that summarizes as much information as the participant will stand for—and as much as your

ability to protect her/his privacy will support. (Sometimes this isn't feasi-
ble; a jumpy out-of-school youth population, for example, may resist providing you with any information, and in order to retain their trust you
may not want to try.) Surveys of participants can help too. A survey of
parents of the children in one after-school program we know showed that
92 percent of the parents were born outside the United States. Talk about
a gold nugget of support for an agency that seeks funding to serve immigrants! And keep records of individuals who want to participate in your
program but have to be turned away. From Meals on Wheels to sixth grade
karate, if your program can't meet the demand, you can show a need.

Anecdotal Information. Many proposal writers shy away from anecdotal information, fearing that it is too casual. But anecdotal information
can be very powerful when used in the right way. It can put a human face
on otherwise cold statistical reports. And sometimes there just isn't any
hard "proof" that a problem really exists—although "everyone knows"
that it does. There may not be actual data on whether the residents of a
senior center are bored, but formal or informal interviews with senior
center staff, participants, and family members may indicate universal
agreement. People may be willing to say things in response to oral questions that they wouldn't say in a written questionnaire.

When using anecdotal information in a grant proposal, be careful not
to insert it haphazardly so it seems fabricated. A good approach is to cite
the individuals you've spoken to—if not by name, then by title or relationship to the community. For example:

> The director of the Starview Teen Center has tried for the last two
> years to get teenagers to join clubs such as chess and current events,
> and take trips to places like museums and sporting events. But he
> has found that they are apathetic and unwilling to do anything but
> play basketball. Two mothers of teenagers here say that their sons
> seem lethargic; another mother says . . .

Although these data are "soft," the problem is very real. It is hard (though possible) to measure "tried to get teenagers to join the chess club," but efforts to get the teenagers involved can be described. Interviewing the Teen Center director is a good way to glean poignant stories that add human interest to a proposal.

Focus Groups. Information gathered from focus groups reflects the participants' dialogue, interaction, and safety-in-numbers venting about a problem. A focus group is just a gathering of people with opinions on or a vested interest in a particular issue, who respond to a set of questions prepared by a neutral facilitator to collect those opinions. The discussion can be recorded on audio or videotape, or by a stenographer; the object is to have a usable record of what is said, for inclusion in a proposal, report, or advocacy document (or all of these). A single focus group can include a few individuals; a more elaborate effort can include hundreds of people who represent one side or many sides of an issue, randomly assigned to discussion groups. Focus groups can help you clarify the problem and craft a solution that is likely to work. Because of the importance of "community buy-in" or "stakeholder buy-in" to the success of any program, focus groups are becoming more and more common.

Grant seekers sometimes make the mistake of expecting the community—the stakeholders—to come to focus group meetings at locations convenient for everyone except the stakeholders. Don't hold such meetings at the university or a hall outside the community, even if someone gives you the space for free. It is crucial to have the meetings in the communities where the problem exists and where the solution will be implemented. To get the maximum amount of information from the greatest number of participants, you should expect to hold more than one focus group meeting, scheduled at different times of the day, on different days of the week, translated into different languages depending on the target population, and offering the services of a sign language interpreter.

Needs Assessments. Needs assessments generally are used to document conditions in a community or population that show gaps in service that you intend to fill. Normally, a community needs assessment is a fairly major project that will be used for many purposes for several years. Ideally, a needs assessment report will include statistical data, anecdotal information, and results of interviews and focus groups (as well as any of the other sources described here). The needs assessment can be as formal as a major research project using validated survey instruments to collect information from a random sample of community residents or target populations; such an approach generally requires consulting assistance—at least—from a university research program, and can be very costly. Before you plunge into such a study, check with your city or county planning office, mayor's or city manager's office, state or local elected officials, other community organizations, or a nearby university library to see if this has been done already.

On the other hand, a needs assessment can be as informal as your own staff members collecting questionnaire responses from your current program participants. The important thing to remember here is what you need the information for: systematic documentation of a gap in services. If you find a community needs assessment that gives you information on all services and needs except health—but you are considering developing a women's health clinic—then it is worthless to you and you had better conduct your own.

Newspaper Reports. Newspapers are convenient sources for all kinds of powerful material that can be included in the needs section of a grant proposal, either alone or supplementing other statistics. Newspapers from all over the world can be read online, either free or for a modest fee, so if you want to know whether the problems you are addressing are more than local, you can see what's happening in other cities or countries.

If you want to provide seniors in your community with information about and help in applying for government assistance to heat their homes in winter, an article in the local paper about the problem, with photographs of elderly people wearing coats, scarves, and gloves indoors, will be as compelling as health department statistics about illnesses and deaths attributable to the cold (use *both* for the most compelling argument). When other data are unavailable (e.g., if your health department doesn't keep such statistics), newspaper articles still can serve as support for your position. If you have the time or staff (or interns or volunteers), review the local papers daily and clip articles that may become relevant to your proposals and your reports to the funders. Sometimes you can use these in an appendix too.

Police Precinct Data. If your program is intended to serve youth at risk of substance use, vandalism, gang participation, or crime; if you want to show the need for an alternative sentencing program for youth or adults; if your focus is on neighborhood crime prevention efforts; or if you want to show a need for any similar crime prevention or intervention program, your first stop is the local police department or precinct. All police departments are required to maintain data on a variety of types of crime, and they usually compile it by geographic area and age of the offender. How it is summarized or released to the public may differ by state or locality. You should find out whether you must apply to the local police station, the central police department offices, or some other department to obtain statistics. You may be required to submit a formal written request, stating how you will use the information, or you may be encouraged to visit the officer in charge of maintaining the data. You may be allowed to photocopy the police statistics or summaries, or you may have to sit in the office and take notes. Be sure you know what the requirements are well in advance of your need for information—and be sure you leave plenty of time for the precinct (or yourself) to collect and organize the information.

School Reading and Math Scores, Attendance Figures, Dropout Rates, and Violent-Incident Reports. Similarly, if you plan to run a program meant to help children or teenagers improve their academic achievement, stay in school, go on to college, or any other education-related initiative, you should be able to show the need through data from the school in question, the school district, the local education agency, or state department of education. If you don't already know which standardized tests are used in your community, or at what grade levels they're given, you should. Show that your target school (or schools) has a greater proportion of children scoring below grade level on these tests than other schools in the district; show that the school (or schools) has a higher dropout rate or more incidents of violence than others in the community. You also may be able to demonstrate from school records that your school has a higher proportion of children in poverty (e.g., a greater percentage of children eligible for free meals) than elsewhere.

Hospital and Health Department Statistics. If your program is intended to address domestic violence, teen pregnancy prevention, alcohol, tobacco, and other drug use, children's asthma, gunshot wounds, or any other health-related issue, your local hospital and state and local health departments will be good places to start. If the particular institution does not keep data on a particular problem, staff there will be able to refer you to appropriate sources.

The Literature. Yes, relevant and up-to-date research, trends, and literature are the types of information included in college and graduate school research papers, but you are generally not expected to scour every esoteric journal or conduct far-flung searches for your proposal. But it helps your cause if you know what the trends and issues are in your area of interest. And why wouldn't you want to know this?

Let's say, for instance, that the literature on nurturing is controversial (some may think there is a subtle "family values" message that encourages parents to stay at home). It would be important to know this and cite it. Suppose that recent trends in the attitudes toward latchkey children indicated that, rather than being disenfranchised and at risk, these children developed strength, character, and resiliency. You would acknowledge this in the proposal, and offer other reasons why it's still important to run a program for these children.

Most important, being familiar with the literature—which is another way of saying the prevailing or conventional wisdom, the accepted thinking—will help you design, refine, and enrich your program. It will afford you the opportunity to study best practices and see what kinds of program elements have been more or less successful. This component of your needs section leads you into describing your program idea. What, if anything, has been tried in your community to address the problem that you have identified? Why do you think these efforts have failed? Why will your program not repeat past mistakes? Why do you expect the "stakeholders" to "buy in"? Even a brief review of the literature can help you address these questions in your program and proposal.

Here again, a search engine such as Google can help you get this information. Thanks to the Internet, there is no longer any good excuse for ignoring trends and research on a full range of issues.

Stop for a Minute: Do I Have to Identify a Need or a Problem If I'm Looking for a Grant to Study Abroad or to Make a Movie?

No. Individual grants are different. They may be connected to a college or university. As we discussed earlier, grantmaking decisions may rely on your portfolio of work, your experience, and other documentation. The National Endowment for the Arts application that we talked about in Lesson 3 explicitly requires that grant seekers have had their work published a certain number of times in specific types of publications. You need only show that you meet their guidelines.

What If the Grantmaker Has Identified the Problems *for* Me?

Although foundations tend to provide funding in certain topic areas (such as youth, parks and open spaces, AIDS prevention, the arts) that are spelled out in their annual reports, they generally don't tell you how to identify or solve problems within the areas that they fund. You could apply either to a "youth" or an "aging" funder with your intergenerational program for fifth graders and senior citizens. You know the types of projects the funder supports because you have read the annual report and the website. You know the topic areas the funder supports. It's up to you to describe the problem and explain why the program you've developed will more than likely solve it. It's also up to you to describe the need for your program in a way that clearly shows how it fits the funder's priorities.

Unlike most foundations, federal government agencies and large national foundations spend a good deal of time spelling out a problem in the application package, usually citing research on a problem of national importance that they expect the grant seeker to solve locally. In the Safe Schools/Healthy Students initiative discussed in Lesson 3, the problem to be solved involves the perceived danger that schoolchildren face both in school and out of school. The Innovations in American Government Awards program (also discussed in Lesson 3) asks about both your problem and your solution—as long as the solution can be replicated in other cities and reflects an innovative public-private partnership.

Another Intangible. This is a good time to mention again that you shouldn't seek a grant to solve a problem that you don't have or is not a high priority for your organization. Too many not-for-profits are so desperate for money that they may try to get any funding that's available, even if it's not directly related to what they really want to do. A child care agency in dire need of money might apply for funds to provide homemaker services. An arts organization in serious financial trouble might apply for a grant to provide substance use intervention.

Even if such organizations genuinely believed they could offer these services effectively, this fundraising approach could endanger their organization's mission by moving into areas that are outside its experience and fundamental concern. But what is more likely to happen is that the grantmaker will see this as a ploy to get money, not an honest attempt to solve a compelling problem. The need for support may be very, very real and very, very compelling. And the grantmaker may understand this and sympathize. But an honest request for funding from sources that are appropriate is a far better approach than scattershot applications to anyone and everyone who offers grants.

Pop Quiz

Multiple Choice

Select the best conclusion to each of the following statements:

1. Grants are usually given to organizations that can demonstrate
    a) longevity of five years or more
    b) continuity of leadership (same leader for no less than two years)
    c) creativity in juggling their mission statements
    d) compelling need

2. Which of the following is not a good example of the kind of data you might include in a grant proposal?
    a) police precinct data
    b) anecdotal information (e.g., stories about a client's need)
    c) focus groups
    d) your own intuition

3. The best example of a needs statement is:
    a) According to police precinct data, 50 percent of youth between 15 and 19 in the Bayside neighborhood have been arrested.
    b) According to the Area Agency on Aging, 75 percent of senior citizens in the South Senior Center are immigrants who don't know if they can receive any benefits.
    c) Three clergymen in Bayside expressed their concern about the drug problem.
    d) All of the above are good examples.

4. How many footnotes should there be in a typical needs section of a grant proposal?

a) No more than 5

b) No fewer than 10

c) At least 1

d) As many as you need to make your case

LESSON 9:
Goals and Objectives: What Do You Hope to Achieve If You Get the Money?

OPENING REMARKS

I can't tell you how many conversations I've had with managers, program planners, proposal writers, and others about goals and objectives. Over and over, even from the most experienced individuals, I hear the same questions. What is a goal? How does it differ from a mission? What is an objective? How does it differ from a task? And how do I figure out what mine should be? They know what they want to achieve, but they're intimidated by this formal way of expressing it. No wonder the goals and objectives section of a grant proposal is the one that proposal writers often think they can just gloss over.—ASF

LEADING QUESTIONS
So—What Are Goals and Objectives?

Goals normally refer to broad, long-term intentions. Although goals are similar to a mission statement, the latter usually suggests the overall purpose for an organization's existence, for example, to work to improve the lives of children. Goals normally pertain to issues you want to address, for example, to improve the education system in this community.

Because goals are broad statements of intention, a particular goal probably won't be met within the time period of a proposed grant project, and probably can't be met through the project alone, if at all. Everyone, proposal writer and grantmaker alike, is aware of this. For example, eliminating youth violence is a goal that, realistically, may never be achieved completely, and certainly not by a single organization or program within a year or two, because it is affected by factors that are numerous, complex, and to a large extent outside the control of most possible interventions. A proposed program, say, a youth mediation program, may be only one of many possible steps toward reaching this ultimate goal.

Objectives should be thought of as outcomes that can be expected from the project itself. Whereas the accomplishment of goals may or may not be subject to measurement, objectives must be concrete and specific, measurable, realistic, attainable, and time-bound. We'll show you how to do this a little later in the lesson. Creation of such clear, measurable objectives is necessary to the development of an appropriate evaluation plan, which we'll discuss in a later lesson. (As you can see, each section of a proposal is connected to the other sections. One person can't write the goals and objectives, another the evaluation plan, and another the budget.)

Everybody Says I've Got a Great Program Here. So Why Do I Need to Talk About Goals and Objectives? Why Can't I Just Talk About the Great Program?

A good program speaks for itself, doesn't it? Let's be blunt: As great as the program seems, if you haven't thought through what it's really supposed to do, you may be wasting your time and money (and your funder's)—or you may in fact be doing more than you think, only in the wrong arena. Too often people design a program that has little to do with a problem they've identified, and nothing to do with solving the problem. Maybe this is because the program is what their staff members are good at; maybe it's because clients are asking for it; or maybe it does address a problem, just not the one they think they're addressing. But they won't really know that unless they do some systematic assessment. And when they seek funding for this program, or when they have to report on it to get a renewal grant, they'll have a hard time making the case that it has accomplished anything substantive.

DISCUSSION

Because so many proposal writers take a "let's get a grant to pay for our excellent programs" approach—and may have succeeded to some extent when the economy was better—it is not surprising that the idea of methodically moving from a well-documented problem through measurable objectives to a well-designed program seems like a lot of needless work. But what is a good program if it doesn't achieve desired outcomes? If your first grader spent three hours each week in a delightful Saturday reading program, would that delightfulness be enough for you if the program didn't improve her reading ability? And what if you were paying $5,000 a year for the program? Would you even use the word "delightful"? Come to think of it, what does "delightful" actually mean when placed next to the words "reading program"? That the classroom is colorful and festively decorated? That the instructor has a winning smile? That the children are adorable and well behaved? Remember Rule 9 in Lesson 6, about meaningless adjectives? "Delightful" may have a place in a reading program, along with many other important elements, but it has no place in a grant application. Let's look at some examples of concrete objectives.

- "Delightfulness" of a program cannot be measured—but scores on reading tests and attitudes toward books and reading can. So one obvious measurable objective for a weekend reading program would be an improvement in reading scores by the end of the year. Because reading scores are affected by many variables—everything from the child's physical and mental health to things going on in the home—a weekly program cannot be expected to magically raise scores, say, by a full grade level. But it should be expected to raise the average scores for all the children by at least a small measurable amount.
- A second objective for the reading program might be any measurable improvement in children's expressed enjoyment of reading

(attitudes toward reading), on a standardized, validated attitudinal survey.

- Objectives for a mediation program for at-risk youth might include a positive change among program participants, by the end of the first six months or year, on a standardized measure of attitudes toward nonviolent conflict resolution; a reduction of 50 percent in violent incidents among the participants by the end of the project; and a 60 percent increase in school attendance in that population during the same period. (Notice that we said "objectives." There are three different objectives mentioned here—and each is measurable.)

What About the Grantmaker's Goals and Objectives?

There are two layers of goals and objectives to think about, and each layer is significant: First, the goals and objectives of the funder, whether stated or unstated, must be understood, and then the goals and objectives of the grant applicant must fit cozily into the context of the funder's requirements.

Many foundations approve funding for a range of programs, letting the prospective grantees decide what goals and objectives they hope to achieve. But government agencies, and many larger foundations, usually have stated or unstated sets of goals and objectives that they expect the applicant to address. If the program announcement or guidelines spell out the goals and objectives for a federal grant program (say, to reduce incidents of domestic violence in an immigrant community), or if the goals and objectives are stated or implied in the background or legislative history of the program (the Violence Against Women Act), the proposal that is submitted should incorporate those goals and objectives into the applicant's own plan.

For example, depending on their perspective, goals, and target populations, some grantmakers expect to see an increase in arrests by the time a funded program is over (because of more police vigilance in a certain community); conversely, some might call for a decrease in arrests at the end of the program (because of a reduction in crime). Some funders expect to see that program participants apply to college in significantly higher numbers than nonparticipants. It is important not to lose sight of the goals and objectives of the grantmaker because the money will be allocated to achieving them. Sometimes these goals and objectives are the result of extensive research in a field previously funded by a government agency; often too they are part of a political agenda. If a presidential, congressional, gubernatorial, or mayoral candidate runs as the "education guru" or the "crime buster," campaign promises may be fulfilled through grants to programs intended to fix the problems the candidate complained about during the campaign.

But even if proposal writers are working with the goals and objectives stipulated by a funding agency, their own goals and objectives should emerge clearly as a logical response to the proposal's statement of need, not as a rote response to a funder's demand for specific goals and objectives. We are completely in favor of using the grantmaker's own language as often as possible in a proposal (in the text and in the subheads), but it must be used within your own specific context or the proposal will fail.

With all this talk of using the grantmaker's own language, it might be a good time to go back to Lesson 3 and revisit the various application packages to see what we mean by language. To reiterate, both foundation and government program officers generally have worked long and hard on the research and policymaking that goes into crafting a program announcement, application or proposal guidelines, or requests for proposals. There is nothing pandering about reflecting either the grantmaker's language or research or perspective in your grant proposal, if you agree with the approach. If you disagree with the funder's premises or priorities—either politically or philosophically—then don't apply for the grant!

"WE'RE AT THAT AWKWARD STAGE OF TRYING TO EXPLAIN A COMPLETELY ACCIDENTAL DISCOVERY AS OUR INTENDED OBJECTIVE."

How Do I Make My Program's Objectives Fit with Those of the Funder Without Losing the Whole Purpose of the Program?

You don't! Remember, you are not going to do anything different from what you believe is needed to solve the problem you have identified. You are just going to think about how you may describe your program and your intended outcomes to make it clear that they will meet the funder's own objectives too. Before writing your objectives, carefully check what the application package says about the program requirements. Have specific objectives been identified that you are expected to address and achieve? What is the problem that the program has been designed to fix? And finally, what elements of the program are likely to alleviate the problem?

The Safe Schools/Healthy Students application package discussed earlier, for example, requires that objectives be reflected in six different areas—a safe school environment is one of the six safe school policies. Applicants are expected to "develop performance indicators that link to proposed goals and objectives, and include levels of performance for each indicator, time frames for achieving levels of performance for each indicator, and source of data for measuring progress." For this grant, you can't choose a couple of the six areas that are targeted. If all six aren't right for your community, then don't waste your time.

Again, your intention is to understand what the funder is getting at. Why has the money been allocated? What does the funder hope and expect will happen by the conclusion of the project period? Sometimes proposal writers are so anxious to win grant funds that they overlook the funder's goals and objectives in expressing their own. If a grant from a local foundation is earmarked for programs that will decrease the number of students who drop out of high school before graduating, for instance, you certainly would approve of a reduction in the dropout rate. But you're concerned right now with getting money to pay for a collaborative after-school basketball project. If you only give lip service to the dropout problem, you may be missing the ways in which this basketball project can successfully address the escalating dropout rate in your community. If you think about the design of the after-school basketball project as a solution to the dropout problem rather than merely as "an excellent program," you certainly will come up with a number of worthy measurable objectives that the program should be expected to achieve, and you may want to add some programmatic elements to achieve them.

We can think of three objectives for a collaborative after-school basketball project for at-risk youth, including a reduced dropout rate for participants (there are many more).

- *Objective 1: Improved Behavior.* By the end of the first six months of the project, participants in the after-school basketball project will demonstrate improved behavior in school as a result of project requirements and activities, as measured by incident reports and teacher observations before the league started and six months later.

- **Objective 2: Reduction in Violent Incidents.** By the end of the basketball project, participants will demonstrate a 50 percent decrease in violent incidents as measured by school incident reports.
- **Objective 3: Improved School Attendance.** By the end of the basketball project, participants will have a 40 percent better school attendance record than students who did not participate in project activities.

These measurable objectives may seem surprising. Maybe when you started thinking about the basketball project you imagined teenagers coming to the gym, changing their clothes, getting out on the court, and starting the game. But if you receive funding to reduce the dropout rate and you hope to achieve that objective, then while the teenagers are "just" having a good time playing ball, adding some elements to that basic scenario could achieve it. And the popularity of the activity—basketball—could help you introduce these elements without losing participants.

For example, if you require the ball players to arrive by 3:15 PM or be benched for that day, you are teaching them promptness and responsibility without necessarily saying so. Before the games begin, you may feature a discussion period (with light refreshments), led by a popular "coach" who is actually a social worker with experience working with at-risk teenagers. The coach might ask the students to talk about their day in school and any problems that they experienced, and use peer counseling techniques to help them resolve these problems. Discussions on sportsmanship, fair play, and following rules could be emphasized during the games, with team penalties enforced for roughhousing and offensive language. On some occasions the games could be followed by a potluck supper, with the families of the ballplayers included.

Or, instead of discussions before the games, you might run a homework help program, with tutors from a nearby college who are studying to be teachers (and who also might serve as coaches), as a condition of playing.

What started out as a simple after-school basketball project has evolved into a program with a very outcome-directed twist. Every activity associated with the basketball project is part of a master plan that expects to solve a compelling problem and achieve measurable objectives. And it in no way detracts from the teenagers' fun.

Once the objectives are decided on—with the participation of program staff with the required expertise to help you assess whether the objectives are realistic and optimistic—it is much easier to design a comprehensive program. If you try to design a program without objectives guiding you . . . well, forget about it. It just makes no sense.

Pop Quiz

Multiple Choice

Which activity would be most likely to achieve each of the objectives listed below?

1. To increase school attendance for teenagers who are truant:

    a) Send warnings home to the parents each time the student is absent.

    b) Provide student stipends based on good attendance records.

2. To decrease feelings of loneliness and depression among seniors at a senior center:

    a) Stock the senior center with extra televisions in every room.

    b) Develop a program that brings young children to the senior center to join seniors in an intergenerational arts program.

3. To make the streets in your community safer:

    a) Ensure a greater police presence.

    b) Start a block watch committee.

    c) Both of the above.

Realistic/Unrealistic?

Which of the following objectives are realistic for a one-year career education course for unemployed adults?

1. Sixty percent of the participants will remain employed for three years after the program ends.

2. Participants will show improved attitudes toward work after completing the year-long course.

3. Participants in the one-year program will attend an average of 85 percent of the sessions.

LESSON 10:
Developing and Presenting a Winning Program

OPENING REMARKS

I was working with the director of a youth program who wanted a federal grant for educational support for young women. Because he didn't have time to work on the proposal with me, we met briefly to discuss his plans. Then I constructed what seemed like a responsible program to meet his objectives for the young women as well as the objectives of the funder. But I made some assumptions that we had not discussed directly. The request for proposals required intensive work with participants, although the grants would be small. I designed a small program addressed to the age group we had agreed on, showed how it would fit into an existing program, and specified that a small number of new staff would be hired to work with the small group of young women who were identified as most needing the help. It turned out that the director had envisioned the grant supporting a much larger number of existing staff, working with all of the young women in that program. When he finally had time to read the draft, it became clear that we had to start over or scrap the proposal entirely. Unfortunately, because of the limited time left to revise the plan, the latter was the end result.—ASF

LEADING QUESTIONS
Okay, I've Identified a Need and Set Out Some Goals and Objectives for a Program I Think Will Meet That Need. Now What?

It's finally time for the meat, the heart, of the grant proposal. The program description, or program plan, should show that you have a thoughtful, workable solution to the problem that you described in the need statement. A clear and detailed description of the proposed program must be strongly supported in several ways. And, as the example above demonstrates, these details must be worked out (and sometimes argued out) in an ongoing, close partnership between the proposal writer, who understands the scope and limitations of the request for proposals, and the program supervisor and project staff, who understand the population to be served, the needs to be met, and their own objectives for the funding.

The Program Description Must Match the Funder's Priorities. The program description should explain what you intend to do and clearly address what you know about the funder's priorities. As we've said before, whenever possible, use language from the grantmaker's guidelines to describe your own program, to show readers that the proposal focuses on the grantmaker's concerns as much as your own.

Note again that this is not—indeed, must not be—a matter of changing the way your program operates in order to meet the guidelines. When organizations change their programs to chase funding rather than because they see the need or because they have thought of a better way to do things, they can lose touch with what they're working for. Rather, describe your program in a way that lets the reader see how it fits into the funder's priorities.

The Program Description Must Address Your Problem. Next, your program description must show exactly and realistically how the program will solve the problem you have identified. You need to include enough details to demonstrate that the planned activities, the number and type of staff, the number and type of persons who are to receive services, and the time frames for accomplishing your objectives are realistic, and that the program you have designed has a good chance of succeeding in achieving those objectives.

The Program Description Must Be Consistent with Other Parts of the Proposal (Not to Mention Clear and Well Organized). Consistency across all components of the proposal is extremely important. If one of your objectives is to deliver 80 additional meals a day to homebound individuals, you must be able to show exactly how you plan to accomplish this. How will you route deliveries to accommodate your full roster of old and new recipients, and still deliver the meals while they're hot? Will you use an existing van for one or more additional routes? Will you purchase an additional van, and if so, is that part of the current proposal, or do you have other funding sources for it? Will you hire additional staff to prepare and deliver the meals, or will you use existing staff and volunteers? How many of each, how do you arrive at that number, and how will you re-arrange the time of existing staff to squeeze in any additional meals that they need to prepare and deliver? Who will supervise them? How will you train any new workers to serve your target population?

In later lessons we discuss additional elements of your proposal that must be consistent with the objectives and the program, including evaluation and budget; for the moment, remember that you also need to know how much the extra 80 meals a day will cost, how much of that expense you are asking for in this grant proposal, and where the rest of the money is coming from.

The Program Description Must Show How the Proposed Program Will Fit into the Organization. You may not just be adding 80 additional meals, but rather creating an entirely new program, which cannot be "added on," no matter how needed, but instead must be fully integrated into the organization. If the Meals on Wheels program is new, you also must discuss issues like who will manage it, where it fits in the overall organization structure, what other programs should be linked to it, and for what purposes.

Whether the funding agency requires it or not, system-wide changes may be an outgrowth of many grants, especially very large ones, and you need to describe what changes you might anticipate and how they would be managed under the proposed program. For example, the Safe Schools/Healthy Students initiative provides enormously important "extras"—worth about $3 million—to a local school district. But these extra programs, services, and staff members cannot be slapped onto the district's structure like a sloppy coat of paint. The grant programs must become an integral part of the school district, linked to all the other instructional, recreational, criminal justice, parent involvement, and mental health activities being conducted in the district's schools. You will need to show in your grant proposal exactly how you plan to achieve this.

It Seems Like a Waste of Time to Do All This Planning When We Don't Know If We'll Even Get a Grant. Why Can't I Figure Out My Plans Once I Win the Grant?

Writing a proposal that doesn't include a detailed, specific plan of operation is like a builder trying to build a house without blueprints. Program plans are the blueprint of the program and the proposal. The reason that proposals generally follow a path that begins with a compelling, documented problem to be solved, followed by measurable objectives, is to make sure that the activities—the plan of operation, the blueprint, the meat of the grant—are designed to increase the chances of achieving the objectives.

A person who wants to start literacy classes for immigrants probably recognizes a need or problem that confronts immigrants in her community. She sees a literacy program as a good solution to the problem. We hope that she also recognizes the need to spell out measurable objectives that can be achieved through the program. Maybe she wants 60 Spanish-speaking immigrants to learn to read newspapers and be able to fill out forms written in English. Maybe she wants the participants to be able to apply for, and get, jobs, or prepare for the citizenship examination. Maybe she hopes they'll learn how to read labels on the food they buy for their families at local supermarkets. The objectives frame the way that activities will be designed to achieve them.

Without linking activities directly to objectives, proposal writers can get carried away. Suddenly they may find themselves proposing to take participants in their programs to the theater as a way to learn English. If you don't look carefully and repeatedly at the objectives as the activities are being planned and developed, the program elements are likely to be haphazard and random. They may be fun, like going to the theater, but what outcomes are they achieving? (And if you think the theater outings really will achieve your objectives, why would a funder give you money for the theater without knowing why you are going?)

How Can I Know Whether Certain Activities Will Achieve Objectives?

As we said earlier, this should be the easy part. You, the development department's only proposal writer, may have absolutely no background in literacy programs, no knowledge of immigrant cultures. Or you, the program person and writer, may have a lot of knowledge about literacy or about immigrants and their cultures; this may be your area of expertise. But no matter what the programmatic expertise of the person writing the proposal, individuals with experience, background information, and commitment to the community certainly must be deeply involved in the development of the program and the fleshing out of the activities. They're the ones who know what activities are likely to work to meet the objectives—and they're the ones who will have to run the program and who will be responsible for the results.

What's in a Program Plan?

The program plan must address everything that will occur from the time a grant award is announced to the time the money is received, and to the end of the funding period (and beyond).

Time Line and Staff Responsibilities. Construct a time line, whether or not the application requires one. The time line should include absolutely every activity that you must undertake to establish, implement, and evaluate the program. What will you do in month 1? Who will do it? Can you do more than one thing in the first month, or will you be spreading yourself too thin? Here is a sample time line for the literacy program for Spanish-speaking immigrants (by the way, notice our use the active voice, as discussed in Lesson 6):

- *Upon notice of a grant award:* Agency director recruits project director through advertising on the Internet and in local newspapers, notices to relevant organizations, flyers in local schools. If appropriate, agency director begins to form an advisory board for the project.
- *Month 1:* If not completed before proposal was submitted, advisory board initiates community literacy needs assessment using focus groups, surveys, and questionnaires. With input from the advisory board, agency director hires project director.
- *Month 1 to Month 2:* Project director takes the lead in working with the advisory board; begins recruiting project staff. Project director and advisory committee collect relevant curricula from appropriate sources, review, and adapt to serve the needs of the program. If necessary, staff members develop a new curriculum.
- *Month 2:* Project director, with advice from the advisory board, completes hiring project staff. Project director sets schedule for classes and ensures that space is available.
- *Month 2 to Month 3:* Project director, advisory board, and program staff begin to recruit participants and develop or modify evaluation materials. Staff members reproduce materials for classes.
- *Month 3:* Project director, advisory board, and staff recruit 60 participants to join the program. All participants take pretests of English literacy skills and are placed in groups with comparable skill level.
- *Months 4 to 11:* Program staff teach literacy curriculum to groups of 15 students in a class, each class meeting two evenings a week at the Fifth Street YMCA. Staff serve refreshments before class. Project director reviews students' work to assess participants' progress monthly.
- *Month 12:* All participants complete posttests of English literacy skills. Project director and advisory board will analyze changes in

test results to measure program effectiveness, and project director prepares a final report to the funder.

The time line need not be described in a list like the one above; it may be in paragraph form, with one or two sentences for each activity. All of these activities may be summarized simply in a chart like the following, either in the text, if there is space, or in an attachment. But don't omit the narrative description of when things will occur and who will do them.

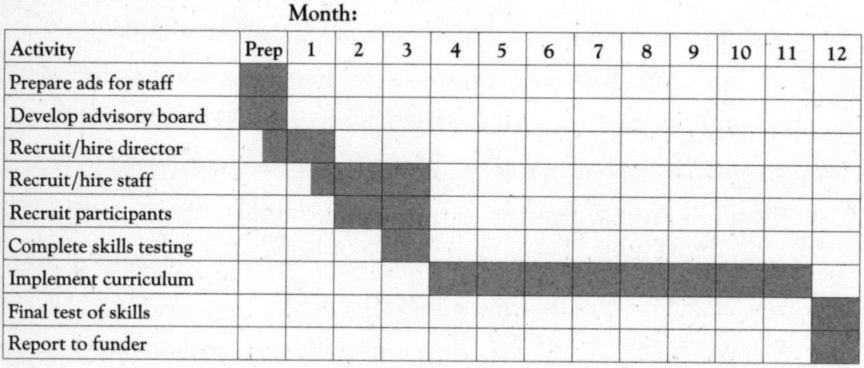
Month:
Activity
Prep
1
2
3
4
5
6
7
8
9
10
11
12
Prepare ads for staff
Develop advisory board
Recruit/hire director
Recruit/hire staff
Recruit participants
Complete skills testing
Implement curriculum
Final test of skills
Report to funder

Job Descriptions. You may or may not need to submit job descriptions with every proposal, but your plan should include detailed descriptions for each staff member who will be hired through the grant. In the example above, who are the necessary staff members, and what are the necessary experience, qualifications, and responsibilities of each? If there will be workers other than the project director and teachers of English for speakers of other languages (say, a clerical worker to maintain student records), what are the necessary experience, qualifications, and responsibilities?

Staff Recruitment Plan. This plan should define how and where job postings will be distributed. (Nationwide or local? Internet sites or newspapers? Which ones? College placement offices, newspaper advertisements, flyers distributed throughout the community? Are trade union contract issues involved in hiring?) It should include everything you will need to do to get started once you know the grant funds will be available. Some grants require a lengthy contract process, so if you don't start addressing recruitment until the money becomes available, you'll be so delayed in implementing the program that you may have a difficult time conducting all the activities you mention in your proposal and spending the money on schedule. This is especially true for local governments, where the hiring process can take considerable time (see the discussion below on government recruitment and hiring).

Advisory Board Recruitment. If you don't have established relationships with people you think should be advisory board members, now—before you start to implement the program—is the time to call or write letters, describe the project to them, and invite them to join the advisory board if the grant receives funding. If the project is a collaborative one, the advisory committee may simply be members of the various organizations you're working with who have assisted in the development of the program. But the role should be formalized.

Government Agency Recruitment and Hiring. If you are writing a proposal on behalf of a city, school district, county, or state government agency, you may need to start the procurement and hiring process as early as the time the grant has been submitted. Many cities have rigorous and complex procedures for subcontracting with not-for-profit organizations and for hiring staff; these procedures may be completely different from procedures for not-for-profits, which are relatively simple. The best way to plan ahead is to decide while you are developing your grant proposal what staff members you need and which agency personnel lines are appropriate. Check with your budget or contracting office to see how you can hire staff most expeditiously and receive contracted services so that grant funds can be spent quickly. Do this now, before you even apply for a grant. We mean it. You don't want to get all tangled up in bureaucratic red tape as you're trying to get your exciting grant-funded program off the ground.

Participant Recruitment. Don't take participant recruitment for granted. Some grant recipients are surprised to find that offering a great new program to a target population with a clearly demonstrated need doesn't always bring the participants flocking to the door when the program opens. You need to explain in your program plan what methods you will use to recruit participants, how you will ensure that the program will grab and hold their interest, and how you will keep them coming back. Will you conduct extensive outreach in the media? Will you ask professionals in your field (physicians, schoolteachers or counselors, social workers, youth workers, senior center staff) to make referrals to your program? Is a proposed activity so popular in your community that it will keep every participant engaged for the entire time? If you're not sure that it's that popular, will you pay stipends? Give a gift certificate or a pizza party or a job to everyone who completes the program successfully? Provide child care?

Marketing Plan. While working on your proposal, think about how you will sell your program to the community—not just to those who will directly participate and benefit. Will you invite reporters from community newspapers and local radio and television stations to visit? Will you send out short press releases describing the program or announcing an existing program's expansion? Funders ask about community buy-in or stakeholder buy-in. Although they sound like clichés or buzzwords, that's exactly what you want to achieve. You want the community to take ownership of your program—to brag about it—to feel secure knowing it's up and running. We've mentioned buy-in often; it's important.

How Do I Make Sure That the Plan of Operation Covers Everything?

If you view your grant proposal as a marketing tool—to sell the seriousness of your problem and the wisdom of your solution—then the activities are the key to your sales pitch. For each of your objectives, you should have one or more activities that are clearly designed to accomplish that objective. Let's say one of your objectives for that "delightful" weekend reading program is to improve attitudes toward reading as a result of the program. What will happen during the program that will improve attitudes toward reading? Maybe some famous people can visit and discuss their own attitudes toward reading. Maybe a well-known local author would agree to discuss her reading history. You might take the children to visit the library, or to a place where books are bound. Popular athletes may promote reading. None of these activities are necessarily likely to improve reading scores, but they very well may improve attitudes toward reading, which may be a good first step toward improving the scores.

No matter how many objectives you propose to achieve, specific activities must be described for each one. Be as detailed as possible. Instead of saying "athletes will read to children," say "football players from John F. Kennedy High School have agreed to read to the children; the football players will receive community service credit for their participation." If possible—and that depends on space and other limitations—a letter from the high school principal should be included in the proposal package, describing the football players' involvement in the program. The more details, and the more partners who have signed on (like the principal and football players of John F. Kennedy High School), the more likely the program is to receive funding.

Pop Quiz

True or False?

1. Activities are the least important part of the grant proposal.
2. Too much detail in describing your program distracts the reviewer.
3. Use terms you know the grantmaker will understand and appreciate in describing the program.

4. Funders prefer that you propose only about half of the activities you expect to conduct so there's room for change.

5. Try to write in generalities just in case you change your mind.

6. Make sure you list specific activities for each of your objectives.

7. Write the activities first, then frame the objectives based on what you plan to do.

8. Time lines are baloney; they waste precious space in a proposal.

9. Funders understand that the person who writes the proposal may not know too much about activities; they'll be sympathetic if you're vague.

10. It is a good idea to do some grant-related work as soon as you know that you've won the money.

LESSON 11:
Finding Partners and Building Coalitions
(The MOUs That Roared)

OPENING REMARKS

A woman called me to ask where she could get a grant to fund her "fabulous" idea. "I want to start a summer program that takes at-risk kindergarteners and high-achieving inner-city teenagers to camp in the Catskill Mountains for three weeks," she explained. "The teenagers will be camp counselors and work on reading skills and social skills with the young children, along with sports and arts and crafts. In return, the high school students will get a stipend and community service credit, along with three weeks of fresh air. Participation in this camp will look great on their college applications and we may get some good students interested in teaching or social work."

A great program, right? But when I asked her if she had gotten support from the local schools, community groups, churches, parent associations, or anyone at all, she gave me this quizzical look as if to say, "Why would I do that? I simply need a grant to pay for the idea." —EK

LEADING QUESTIONS

No matter how well designed you think your program is, before it can evolve into a winning proposal, you must have at the table the right people with the right attitudes and the right expertise and knowledge representing the right organizations. "At the table" is sometimes a polite (but inaccurate) way of saying that a lot of different organizations support your idea but are doing nothing to demonstrate that support. To turn a good idea into a winning program, the right partners really have to be actively involved. At a real table. And they have to be there willingly and maybe for a number of weeks or even months. Designing a high-quality program is not something that can be done quickly by someone like the woman with a fabulous idea in the opening remarks box.

Is This Where Collaboration Comes In?

We have mentioned collaboration throughout this book, and we'll continue to mention it in the next lessons. Collaboration is one of those words that everyone throws around, assuming that it's simple to do, as natural as breathing. In truth, collaboration does not come naturally to most people because it goes against everything we have learned and believe. In *No More Teams!* Michael Schrage* reminds us that although most Americans say they want to be team players, they'll grab their bats and balls and head for home unless each of them can be team captain. Americans usually respect rugged individualism, often viewing people who believe in working together as wimpy idealists or non-self-starters who don't have an original bone in their dreary, bureaucratic bodies. Yet whether it is in the operating room, the boardroom, the basketball court, or just about anywhere else, people who have a genuine problem and a limited amount of time to address it need to work together to come up with a solution. Schrage says: "The act of collaboration is an act of shared creation or shared discovery. James Watson, who won a Nobel Prize with Francis Crick for their discovery of the double helix, put it simply: Nothing new that is really interesting comes without collaboration."*

Because collaboration is a lot easier to say than to do, most people have no training in how to be a valuable partner, occasionally leading critics to complain, as some have done recently about President Obama, that someone is being "too inclusive." But true collaboration means leaving a lot of baggage at the door. It means coming to the table—yes, really sitting down and talking face-to-face—with an open mind and a commit-

* Schrage, M. (1995) *No More Tears! Mastering the dDynamics of creative collaboration.* New York: Broadway Books, 1995.

ment to solving a problem in an honest way. And a commitment to finding the best possible solution to the problem, even if that solution doesn't necessarily benefit (financially or otherwise) all the partners at the table. This truly is not easy.

Why Is Collaboration So Important?

Because most of us don't really understand collaboration, we tend to be skeptical about its importance, sometimes viewing it as mere jargon. But it is important to collaborate for two reasons. First, the more people with expertise and diverse points of view who are sincerely committed to developing a solution to a pressing problem, the more likely it is that the solution—the program—will be well developed and of a high quality. Second, the more individuals and organizations involved in developing the program, the more individuals and organizations who will actually support the program, agree with the need for it, and agree that the program they have worked out is really likely to meet the need. And the more people who believe in the program, the more likely they are to promote it, recruit participants, and give it good publicity by enthusiastic word of mouth.

What Makes Collaboration So Difficult?

Most people think they want to work together, think they're collaborative, and think collaboration is a good thing. But it isn't easy to leave our preconceived notions, our long-held beliefs, at the door without learning how to do this. It isn't easy to replace our usual roles, responsibilities, goals, and expectations with an entirely new set. For instance, if you represent a not-for-profit organization that works with children, you've probably adopted a particular approach to youth development that you think is the best way to help children achieve their greatest potential. But a new partner may have a completely different—but also very successful—approach. Does one of you have to forgo your tested views in collaborating with the other? Is it possible to incorporate both views? Is there an underlying philosophy that could help you both be comfortable with the details and outcomes of the program?

You and your counterpart, as directors of your respective programs, are both accustomed to making decisions, solving problems as they arise, promoting the program to outsiders. Who will do this now?

And there are other problems, as the following questions indicate.

The Money I Can Get from This Grant Is Barely Enough for My Own Program. Why Do I Have to Share It with a Partner?

This is a very good question, but there's a problem—a big one—inherent in it. Sometimes we only think about collaborating to work on a grant proposal, not to work on significant problems that confront us every day, whether there's a grant to apply for or not. Talk about the need for a culture change, a paradigm shift! Collaboration must become a way of life, a natural response, not just a grant response.

For years, government agencies, schools, nonprofit organizations, colleges, and so on, would independently design programs or promote the same old programs—and submit them to the grantmakers. And often they won the grants. Then grant seekers were told by funders to collaborate on grant proposals and then share resources after grants were won. Public schools were required to include parochial school students in their grant-funded programs. City agencies were told to show which not-for-profit organizations were involved in program development. Nonprofit organizations were told they had to partner with each other, and with businesses and religious institutions, not to mention government agencies. And everyone felt like throwing up their hands and crying, "Uncle!"

The greatest shock about collaborating on a grant was that—gulp—not every partner would automatically receive grant funds from every partnership grant. Collaboration cannot only be about money. If it were, we would probably need a new word to describe it. Collaboration must be seen

as a strategy to make things better by working together in a sensible, methodical manner. But that strategy can include something for everyone—
well, maybe not everyone, but several of the partners. For example, in a
welfare-to-work consortium, the lead agency (funders always expect one
agency to receive the check and be responsible for administering the
grant) may get less money to operate the program itself, but a bit more for
administrative costs. Or one partner may take on an element of the program for which it is especially prepared (perhaps a school or a nonprofit
GED program handles the literacy component) and refer participants to a
second partner for another element (say, job training), to another for child
care, and to still another for job placement. Each partner may receive a
different amount of funding, depending on the cost or the partner's ability
to contribute in-kind services or other support. In better economic times,
some partners may be able to absorb their piece of the project into their
own ongoing operations. A long-term collaborative approach can ensure
that as different grant opportunities come along, the other partners will
benefit, with the full support of those who get funding in this round.

That said, there still may be times when a collaboration for a particular grant just doesn't make economic sense to any of the partners. A funder may require a collaboration in hopes that it will cost less than grants
to individual organizations, even when it is clear that the collaboration
actually could increase the project's cost. Although some grantmakers
consider the extra costs associated with creating and sustaining a collaboration and provide a bit more money to support this work, in the current
economic climate it is very possible that there are no resources available
within any of the partner organizations—or in the grant—to pay for the
work involved. Although collaboration may indeed be the best way to
get things done in the long term, sometimes the partners have to decide
not to pursue a particular funding opportunity. And we think you should
let the grantmakers know why.

But We Provide All of the Services That Are Called For in the Request for Proposals; Why Do We Need a Partner?

This is another good question. Our position is that sometimes you should not pursue a grant that requires a partnership, especially if you believe that the amount of funding provided could not support the program that you and your partners would have to implement jointly. But very often a funder who is asking for a community coalition or partnership is looking for results that a single agency cannot possibly achieve. It is rare that a single agency really offers all of the services that the grantmaker envisions in such a request for proposals. For example, a coalition of health providers and social service providers may have a better chance to have an impact on children's asthma than any one of them alone.

DISCUSSION

Increasingly, government agencies and many foundations are calling for collaborations among not-for-profit organizations, or between nonprofits and businesses within a community, or between community-based organizations and larger institutions like a university, a city agency, a hospital, a board of education, or a national or regional nonprofit. Sometimes a group of grantmakers themselves form a consortium to pool their resources, again believing that they can have a greater, more widespread impact this way. If a partnership is called for, ignoring this requirement is fatal to a proposal.

All nonprofit organizations of any size should be reaching out to other organizations in their field of interest and/or in their community, even if these organizations have been competitors in the past. They should be discussing ways of working together productively to address issues of mutual concern. It may be necessary for organizations whose programs overlap to rethink which of them will provide which services. All of this takes time, usually much more time than is available between the time a funding announcement appears and the deadline for proposal submission; this is why collaboration should be ongoing and not only grant related.

Although the lead agency in almost all partnership arrangements must be a government agency, a school district, or incorporated as a 501(c)(3) organization with tax-exempt status, smaller organizations that are not incorporated may be important partners in a project and may strengthen a proposal by demonstrating a true community partnership. This is a good way for small grassroots organizations to become known to a wider audience than just their immediate neighborhoods, which is important to their own fundraising efforts.

If you do not presently have relationships with other community organizations, you should be approaching every sector of the community, from churches to merchants, from tenants' associations to civic and immigrant associations, from schools and school districts to hospitals and health centers, to discuss ways you might work together. If there are existing task forces (such as a task force to combat drug use among teens or one to address domestic violence in a certain immigrant community), join them. If you can't join, see if you can observe meetings or even become part of working groups that may form. If there are none, talk with other agencies about forming one.

City agencies with sites in the community should be approached. Elected and appointed officials at every level of government also should be included in discussions. If you're not a member of the local Lions Club, or Kiwanis, or chamber of commerce, consider joining. The broader and more diverse the representation within a community, and the more convincing the coordination and integration among partners, the stronger the proposal and the better the chances for funding.

And even if you're not currently seeking any funding, you'll be pleasantly surprised at how much support community organizations can provide for one another. Maybe the Rotary Club will throw a holiday party for the children at your day care center; maybe a bank will provide a meeting room for a class in English for speakers of other languages; maybe the school board will find money for snacks for children in the after-school program.

How Do We Show the Funder That We've
Worked Together on a Grant Proposal?

Some (not all) grant applications that require collaboration also require documentation of the development of a collaborative program. Notices of meetings, lists of those invited, attendance lists, agendas, and other such documents may prove useful; you should start and keep a file.

Letters of commitment (also called memoranda of understanding, or MOUs) spell out the ways groups will work together, refer clients, participate on advisory boards, and so on. MOUs are an important way to document a partnership, replacing the bland, redundant "support" letters commending the program that organizations so often attached to their proposals in the past. MOUs should be included in a proposal package, if they are allowed. They should be considered minicontracts. Normally they will be presented in an appendix (and are discussed in more detail in Lesson 16); occasionally you will be asked to put them into the body of the proposal. In any case, a paragraph or two about the partners should be included in the proposal narrative.

Reviewers generally can tell if a collaborative effort has been thrown together for a particular grant, especially if they are familiar with your community. Again, outreach and discussions about possible joint efforts should begin now.

When a collaboration is proposed in a funding request, each partner's activities, roles, and responsibilities should be addressed with the same level of attention, and their interactions must be presented fully and in detail. For example, for the welfare-to-work consortium mentioned earlier, details of each partner's contribution would be described, along with the ways in which each partner would identify, refer, and provide support to participants and interact with the other partners in the consortium. Which partner or partners would handle job training? How, and from which other partners, would clients be referred for training? How, and to which partners, would clients be referred for job placement, child care, social services, GED preparation, or college courses?

Government Collaborations. For grant seekers representing local government agencies, collaborations can present a more complicated set of issues. Many government agencies, because they are responsible for specific services like transportation, sanitation, or housing, are inexperienced at working with one another, let alone with "outsiders" like schools, not-for-profit organizations, colleges, and hospitals. Collaboration among government agencies involves not only potential competition for dollars, but competition for credit, for attention, for praise—maybe from the mayor, the governor, the press. If the police department collaborates with the health department to strengthen the latter's application, and this helps win the grant, then where is the police department when the press conference is held? The answer is that all partners should be viewed as teammates, integral to the winning of the grant—and included in the press conference to announce the grant! When a baseball team wins the World Series, the player who hit the tie-breaking home run—or the team manager or team owner—isn't honored alone. All teammates, managers, and coaches are honored together.

Many not-for-profit organizations shy away from working with government agencies or with large nonprofit institutions like universities and hospitals because they are afraid they'll be swallowed up—disregarded and disrespected by the larger, more powerful agencies. And we've seen this happen. It is critical that the larger organizations, which usually take the lead in the proposal process and manage the grants when they are received, work to keep the process and lines of communication open to avoid shutting out the smaller groups. Timely input and ongoing support from those closest to the community can make or break a project.

So, as we've said, learning to collaborate—learning not to act like Big Brother or the King of the Road—is important for government agencies. If you want to solve your compelling problems (and win competitive grants), you have to view not-for-profit organizations of all sizes as real partners. And not-for-profits must, in turn, stop viewing government with the same reserve (at best) or distrust as in the past. State and local agencies must be seen as the valuable resources they are—both to enhance grant proposals as partners and to provide useful data, statistics, insights, and experience in implementing programs.

As George Bernard Shaw once said, "Success comes from taking the path of maximum advantage instead of the path of least resistance."

Pop Quiz

True or False?

1. Collaboration isn't that hard—we're all essentially team players.
2. Every organization that collaborates on a grant application should, without exception, receive at least some money once funding is approved.
3. If a grant doesn't require collaboration, don't ever do it.
4. City agencies like to collaborate with city agencies, schools like to collaborate with schools; it is when they have to cross sectors that problems rear their ugly heads.

Short Answer

1. The best way to actually prove that you collaborated with other groups on a grant proposal is to include _____ and _____ in your application. (Give two examples.)
2. List five different sectors of the community that might collaborate on a winning grant. _____, _____, _____, _____, _____
3. What are some synonyms for "collaboration"? _____, _____, _____

LESSON 12:
The Evaluation Plan:
How Can You Be Sure If Your Program Worked?

OPENING REMARKS

I was evaluating a grant-funded program designed to help a small number of families in shelters find (and remain in) permanent housing by providing intensive, long-term assistance. A variety of measures showed that it was a very successful program; for example, the families remained in permanent housing much longer than families without this assistance. But staff interviews indicated that the staff felt overwhelmed and burned out by the amount of work they were doing and thought there was a need for more staff. A review of the case files showed that they were overworked, but not because they had to be. It turned out that in addition to the small group of clients who were their primary focus, they were providing short-term help or information to hundreds of other families in the shelters. Among other recommendations, I suggested that the program managers either rethink their objectives—and possibly hire additional staff to do the short-term assistance— or retrain staff to focus only on the smaller group that was the original target population. —ASF

LEADING QUESTIONS
I Have Four (or Three, Two, or One) Programs to Run. Who Has Time for Evaluation?

First of all, you'd better make time if you ever want another grant from the funding organization that asked for the evaluation. In the wake of those corporate scandals at Enron, Global Crossing, and Worldcom, Congress passed new laws concerning transparency and accountability in the private sector, and has been working to apply these regulations to the nonprofit sector. Foundations and government funders, often under pressure from their boards or the legislative bodies that set the rules for government programs, increasingly are looking for proof that their grants make a difference and are not "just an employment program for the workers."

Besides, as you'd agree if you had time to think about it, you really do want to know whether the programs that keep you so busy are operating the way you want them to, are meeting your objectives—and are worth the effort. Too many people wait to think about evaluation until the report is due, which is a sure-fire method for creating serious headaches for everyone involved with the program and is no way to measure the success or failure of a program. Remember: Programs aren't funded and conducted to look good in reports. They are designed, funded, and implemented to address compelling problems or conduct individual projects. Well-designed and well-executed evaluations tell you if you've been successful.

The best time to think about the evaluation is when you're first designing a program, when you can select those outcomes and indicators that will satisfy you that the program is working, whether or not the grant application actually requires an evaluation plan. If the information is carefully and systematically collected, and it convinces you that you're getting the results you intended, it almost certainly will be sufficient to convince the funder as well. And every grant proposal should discuss how a program will be evaluated. It's common sense (we hope) to describe to a funder how you will know if the program is working and has worked. Don't let the absence of an evaluation requirement stop you. Your evaluation plan can be addressed along with your measurable objectives or in your program description.

My Staff Members Work Hard. They Know If Programs Are Working. Why Do They Have to Have Someone Evaluating Them?

People don't like the feeling that someone is looking over their shoulders monitoring everything they do. But this really is not what an evaluation is about. Almost all program staff members and managers we've ever met are interested in how well their program is doing, and whether their teenagers or seniors or children or students of English for speakers of other languages are getting something out of it. More important, the staff wants to know whether the participants are getting what the staff members hope they will get out of it. And almost all staff members and managers truly want to know how they can improve their programs. The purpose of an evaluation is not to judge an individual worker but to consider the entire program and determine what works, what doesn't, and how to fix what needs fixing—and sometimes, as in the evaluation described in the opening remarks, to reduce the amount of work a staff person is doing!

I Work for a City Government Agency. Of Course We Know How to Run Grant Programs. But Federal Applications Ask for Such Complicated Evaluation Plans . . .

If a government agency is giving grants for hundreds of thousands of dollars—often millions of dollars—of taxpayers' money over one, two, or three years, why wouldn't it expect to see the most rigorous, methodical evaluation plan? Proposal writers, like program staff, sometimes take offense at the whole notion of evaluation, as if the funder is prying or being just plain nosy. The evaluation plan should be viewed as an important element of the proposal, linked in an orderly way to the objectives and the activities planned to achieve the objectives. As the program is developed, the evaluator should be involved in the process of identifying realistic measurable objectives.

Whoa . . . You Said "Evaluator"! Do I Need to Hire—and Pay for—an Evaluator?

The answer to this question depends on your organization's capacity to develop meaningful evaluation plans and conduct meaningful evaluations, whether you are a not-for-profit organization or a government agency or a school district. Often federal or state grants require that the applicant spend a specific percentage of the grant funds on evaluation activities. That's usually a Big Hint that you should work with an outside evaluator—either a local university, an individual consultant, an evaluation organization, or a state or city agency that conducts evaluations.

Most evaluators who work with government and nonprofit agencies understand the grants process and are willing to help develop the proposal (and the evaluation plan) "on spec," meaning they get money only if the grant is funded, even if they donate considerable time to the planning process. If the evaluator expects to be paid to participate in the development of the proposal for a grant, this is probably not the right evaluator for you. (It wouldn't be the right evaluator for us.) It is reasonable for not-for-profit organizations and government agencies to try to find competent evaluators who do not view a grant as a cash cow. Evaluators should be as much a part of the program development team as every other partner, helping to define and refine the objectives in measurable terms and devising a comprehensive plan that should be included in the grant proposal.

Some evaluators—especially if they are from universities—may be willing to donate space for meetings and activities, recruit student interns, or provide professors' expertise for all facets of the program. In this way the evaluators become real partners, collaborators, not just hired hands.

The cost of conducting the program evaluation should be outlined in the budget; sometimes a separate evaluation budget should be attached, explaining how many people will be conducting the evaluation, and in what capacity, along with other relevant details. The evaluator should be able to help with this too.

DISCUSSION

An evaluation, like a needs statement, can range from the simple collection of information on a few indicators (e.g., attendance; demonstrated improvement in a skill; or other concrete measures) to extremely complex research projects to determine the long-term outcomes of the program or to compare it with other programs to determine which is most effective. Evaluations generally are of two types: process evaluation and outcome evaluation.

Process Evaluation. *Process evaluations*, sometimes called *formative evaluations*, are used to assess the functioning of the project and provide feedback to allow for program corrections. Process evaluations consider such questions as whether activities are occurring when and where they should, who is receiving the services, how well they are being implemented, whether they could be done more efficiently, and whether participants are satisfied.

Process evaluations generally make use of qualitative methods, which might include focus groups, personal reports, observation notes, case files, surveys, and interviews. You might use this type of evaluation during the first year of a new program, or you might maintain some form of process evaluation throughout the life of the program to keep it functioning at the highest level.

Outcome Evaluation. As the name indicates, *outcome* (or *summative*) *evaluations* measure outcomes, program effectiveness, and the program's impact on the problem that it is designed to address. The questions that outcome evaluations raise include whether program objectives have been achieved; whether the target population has changed as a result; whether unanticipated results have occurred and whether they are desirable; what factors may have contributed to the changes that have occurred; how cost-effective the program is compared to others with the same objectives; what impacts the program has had on the problem; and what new knowledge has been generated.

Outcome evaluations generally, but not always, are formal in approach and designed according to professional research procedures. They use primarily quantitative methods, but may draw on systematically obtained qualitative data to help explain the research findings. Such evaluations probably would involve "before and after" measures of attitudes and/or behavior and/or knowledge of members of the intervention group (the group that experiences the program) and at least one control or comparison group (which does not receive services, at least until a later time).

Keep in mind that a program's impact on a broad population or community might require multiple measures over time and might be well outside the scope of your project or your ability to evaluate. For 15 years or so in the 1980s and 1990s, crime was down nationwide. It is creeping back up in many locations, and it takes the resources of many different research institutions to determine what factors even need to be examined to determine why it is increasing—and whether programs like your teen center are part of the reason your area is not feeling the same impact.

Which specific data collection methods are used depends on the nature of the evaluation and the questions to be answered. They may include standard attitudinal or behavioral measures that have been tested on similar populations or they may be developed and tested for the specific target population. Questionnaires, observations, systematic collection of data from various sources, and similar techniques may be used.

Okay, Evaluation Is Useful. But How Much of the Evaluation Design Do I Have to Put into the Proposal?

At the most basic level, unless you're writing a proposal for a huge grant that requires an external evaluation—in which case the evaluator will write the section—you often just need to let the reader know that you care about outcomes, want to know if you've succeeded, and have thought carefully about how you will know if you've succeeded. If you can make the case that collecting a few pieces of information, and looking at changes in those indicators between the beginning and end of a program, will tell you whether the program has worked, and if that information clearly relates to your objectives, the reader probably will accept this as a reasonable effort at evaluation. Some examples might include children's reading scores before and after a semester of tutoring in an after-school program; youth workers' ratings of sixth graders' improvement of social skills as well as acting skills in the drama group; the number and percentage of teenagers' acceptance to college after the college-bound program and the number and dollar value of scholarships they receive; responses to two or three questions about older persons' feelings of depression or loneliness before and after they've engaged in a discussion club for a few months; or a few questions testing a teenager's knowledge of the effects of tobacco, alcohol, and other substances on the body.

At a slightly more sophisticated level, some basic principles that underlie the evaluation section of a proposal will be at the back of a reviewer's mind.

- *The linkages between the activities (program components) proposed and the expected outcomes of the program must be clear and explicit in the evaluation design.* This linkage is spelled out in the program objectives. Here's an example: By the end of the project, 80 percent of the 21- to 24-year-olds who participate in a comprehensive work-study program will pass their GED exams. The GED scores of the work-study participants will be collected and analyzed.

- *"Dosage," the actual amount or level of services provided, can influence outcomes.* For example, children who participate for two hours several times a week in a tutoring program may show better results than children who participate for an hour once a week—or may not, which has implications for program planning. Another word for dosage is *intervention*: what (and how much) is actually received by the target population that will likely yield a certain result that can be measured.

- As suggested by the last example, *negative findings can be just as important as positive results* because they help in understanding why a program did not work and how it might be modified to be effective.

- *Qualitative data* (informal interviews, for instance) *can be as useful in determining the effectiveness of an intervention as quantitative data* (scores on standardized tests).

Reviewers will look at the evaluation section to see if it answers several important questions beyond the obvious, How did the project work? Were the specific objectives achieved? Which ones were or were not? Were the activities that you planned actually conducted the way you planned? (You may have planned for four workshops to take place in the evening but revised that plan when too few people wanted to come out after dark. Instead, you ran the workshops on Saturday mornings, and you provided child care so people could attend—which greatly improved attendance.) Were there any unexpected world, national, or local events that seemed to affect the success of your project? What did you learn from them? Did the staff members who were hired to run the project follow the job descriptions stipulated in the proposal? Was there community and/or organization buy-in—and if so, how do you know? Could the project be replicated by other organizations in your town or across the country as it is, or should elements be changed for replication purposes?

This Can Be Serious Stuff. As we discussed earlier in this lesson, many grants, especially those from the federal government or large foundations interested in funding demonstration projects, require systematic outcome evaluation of the funded project to demonstrate whether the program has had an impact, and why or why not it had an impact. In many cases the funding agency expects, or even requires, that the grantee hire an external evaluator, and tells you in the guidelines to build in the costs for the evaluation.

If you think you may be interested in seeking funding to test a model program that you have created (or are replicating), you should establish a relationship with a college or a consulting group that has experience with the federal funding agency or experience evaluating the type of program proposed. As we said before, the earlier an evaluator becomes involved, the more useful the evaluation plan will be and the stronger the proposal is likely to be. Ideally, the evaluator will help you formulate realistic goals, achievable objectives, and even appropriate activities that can be expected to lead to the results you hope to see. The relationship between you and the evaluator is a special type of collaboration.

"WHEN I NEED SOMETHING TO CHEW ON THAT'S NUTTY AND SUGARY-SWEET I READ ONE OF YOUR PROPOSALS."

Pop Quiz

True or False?

1. Evaluation is only necessary for large government grants.

2. Process evaluation looks at how many, how much, how well, and how often.

3. A large, multiyear grant should have only an outcome evaluation to tell you what the program's impact was.

4. If a grant application requires an outside evaluator, you have to hire a consultant to help you with the evaluation section of the proposal.

5. An evaluation has to be a formal process using an academic research approach.

6. An evaluation considers only statistical data.

7. Whew . . . the grant application doesn't require an evaluation plan . . . so I'm off the hook.

8. The best time to think about evaluation is at the very beginning—when you first begin designing the program.

9. Small demonstration projects don't need to be evaluated.

10. Frankly, you should always work with an outside evaluator, even if you are applying for a $5,000 grant.

Essay Question

1. Describe three important things that you can learn from an evaluation.

LESSON 13:
The Budget: How Much Will It Cost . . . and Is the Cost Reasonable?

OPENING REMARKS

As I was reading a proposal that a municipal government agency was about to submit to a foundation, I noticed that the budget seemed awfully high for a relatively modest project. Nothing in the program description or objectives seemed unusual, and I was anxious to see what in the world was going to cost all that money. Was there a conference in Maui that 10 staff members would attend? Was the commissioner planning to buy an SUV or something? When I finally got the budget narrative, I saw it right away. The project director of this relatively modest little program was expecting to be paid an annual salary of $120,000. No one preparing the proposal had a problem with that amount of money . . . hey, it's a grant, right? (P.S. They changed the salary but they didn't get funded.) —EK

LEADING QUESTIONS
How Do I Figure Out How Much Money to Ask For?

We're pretty far along in this book, yet we haven't focused on the budget . . . hmm. We've alluded to the budget in every lesson, emphasized its importance, but only now are we focusing on it. Don't for one minute think that you should wait this long to focus on your proposal's budget. You should be considering costs as you lay out your objectives, design your program, build your collaborations, and think about staffing, evaluation, and everything else.

The budget must be consistent in every respect with what you've said you are going to do. Many proposal writers provide excellent needs statements or program descriptions but offer budgets that appear inflated at one extreme or inadequate to carry out the necessary program activities at the other. Some proposal review criteria include points for what is called the *appropriateness* of the budget. The individuals who will be reviewing your proposal often have run programs or agencies like yours, although probably not in your city or town. They already know what's realistic and will react favorably toward your proposal if your budget does not overstate or understate the amount of money you will need to do the job. And with money scarce, it is more important than ever to justify every expense—to yourself as well as to the prospective funder. To develop a realistic budget and explain all proposed costs, you need to know:

- Exactly what staff and other costs are required to do the job?
- How many people—professional, clerical, full- and part-time— must be hired to implement the program?
- What skills, education, and experience will each project staff member need to have?
- What is the usual salary that such a background can command?
- Do you need to pay rent? For how much space? Why do you need that space?
- Is any local or out-of-town travel involved? For what, and how often?
- What equipment and supplies must be purchased for the program?
- Are there any costs involved in staff training?
- Will there be any stipends for participants?
- Do you need to hire consultants? If so, what will they do, and how much time will they spend on these activities?

You also have to decide what you *don't* need funds to pay for. Can your agency's secretary handle typing the newsletter you'll develop to publicize the grant-funded program? (Does your agency even *have* a secretary?) Can managers donate any time to making sure the program is working well at the beginning? Do you have volunteers or interns available? Can your own staff conduct training for new staff? Again, be realistic. If adding responsibilities to the workload of existing staff will burn them out—don't do it!

There are two key budget questions you need to ask:

Is the amount of money I'm asking for really sufficient to achieve the objectives I've proposed? This is an important question because your objectives often get lost in the shuffle of the activities you're planning. Why are you developing the after-school or weekend reading program? If you hope to increase reading scores, you probably want to hire licensed reading instructors, who command a relatively high hourly rate. If you hope to get children excited about books but have no intention of measuring reading scores before or after the program, then you may be able to hire young, enthusiastic college students who would expect to earn significantly less per hour. Remember that the proposal process works backward and forward: When you craft your objectives, you must keep budget parameters in mind. If the grantmaker is providing a finite amount of money for a lot of required activities, make sure that you don't set unrealistic, unattainable objectives.

Is the amount of money reasonable or outlandish—or somewhere in between—for the things I want to do? The question is much more than a nuance or a matter of semantics. Grant seekers sometimes view grants as opportunities to hire additional staff and purchase equipment and supplies that couldn't be afforded otherwise. Others may "lowball" their cost projection in order to win a grant. But reviewers of government proposals and foundation program officers have been around the block, and they are looking for a budget that's not too high, not too low, but *just right*. What would a reader say about a $2,000 computer, when perfectly good PCs are available in the stores for under $500? Is $30,000 a reasonable yearly salary for a master's-level bilingual social worker in my area, or do I have to allow at least $15,000 more?

We Don't Have Any Money to Pay for the Guy Who Keeps This Place Clean. Can I Ask for His Salary in This Proposal?

Probably not. But it's a very good question. The issue of who will fund support services such as secretaries and custodial staff is discussed endlessly by grantmakers as well as grant seekers. Most funders rightly want their money to be spent on activities that directly benefit the intended target population.

But many grantmakers are becoming aware that unless somebody pays for the person who cleans up, or who answers the phone, or handles payroll, or maintains the files, or tracks and orders supplies, these jobs will fall on higher-paid professional staff, often to the overall detriment of the funded programs and intended recipients. So if you can show that the custodian plays a role in the operation of the program for which you are requesting a grant, or provides a less costly service than you could otherwise obtain, you may be able to receive the portion of his salary that is directly attributable to that role. For example, say you run an after-school arts and crafts class at your community center, and you have to leave the room clean for the senior citizens' exercise class the next day. You might require your art teachers, who are paid $15 to $25 an hour, to spend an extra half hour to an hour cleaning up each day, or you might make the case to the grantmaker that it is more efficient to pay a custodian $10 an hour to do this. Clearly this doesn't solve the problem of where the rest of the custodian's salary comes from, but it does help a bit. The key is to make your case. Don't try to slip unexplained expenses into the budget.

Local government agencies and school districts do not generally have to ask for funding to pay custodial salaries. They usually can provide cleanup, clerical support, and other important services as part of their everyday activities, as an in-kind contribution. Usually the grant-funded program is a drop in the bucket compared to the overall municipal agency budget. That's why it is smart for government agencies to be very generous with in-kind contributions. Grantmakers of all kinds (government and foundations) might have a difficult time sympathizing with a munici-pal agency that claims it has no one on staff to type some letters or to clean up at the end of program activities. Nonprofits, on the other hand, which often need every penny of the grant money to survive, must be re-sponsive to specific funders' requirements about what they will and will not fund.

All grant seekers want to know what is an allowable cost and what isn't. Is a custodian allowable? Rental space? Construction costs? Am-bulettes? Vans? T-shirts? In most cases the best way to find out what you can and cannot use grant money for is to read the application package carefully. (You've heard this before?) The Safe Schools/Healthy Students application discussed in Lesson 3, for instance, requires applicants to spend at least 7 percent of the funding on a yearly evaluation and another $300,000 to ensure that the schools are safe. Safety could mean a security guard, police officers, metal detectors in the school, and/or a police pres-ence on the streets near the school. If the application says nothing about what you can and cannot use the money for, and you're not certain, call the funder. Don't automatically assume any element of your program will—or won't—be an allowable expense.

But We Really Need a Full-Time Custodian. Couldn't I Pretend We Need a Few Extra Youth Workers but Pay for the Custodian Instead?

In a word, *no!* Even if doing this were ethical, it's just plain stupid. As we've said before, whether at foundations or government agencies, the program officers responsible for the grant you are applying for are very well aware of what it takes to run a program for 50 children or 200 elderly people or 12 physically challenged teenagers. In many cases they've been there themselves, running programs and writing their own proposals for funding. In other cases they've been reviewing proposals and visiting and evaluating programs for many years. They know the realities and they know the tricks. They can be very supportive if they see a strong, honest case for the costs of your program, and very annoyed if they think you're trying to fool them.

DISCUSSION

Much of what we discuss in this lesson is just common sense. If you've ever prepared a budget for your organization, you probably are familiar with most of the terms and examples we're providing here. Just remember that each budget item must be calculated and described in a way that clearly and adequately addresses program needs for staffing and other costs—and demonstrates that each and every activity can be properly performed with the amount of money specified in your budget.

The key to developing your budget is to think through all of the real costs of operating the program and to show exactly how each budget line relates to program implementation. Even if you are not required to present a formal budget narrative (a section in which you provide a verbal description and justification of each budget item), the budget must flow from the proposed activities and reflect realistic estimates of what is required to implement the program. It should be comprehensive and detailed enough to demonstrate that you fully understand and can justify all likely costs. And, working back and forth between the budget narrative and the program, you should be sure that every item that appears in the budget/budget narrative is accounted for in the text of the proposal.

The Budget Reflects the Program. There may be several different ways to develop programs and budgets that address the same objectives. For example, an organization might plan a program to tutor 100 sixth graders after school during the course of a year. The budget might reflect one of several different choices you could make for implementing the program. You might use 50 tutors (each working two days a week with two students) or 25 tutors (each working one day a week with four students). The tutors might be volunteers who are given transportation costs, or they might be paid by the hour, or they might be given a flat stipend for the year. Whichever strategy is selected (and justified in the needs section and the program description), the costs of each strategy will differ, and the costs must be explained in some detail in the budget narrative. How much you spend depends on what you're trying to accomplish, and how.

As to the form and content of the budget, not surprisingly, grantmakers require varying degrees of detail. All budgets won't look the same. Federal funding agencies (which tend to provide a lot of money) and state and local agencies (which provide less but have to account to taxpayers and federal funders) expect detailed budgets, with a separate line showing each budget item and calculation of costs.

Budget narratives, or *budget justifications*, describe the budget in words and justify the expenditures, item by item. In a narrative, you will relate each budget item to the activity it supports. One sentence usually is enough for each item. Again, even if the narrative isn't required, developing one helps you make sure you haven't left anything out. You may think it is obvious that a clerical assistant will maintain program records such as attendance, reading scores, surveys, and so on, or that the youth workers will organize and oversee basketball games—or that the basketball program needs to buy basketballs—but you still must explain these things to the funder. If equipment such as a van, desks, computers, file cabinets, and so on, is required, its purpose should be clear in the program narrative, and the budget should indicate how many, what type, and the unit cost.

Foundations want to see program budgets with projected income and costs. In the past they did not usually require a formal budget justification, but some foundations are moving in this direction. Even if a formal budget narrative is not requested, be sure that all of the items in the budget relate to activities described in the program narrative. Whether you are approaching a government or private grantmaker, the numbers in your budget should be as specific as possible. Rounding out a budget item to the nearest hundred or thousand dollars suggests to the funder that you're trying to take a short cut, which is not smart; showing the exact cost of six basketballs demonstrates that you've researched costs and thought about the program in detail.

Sections of the Budget

Program budgets generally focus on four areas. Toward the end of this lesson, we'll show you a very simple sample budget for the literacy program we talked about earlier; it will cover all four of the areas discussed here. All program budgets will have a similar breakdown, though some funders ask for more details or a different format. Some government budget forms run to several pages, and we're not going to review them here. It goes without saying that you should follow the directions and call the program officer if you don't understand an instruction. But all budgets need the following information.

Personnel Services (PS) (also called *personal services*) include the costs of all project staff (not necessarily by name, but by title) and the percentage of their time or the number of hours that they will work on project activities.

Unless the grantmaker specifically rules it out, you may include all of the time that one or more managers can reasonably be expected to devote to the program, whether in setting it up, recruiting, training, supervising the program director, conducting outreach, maintaining partnerships, acting as liaison with the funding agency, and so on. In most cases this will be expressed as the proportion of the managers' time allocated to the program, based on a full-time salary.

Staff should be broken down by full-time or part-time, year-round or seasonal. Although we are oversimplifying here, full time means any employee who works full-time for the agency, even if not all of her time is allocated to the specific program. Part-time, for budget purposes, means any employee who works less than 21 hours a week. The reason for this dis-

tinction is that staff members who work 21 hours or more normally are entitled to every benefit the agency offers, while part-time employees are
entitled only to what is required by state or local law, so the calculation of
fringe benefits differs between the two groups.

Each budget line presents one or more staff members with the same
title. For example, for the literacy program we described earlier, one line
would show the annual costs for a project director at 50 percent of full-
time (she devotes the other 50 percent to a different program), at a specified annual salary; another line would show the total annual cost for
three teachers of English for speakers of other languages, each at 15 hours
per week over 40 weeks, averaging $30 per hour; and the third line would
show a clerk to maintain student records at 50 percent of full-time at a
salary of $22,000 a year.

Staff whose positions will not be funded by the grant still should be
listed if they are working on the project, and their salary should be shown
in a separate column as an in-kind donation. It would be a mistake to
leave in-kind contributions out of the budget. The funder needs to see
the grantee's commitment to the project, as well as the total cost of the
project, for replication purposes. Salaries for a multiyear budget should
reflect anticipated cost-of-living and contractual increases if the funder
allows it.

Fringe Benefits (e.g., social security, unemployment, health and disability insurance, vacation, holidays, pension) are shown on a separate
line and should not be combined with salaries. Because different organizations have different packages of benefits, fringe is estimated as a percentage of the total cost of salaries. As noted earlier, it may be calculated
differently for full-time staff, who receive all benefits in your package, and
part-time staff (less than 21 hours a week), who may receive only legally
mandated benefits.

Other Than Personnel Services (OTPS) (or *other than personal services*), as the name indicates, describes all costs associated with the project that are not staffing costs. They may include the program's share of

rent (for the number of square feet it occupies, or for rental of meeting space when it can't be donated, a gym, etc.); its share of liability insurance or an agency-wide audit; supplies such as paper, photographic materials, sports equipment, and travel. This category also includes consultants—perhaps a theater teacher who comes in to produce a play, a human resources trainer, or a program evaluator; anyone who provides services but is not a regular employee. Of course, you will recruit volunteers and student interns whenever possible; if you pay them stipends, these are an OTPS cost.

If out-of-town travel is planned (say, to take a group of senior citizens to a theater production in another city, or a group of high school students to visit colleges, or for staff to go to a professional conference in another city), the budget should show the actual or estimated train or airfare, the cost per mile for a car, actual or estimated daily cost of hotel and meals, conference or training costs, and so on. Make sure they're allowable expenses under the funder's guidelines. Also, be sure that such costs are in line with any regulations your organization or government agency may have on the books; for example, many organizations have maximum amounts you can spend on a hotel room or a meal.

Indirect Costs (also called *overhead* or *administrative overhead*) are agency-wide costs that cannot be reflected in the program budget but are required just to keep the doors open—the fiscal, human resources, and development departments; utilities; custodial, security, and clerical costs not allocable to any program; and accounting, legal, and insurance costs. This line usually is expressed as a percentage of the total program budget and of course will vary depending on the size and complexity of the organization. The funder may limit the amount that can be charged as overhead, and as a result you may receive much less than your actual costs. In some cases this may be negotiated. Federal agencies, for example, may instruct you that the maximum overhead you can request is 5 percent or 10 percent of the total budget. However, once you receive a

LITZLER

"THIS ONE HAS IT ALL. BELIEVABLE
CHARACTERS. PLAUSIBLE CASE. IN-
DIRECT COST RATE OF THIRTY
PERCENT."

grant, you may go through a process that shows your actual, audited costs in detail, and win an agreement from the funding agency for a higher "negotiated rate" for the following year.

If you are framing your grant proposal budget for the first time, it may seem very technical and intimidating. But it should be no more daunting than doing your household or personal budget. Once you do your first budget, the others will be much easier. And we'd be surprised if there were no one in your organization or on your board who handles financial matters. Of course, large organizations—government agencies, school districts, citywide or national not-for-profits—have entire departments that handle budgetary matters. These specialists will be happy to work with you on your proposal budget. (They are money people. They want you to bring funds into the organization!) If you are a small grassroots organization applying for foundation funding and you need assistance with your budget, see if there is a university nearby that has accounting students willing to help, either for free or a nominal fee. Or call the grantmaker. The program officer may have some good suggestions about where you can go for technical assistance.

You must be brutally honest about your budget. If you fudge here and there—and the grantmaker finds out—well, you know the rest. If you innocently underestimate your proposal costs, you'll find yourself trying to conduct the grant program on a shoestring, which is neither fun nor easy to do. And if you underestimate costs, you decrease your chances of achieving your objectives. So be careful.

Sample Budget for Literacy Program

Personnel Services (PS)	N. Hrs /week	N. wks.	Annual Cost	In-kind
Project director, 50% of full-time at $38,000/year	17.5	52	$19,000	
ESOL teachers (3), 15 hours/week each, at $30/hour	45.0	40	$54,000	
Records clerk, 50% of full-time at $22,000/year	17.5	52	$11,000	
Subtotal Personnel			$84,000	
Fringe at 21% (full time staff)			$ 6,300	
Fringe at 10% (part time staff)			$ 5,400	
Total Personnel			$95,700	
OTPS				
Books, supplies and materials, 90 students at avg. $12/student			$ 1,080	
Printing/photocopying publicity materials			$ 500	
Room rent, 200 sf at $14/sf				$ 2,800
Volunteers (3), 15 hours/week at estimated value of $10/hour				$18,000
Total OTPS			$1,580	$20,800
Project Subtotal (PS + OTPS)			$97,280	$20,800
Administrative overhead at 10%			$ 9,728	
Project Total			$107,008	$20,800

Pop Quiz

True or False?

1. I'm desperate for a new copier for our executive offices. I should include one in the budget of the housing grant I'm writing, right?

2. I'm desperate for new laptop computers so my students can communicate with other children throughout the world. The funder says no equipment costs. But if I explain carefully why they will improve reading scores, it's okay to put the laptops in the budget anyway.

Short Answer

1. If a reading instructor is working on a grant-funded project as an in-kind contributor, what does this mean and how do I show it in the budget?

2. What is the difference between PS and OTPS in a grant proposal's budget?

3. Give two examples of OTPS expenses.

LESSON 14:

Sustainability: How Will You Continue the Program When the Grant Funds Run Out? (and You'd Better Not Say, "I Won't!")

OPENING REMARKS

A recent grant application—the one we've referred to throughout the book, Safe Schools/Healthy Students—asked applicants to explain how "short- and long-term strategies will allow for the systematic development of infrastructure that builds organizational, community, and individual capacity to sustain outcomes beyond the life of the grant."

"How are we going to address that mouthful?" everyone wondered. "Where do we begin?"

Increasingly, sustainability—plans for keeping programs and organizations up and running once the grant period is over—is a topic writers are asked to discuss in grant proposals. Grantmakers, it seems, don't like to think that the grant-funded activities will end the second their money runs out. They want some assurance that additional funds will become available to maintain the program. And can you blame them? —EK

LEADING QUESTIONS
But If I Had Enough Money,
I Wouldn't Need to Apply for a Grant in the First Place!

Obviously, if money were no object, all the programs in the world would be created, enhanced, expanded, and sustained if successful. In the past foundations assumed, often correctly, that a successful program would be picked up and replicated by a local or state government agency.

But now funders at every level, from foundations to the municipality to the state and federal government, assume that you will find someone other than them to maintain a program after their grant ends. Federal agencies assume that local government, or perhaps businesses or individuals, will step in to keep a really good program going. Local government agencies hope the state will take over the funding, or that clients will become eligible for entitlement funding such as Medicare or Medicaid or federal disability insurance, or that clients will be happy (and able) to pay fees for services received when the program works well. We know that this is a catch-22, especially right now. As we are preparing this edition, the headlines are screaming about city and state budgets being slashed; many foundations' investments have been decimated; and organizations (and staff members) we care about deeply are experiencing the effect. Yes, tough economic climates do make it much harder to patch together support for programs you feel are very important. But there still are ways you can show a grantmaker (and reassure yourself) that at least some of the program elements, if not the entire program, will live on.

Show That Other Grantmakers Are Interested in the Program. Earlier we suggested that you keep on file a list of current funders of the agency and your programs. Your program budget could show actual income from other grants as part of the total support of an existing program, or it could show all the other grants for which you're applying to support a new program. If you're a government agency, you should describe the tax levy support that the locality already provides, or any external government funding stream that is or will become available, in order to demonstrate the stability of the program.

Explain That Long-Term Government Support Will Be Available Once You've Developed the Program. As we've said, foundations have always liked to provide seed money for new programs that they expect the local or state government to take over if they prove to be successful. But in times of government belt-tightening, this is an expectation that has limited prospects.

Nevertheless, if you can mention government funding streams that may be available once the program is established, you should do so. One example is an employment program for out-of-school youth. As we write, there still is federal money, usually through a state or local government agency, for this kind of effort, but the guidelines require the grantee to serve fairly large numbers of young people. If you feel you're not ready to jump into such a large-scale effort and want to start small and then expand once the program is up and running by applying for the government grant, your request may fit right in to a foundation's "sustainability" criteria.

In a health program you may know that most of your prospective clients will be eligible for reimbursement through an entitlement program or through private insurance. You may be able to show that once your program has reached full capacity, it will be supported through this income. If you win a grant to provide special skills training to your home care staff, you may be able to sustain the program by selling the training to other organizations that want their workers trained but don't have the resources to do it. If you can demonstrate that your approach will work, the grantmaker may be interested in helping you start up and operate the program until the funding stream is well established. If you are a county or municipal agency, tell the reviewer about prospects that the tax levy budget will cover the funding once the grant period is over. Be open about any difficulties you may encounter while tax revenues are down, but explain which state or federal grants will be available to fund this program, and describe any success you've had in winning such grants. Be sure you make it clear how and when you will apply.

Show Underlying Support from a Larger Program. For example, if your agency operates a teen center with other foundation funding or government contracts or grants, show how the proposed karate program or day camp fits into that structure. If you run a senior center, show how a health grant will provide nutrition courses for the participants. These activities may end when the grant runs out, but because there's an underlying, stable source of funding, it is more likely that you will be able to find other grants or realign your overall program to eke out at least part of what you need to keep a project going.

Demonstrate Your Organization's Commitment to and Experience with Fundraising. Do you have development staff? Describe how that staff will pursue additional funding in the future. Do you have a fundraising plan? Describe it. Have you raised private or government dollars in the past? Explain your past success in raising money to sustain programs that are similar to the one in the grant application.

One organization we know had a program that brought otherwise homebound elderly to a senior center to socialize with each other and with more active seniors. This program started with foundation funding. It had always operated on a shoestring, but because an external evaluation showed that it reduced serious depression significantly among the elderly participants, the agency was committed to keeping it alive, and had done so for more than 10 years. Support was patched together at various times from small foundation and corporate grants, from bits of government contracts when the funder approved, from in-kind contributions, and from the agency's own general operating funds. Proposals for this program consistently demonstrated the organization's commitment to keeping it going, and this commitment did help to win additional grants over the years. Sadly, the program finally had to be closed because of cutbacks in other funding. So we know you can't keep all of your important programs going—there's just not enough general support available out there even in the best of times. But when it's appropriate and possible, tell the grantmaker so.

Consider Asking Participants to Help. We've all become accustomed to the idea that grants from foundations and government would always allow us to provide free services in needy communities. The reality of the current economic crisis may force us to reevaluate this assumption. In Lesson 1 we talked about fundraising approaches that smaller organizations could use before they were ready to apply for grants. In these economic times, even more established organizations may want to look back at some of these alternative income sources. Of course a bake sale won't sustain a program, but contributions from participants in the form of dues, fees, or in-kind donations can help offset the costs. Even in the lowest-income communities, program participants may be able to pay modest fees or offer volunteer assistance in return for services. Some organizations have incorporated "pay what you can" contributions into their programs, with some success. If you are thinking about such an approach, explain this to the funder as part of your plan to sustain the program—and show how a grant can help you do this without denying services to those who can't give anything.

Show How Your Community Partners Will Be Part of the Fundraising Process. Everyone interested in the proposed program—especially if it is a collaborative one—and connected to the organization in any way needs to get together to figure out how to sustain grant-funded programs. It may be possible for some of the partners to provide portions of funding in a few years. If they can't, at least you can show how the effort has been made.

Use Grant Funds for Activities and/or Resources That Have a Life Beyond the Grant Period. Training, for instance. If grant funds are used to provide up-to-date training for your organization's staff, then the newly trained people will continue to do excellent work once the grant period is over. Train-the-trainer courses (sometimes referred to as turnkey training) increase exponentially the number of individuals who receive training. If 10 staff members participate in a comprehensive, intensive, grant-funded seminar conducted by a top-flight instructor with vast experience in the field, and each of them turns around and trains another 10, who train another 10 . . . well, you get the idea. You are training thousands of people for the price of one grant-funded training session. But don't get carried away. The funders are aware that you're trying to maximize your grant dollars—to spread them as thin as possible to get the most bang for the buck. But they also can sense when you are spreading the money too thin, and getting no bang whatsoever.

Resource guides also live on when a grant period is over. Funds can be used to develop comprehensive guides that will benefit the community (e.g., an exhaustive listing of all programs in a city or community that provide day care services—including their requirements, program elements, and ratings would be helpful). The more comprehensive the resource guide is, the more expensive it is to prepare. But it can be updated inexpensively from one year to the next by simply adding or subtracting a page. Professionally produced and edited training videos also live on when the grant has concluded. While costly to shoot, they may be widely used over many years—more than making up for the price.

Coalitions That Develop and Implement Projects Collaboratively May Have a Better Chance of Sustaining Projects. You'll have more potential funders as a group than each has alone. If an after-school program is a partnership among the school district, a few not-for-profits, the city's parks department, and a local college—well, maintaining this program may be easier than if one not-for-profit alone ran the program, especially if the partners are pleased with its success.

Is It a Mistake to Request a Grant to Fund a Program That Really Will End When the Grant Period Is Over?

This is a difficult question to answer. If you're making a film or writing a book or building a homeless shelter that will be funded through a second grant, you may be able to complete it within the grant timetable. But why should a successful program for seniors or teens or young children not be ongoing? If you are very sure that there is no possible source of funding to continue a program, you may feel it's better not to get started and inevitably disappoint the participants when it ends—not to mention having to lay off staff. Remember what we said in earlier lessons about not chasing money if it doesn't fit with your mission? This warning applies to pragmatic considerations as well.

But what if you feel strongly that you must start a program to address what you know is a growing need? You may just be a little ahead of a trend. A few years ago, there wasn't much broad funder interest in programs for people with Alzheimer's, but because of the growing need, some managed Medicaid organizations are turning to these programs as a less costly alternative to nursing homes. You might not have been sure that this would happen when you first realized how necessary such a program was, and you probably would have been afraid you couldn't sustain it if you got a grant to start it up. But if you started the program anyway because you knew how important it was, you might be in a good position to sustain it now.

One way to get a sense of what grants are going to become available is to keep in touch with advocacy groups working to create new funding streams to support programs of interest to your organization—and don't forget to tell prospective funders about the advocacy efforts.

Sometimes, even in an inhospitable economic climate, when current funding is uncertain and the prospects for future funding aren't at all clear, it may be worth pursuing a grant for what is called a demonstration project, a model program that is tested through a rigorous and formal evaluation, which will show the project to be effective or ineffective. If it is effective, it may be expanded and funded through the organization's budget or other outside funding that becomes available just because it has been demonstrated to work. If it is effective in some aspects but not in others, it may be revised and tested again. If it is shown to be ineffective, of course, there is no point in continuing it.

Finally, as a very last resort, you may have to level with the funder. You may have to say you've explored other prospects for support, but there's nothing out there right now that you can point to. But explain how important the program is, what an impact it will have on people's lives. And show how committed you are to doing whatever it takes to keep it going once it's started.

Pop Quiz

Essay Questions

1. Let's say you want to show that you will sustain a literacy program for immigrants in your community if the Love Foundation gives you a grant to cover the first year. How will you convince the foundation that your program isn't a "one-year wonder"?

2. Explain why you might decide to apply for a grant even if you're not sure you can sustain the program.

Short Answer

1. Another good word for sustainability is _____.

LESSON 15:
Capacity: Proving That You Can
Get the Job Done

OPENING REMARKS

I've received many calls from people who wanted help with getting a federal grant. A little discussion revealed that these people were from small, grassroots organizations that were running a well-attended recreational program for children in the area, or beautifying and maintaining a neighborhood park, or patrolling their blocks to prevent drug users from doing business there. But they operated by committee, with little or no organizational structure, financial system, or other mechanisms that would have let them handle large sums of money and the complex financial and programmatic reporting that is required by a federal grant. They did not have the organizational capacity to manage such a grant.—ASF

LEADING QUESTIONS
If I Work for a Not-for-Profit Organization, What Does It Take to Prove My Organization Can Handle a Grant?

In some application packages, especially from a government agency, you may be asked to address organizational capability or organizational capacity, or something similar. It's important to be able to demonstrate that you can manage the money efficiently, implement the program as it's designed, and handle the reporting requirements (which for some government grants are substantial). Even when these questions aren't asked, somehow you need to include at least a paragraph with information about your track record in the proposal, because it is one of the things almost all grantmakers really want to know.

Here's the kind of information you want to provide in order to show capacity:

- The organization's history.
- Your successes in implementing projects similar to the proposed program.
- Your recognition in the community to be served.
- Relationships with partners in past and proposed collaborations.
- Management and staff experience, qualifications, and awards.
- The organization's budget.
- A description of your organization's fiscal control procedures.
- Grants that you have won.
- Some grantmakers ask for letters of collaboration or commitment in this section, or a chart describing community linkages; some ask that they be presented in an appendix.

As we've said before, you can save a good deal of time if you have assembled a file of materials that document your organizational capability, which you can tailor to a specific proposal. Again, the key is to demonstrate that the organization, its leadership, its staff, its partners, and sometimes its board are experienced and accomplished enough to guarantee that the program will operate as planned, that the grant money will be spent appropriately and with appropriate fiscal controls, and that the project has a good chance of meeting its stated goals and measurable objectives. If you have assembled the documents described in Lesson 4, you will have a much easier time persuading a reader that your organization and staff have just the right kind and amount of experience. If you haven't done this already, add to this file a brief history of your organization; its experience in operating all the current programs (the number of years a program has operated, the number and type of clients served in it); any awards or honors the organization or any of your programs has received; brief descriptions of the board members' experience, whether related or not, and their affiliations; and any honors and awards that board members, managers, and staff have received.

Having a presence on the web helps to demonstrate capacity. This is an important way to let prospective program participants (and funders) know what you offer. Posting the relevant sections of your 990 tax forms and your most recent annual report, perhaps even your audit report, demonstrates that you operate transparently—you are prepared for anyone to see this information.

You should be able to describe how the board oversees the organization. For example, how often does the board meet? Does it have committees or working groups that meet regularly? What are they and how do they operate? How often does the board receive reports on programs, and how does it intervene, if necessary, to affect the way the agency or major programs are operating? How does the board maintain oversight of the budget?

It is extremely important to demonstrate that you have fiscal systems in place to ensure the proper expenditure of grant funds. Internally, how are finances managed? Who oversees your fiscal affairs? What staff do you have to track income and payments, and what controls are there over the receipt and expenditure of funds? Which financial software do you use? How often are budget reports provided to management and the board? Is there a regular external audit? Is there a development office? What types of grants do you apply for?

Foundation funders expect you to submit any available agency-wide audit reports and generally require reports on the expenditure of their funds, but they rarely ask for a separate audit just for their grant. Government agencies do conduct separate program audits, but despite the time they take and the wear and tear on your fiscal staff, this can benefit you in the future. Because government agencies generally have strict accounting and accountability requirements, your organization is considered more stable and credible if you have had financial or program audits and received positive evaluations from other government funders. If you have received government grants, have you been audited? Have your procedures been evaluated? Have all of your reports been on time and accepted by the funder? If so, say so. Any information you can provide that shows that other grantmakers have found your organization to be fiscally responsible and programmatically sound will enhance your ability to win new grants.

In the same vein, any internal or external program evaluation reports that you have commissioned can help to demonstrate not only the quality of your programs, but also your confidence in your ability to implement them. Again, it is not usually necessary to submit copies of these documents with a grant application, but it is often useful to describe or refer to them.

If I Work for a Local Government Agency or a School District, What Does It Take to Prove My Organization Has the Capacity to Handle a Grant?

Grantmakers—federal, state, and foundation—have certain expectations about municipalities and school districts that differ from their expectations for not-for-profit organizations. A city's police department or school system is not dependent on a grant to conduct its day-to-day business, but a not-for-profit organization may have to shut down numerous programs if it doesn't receive grant funding.

LITZLER

"COULD WE RENAME THAT SECTION 'ORGANIZATION BACKGROUND' INSTEAD OF 'EXTENUATING CIRCUMSTANCES'."

Because of their size, their responsibility, and the critical services they provide to the community, government agencies are assumed to have the capacity to implement grants . . . but do they? Although a municipal agency or school district may manage enormous budgets, run numerous programs, and employ huge numbers of people, funders need proof that grant programs will be implemented in precisely the manner and time frame spelled out in the grant proposal. They want to see that cities and school systems are not "black holes" into which money is poured—and immediately lost.

To show organizational capability, municipal agencies and schools should, first, flaunt their resources, brag about their leadership and accomplishments, explain their management structure, describe funding streams, and highlight previous grants they have won (and implemented efficiently). Grantmakers may not specifically ask about hiring and procurement, but they would certainly be relieved to know that grant-funded staff will be hired quickly, without obstacles delaying the process, and that contracts and subcontracts will be efficiently organized. If the city has systems in place to speed up grant spending, don't hesitate to mention them.

A time line like the one we developed in Lesson 10 is very important to show funders exactly when grant-funded positions will be posted, interviews conducted, staff hired, and staff given the go-ahead to start working. Time lines that show which activities will take place before funding is approved—even before the proposal is submitted—help prove organizational capacity for a municipal government agency or school district.

What's This "Adequacy of Resources" Question?

Whether you are a nonprofit organization, a school district, or a government agency, you will have to demonstrate a few other things to show you can handle a grant. For many government funding opportunities, you will be asked to describe the adequacy of the resources that will enable you to conduct the grant-funded activities. You can't assume that a reader knows anything about how strong and substantial your organization really is, and what wonderful "extras" you can provide.

In some ways this question overlaps with information you may also have to give when you demonstrate the sustainability of a program and the in-kind contributions you will make available. It's okay to be redundant; in fact, if two questions in the guidelines call for the same response, then you *must* be redundant.

Explain what your physical facility is like and what part of it will be available to the program. Do you have a computer lab? Do you have a library, an auditorium, a gymnasium? Also (and this is where a floor plan may be useful) explain how the space is accessible to participants with disabilities. How many volunteers are available to support program activities? What are community partners contributing to the project?

As you can see, the word "resources" here doesn't just mean money. This is where you brag about all your other assets.

A LAST WORD

A good way to view organizational capacity is to think of a couple of analogies. First, would you hire an assistant for your staff without studying an applicant's résumé; summoning the person to at least one, and maybe many more, interviews; calling a number of references; perhaps requesting a writing sample, and "asking around"? Second, if you worked in a university admissions office, would you accept an applicant into the incoming freshman class without looking at grades, standardized tests, a personal essay? Without speaking to faculty at the applicant's high school, checking references, meeting the student?

So it is with funders. Even in the best of times they want to know as much as possible about your organization's capacity before sending you a check. When they are struggling to make the greatest impact with reduced resources, it's even more important to show them that you can accomplish what you say you will.

Pop Quiz

True or False?

1. An organization's leadership is critical to a funder's assessment of the organization's capacity.
2. Before I apply for a government grant, I have to make sure my organization has the right fiscal controls in place.
3. Nobody cares where my board members work and how much time they spend overseeing this organization.
4. I should expect to put my organization's detailed history, all program descriptions, and staff résumés in every proposal I write.
5. Government agencies should brag about the resources they can bring to a grant-funded project.

Essay Question

1. A grantmaker is on the fence. There are two excellent applicants for one chunk of money. Describe all of the things that were included in your proposal that prove your organization has the capacity to implement the grant and therefore should be the one to get it.

LESSON 16:

Front and Back: The Cover Page or Cover Letter, the Abstract, the Table of Contents, and the Appendix

OPENING REMARKS

When I was a beginning grant writer, I focused only on the parts of a grant proposal that were worth a specified number of points—the items I viewed as questions that called for good answers to get the best possible score. Materials such as the cover letter, abstract, table of contents, and appendix received the shortest shrift—until the first time I actually looked back at a copy of a proposal that I had submitted to the federal government for many millions of dollars. The abstract— the very first impression the funder was getting of my organization (and me)—was a mess. There were grammatical errors. The whole abstract was one long, long, long paragraph. And the information in this endless paragraph was disorganized and unclear. No wonder we didn't get this grant. Now I wouldn't think of sending a proposal off without a perfect cover letter, a crisply written, well-organized abstract, a comprehensive table of contents, and an appendix full of relevant, well-chosen information (if an appendix is allowed, of course).—EK

THE COVER PAGE: MAKING IT OFFICIAL

When you are submitting a proposal to a government agency or a common application form published by a regional association of grantmakers, there is usually a page that takes the place of a cover letter (though cover letters often are included anyway, to be polite). The cover page contains the agency's legal name, address, and contact information (including the executive director or agency head, and a program contact person if different); the employer identification number (the organizational equivalent of a social security number); the number or identifier of the grant you are applying for (e.g., the *Catalog of Federal Domestic Assistance* program number); the amount requested; the project start and end dates; and other items, depending on the agency issuing the application package. You would expect these forms to be standardized (and to the extent that every grantmaker needs similar information, they are). But each state and city will have certain elements that are important to that entity, so we thought it would be meaningless to try to give examples. Indeed, even within a single municipality, the cover forms can differ from agency to agency.

One cover page that is almost universally used at the federal level is Form SF-424, usually with a letter prefix representing the agency (e.g., ED 424 is the cover page for applications to the U.S. Department of Education). We're including this form in Appendix 4 because, like the common application forms, it includes almost everything you will see on any government cover form.

THE COVER LETTER: GETTING OFF ON THE RIGHT FOOT
When Do I Need to Use a Cover Letter?

When you are applying for a government grant and there is a cover page, it isn't really necessary to add a cover letter, which probably will be discarded anyway. But for all foundation proposals, even when there is a cover page, and for some government proposals that don't include a cover form, we recommend a cover letter. It should be brief—not more than half a page—one page if it substitutes for an abstract or program summary. It should give a one- or two-sentence statement of what you're requesting in the enclosed proposal and one or two reasons—based on the foundation's priorities and interests—you're applying to this foundation. This is especially important if you are new to the foundation.

If you're not including a formal program summary or abstract, use the cover letter for this purpose (see the next section and Appendix 4 for some pointers). In this case, include one or two sentences each about the need, the objectives, the program, the partners if it's a collaboration, how you plan to evaluate the program, the cost of the program, and the amount you are requesting.

If a program officer has been helpful to you in developing the proposal, you should mention this—and note that you've tried to include information that you discussed with him or her. If you've had a grant from this foundation before, mention how important that grant was to your community. (Remember that grants aren't about you, they're about the needs you are trying to address.)

Keep the letter short, to the point, and polite. And that's it!

THE ABSTRACT:
MAKING IT EASY FOR THE PROGRAM OFFICER

An abstract (sometimes called a summary, program summary, or executive summary) is the first thing a reader sees and may be your most important marketing tool. But because you can't really prepare it until your proposal is nearly finished, there's a tendency to rush through it seeing it as less important than the rest of the proposal. And if a grantmaker doesn't ask for an abstract, many writers assume it's not necessary and breathe a sigh of relief about having one less thing to worry about. But if you can slip a summary like this into your proposal, you really will be a little bit ahead of the game.

Isn't an Abstract Redundant? The Proposal Explains the Program in Great Detail, So Why Summarize?

The abstract gives the program officer something to take to the foundation board, or gives the government agency something to take to its congressional oversight committee to show how the money is being spent. The abstract summarizes the proposal in a page or two. It can be read quickly, yet it gives the reader—the reviewer—a good sense of the need, the program, the applicant, the goals and objectives, and the budget. The abstract is a work of art! (Stop laughing. To a proposal writer, this is art.)

If you were a funder, you'd want the applicant's abstract to include a little more than just a summary of what the organization (or individual) plans to do with the money, although you might not say so in the application guidelines. As noted, foundation program officers often use abstracts to summarize the proposals they plan to recommend to their boards. Government agencies may use them to demonstrate to elected officials that the grants went to projects that were intended under the legislation that authorized them. When a funding agency asks for an abstract or an executive summary, it often specifies how long this item should be (e.g., two double-spaced pages; half a page; 250 words) because this, or something similar that the program officer prepares, is the document that is going into his or her report or recommendations. So within that limited space you must be sure to cover most of the following information briefly. (The key word is briefly; you may need to cram each item into a single sentence.) As you'll see, it closely tracks the components of a proposal and the outline we worked on in Lesson 7. (Another example is given in Appendix 4.)

- A description of your organization, agency, school district, or school. What are you? Where are you and what area do you serve? What services do you provide? To how many people? How long have you been in existence?
- The compelling problem you are addressing in your proposal. If you have room, you should give a taste—a *taste*—of the research and statistical information that are included in your needs section.
- Description of your program, explaining that it will address the problem you've identified by targeting a specific population and achieving the objectives that you briefly summarize. What activities will you conduct? Who are your partners? If all a funder wants is a two- or three-sentence summary of the program alone,

you should be sure that this summary is finely honed and includes all of this information.

- Description of your evaluation.
- Overall cost of the project, the amount of the request, and, as appropriate, your organization's contribution to the project cost and other funders who are supporting the project through either cash or services.

Sure it's a lot of information, but you must keep the abstract to the page or word limit the funder indicates. That's why you can't just dash it off at the last minute.

What's the Difference Between an Abstract and a Summary? None, except possibly length. We tend to think of an abstract as a little more complete and formal in style, and it's the term you may see more often in a government request for proposals. We think of a summary as shorter (often just one paragraph), perhaps less formal, and the term that may be used more often by foundations. But the information contained in each is basically the same.

TABLE OF CONTENTS:
THE READER'S TRAIL OF BREAD CRUMBS

If your proposal is only a few pages long (say, up to the five or six pages that many foundations ask for), and if you've done a snappy abstract or summary paragraph, you won't need a table of contents. But for longer proposals, such as those for national foundations and government agencies, this road map can be very helpful. It tells the funder that you've covered all the items in its application guidelines or in a request for proposals. It helps a reader or reviewer flip back to something he or she read earlier to check a fact or answer a question. It's useful to the reader, and anything that makes the reader happier is good for you. We suggest that you take the time to create a table of contents, even if the guidelines don't require one.

Think back a minute to Lesson 3, on application packages. Remember that we said you should answer all the questions and instructions, in the same order the grantmaker lists them? In Lessons 3 and 7, we suggested that you use an outline. Subheads would include the keywords mentioned in the instructions, to demonstrate that you are responding to the required topics. So it should be pretty easy now to create the table of contents: Just go back and list the titles of the major sections. (Don't get carried away and make the table of contents three pages long; you can stop with the major subheads.) Include the titles of appendixes or attachments too, so the reader can see instantly that they're all there and where to find them.

And the reason we're mentioning this at all—you may be thinking, "a table of contents, oh, come on!"—is because it's another intangible: something that makes your proposal better but is not necessarily mentioned in the guidelines or application. A table of contents will allow you to check that you've answered all the questions and that your subheads show continuity and are relevant. And as you prepare your table of contents, you'll notice if any of the sections of the proposal seem a little skimpy and need more work.

THE APPENDIX: IT'S NOT JUST A USELESS ORGAN

You say you have only five pages to make the case for a large foundation grant, and there's important information about awards and honors your agency has received that you have to stuff into those five pages to prove you are the stellar organization the foundation is looking for? You say you've developed an extraordinary partnership with four other organizations in the community to solve a problem you've all been wrestling with on your own, but you don't have space in the proposal to do more than describe the partners in a few words? The appendix is not a useless organ. Here's where you get to show off without occupying vital space in the proposal narrative.

I've Seen Those Huge Stacks of Paper That People Call Appendices. Aren't They a Waste of Paper That Nobody Ever Reads?

We think this is the wrong way to look at it. The appendices let you demonstrate a lot of things that don't fit into the body of the proposal. For example, the narrative may mention that you have a diverse board of directors, but the list of the names of your 15 or 20 board members, with their business titles, other nonprofit affiliations, and so on, paints the picture more concretely.

The list also allows funders to determine whether there is any connection with board members that may enhance the prospects for a grant or whether there may be a potential conflict of interest. For example, some corporate foundations prefer to give grants to organizations with which their employees or employees' families are connected; others— and some government funders—avoid this type of connection. Or you may talk in the capacity section about how financially stable and enduring your organization is; the audit report in the appendix documents this. As we said in the last section, if you include a list of appendices in the proposal's table of contents, readers will know where to look for whichever pieces of information they consider most important. And there are lots of things they consider important. The appendices for foundations and those for government agencies overlap to a very large extent, but foundations sometimes ask for a bit less information. We'll start with the foundations.

Attachments for Foundation Proposals

What should be attached to a foundation proposal? You will notice as you read foundation guidelines, especially the common application formats published by some regional associations of grantmakers, that foundations usually refer to attachments, not appendices. At the risk of being boring, we have to repeat: Start with the guidelines and make a phone call if anything isn't clear. If you did the homework we suggested in Lesson 4, all you'll have to do now is reach into a folder and pull out the specific documents that most foundations ask for.

The common application formats have a section in which they list attachments. Even if you're not using one of these formats, it makes sense to have a section at the end of your proposal—however short—in which you list the attachments in the order in which they appear. Following are the attachments that are most often requested.

- *Documentation of Not-for-Profit Status.* Almost all foundations ask that you attach the 501(c)(3) and IRS determination letter.
- *Agency Budget for the Current and Often for the Previous Fiscal Year.* Some foundations also ask for the projected agency budget for the next fiscal year.
- *Project Budget.*
- *List of Other Funders for the Project.*
- *Most Recent Audit Report.*
- *Tax Return Form 990.*
- *Most Recent Annual Report.* Foundations understand that many nonprofit organizations don't publish an annual report. But you should note this when you describe the attachments so the reader doesn't think you just forgot it.
- *Brief Biographies and/or Résumés of Key Staff.* Normally what's expected is a page with one-paragraph summaries of the experience and qualifications of the executive director and/or senior manager responsible for the project, the project director, supervisor, or coordinator, and any professional staff members who are critical to its implementation. Some grantmakers want to see the résumés too.
- *A List of Partners If the Proposal Is for a Collaboration.* Foundations don't usually ask for commitment letters or contract letters, but it may be worthwhile to include them if you've developed

them. Nor do foundations usually require attendance lists or minutes from partnership meetings, but if this is an important element of your proposal you may be able to strengthen your chance of winning a grant by documenting the development and current operations of the partnership.

- **Other Attachments.** Foundations often like to see a few (a few!) news articles about the organization, or the executive summary of an evaluation that's been done on the program to be funded. Most foundations do not want to see videotapes. If you happen to have a tape that you think effectively documents the program you want funded, and if the guidelines don't prohibit it or request it, call first to see if there's any interest in seeing it.

Attachments for Government Agencies

As we have said so many times that we're sure you're sick of hearing it by now—but we'll keep saying it—the single most important activity in

"THE HUMANITIES FOUNDATION WAS TROUBLED BY THE PATHOS OF YOUR AUDIT FINDINGS."

preparing an application is to check and recheck what the guidelines say the funder wants. Most government application forms or announcements tell you exactly what you must attach. Some recent applications have stipulated how many pages long the appendix can be, without even hinting at what information should be included. The types of attachments that you might include are exactly what you would submit for foundations, with a few additions.

- **Certifications and Assurances.** Most government agencies require that you agree to a number of conditions that become part of the contract once you win a grant. Examples include agreements that you are or will be in compliance with all relevant laws, such as fair labor standards and equal opportunity laws; environmental standards; that you disclose all lobbying activities; maintain a drug-free workplace; and so on. Most of these forms have to be signed by a board member and/or the executive director, the agency head, or the school superintendent, so get them completed well in advance of the day the proposal has to go out. More than once we've chased around getting the right signatures at the last minute, when, of course, all the people we needed were at important business meetings, at funerals, or out of town.

- **Documentation of Partnerships.** If the proposal represents a collaborative project or a partnership, documentation for a government proposal is usually much more stringent than for foundations. Here you must include memoranda of understanding (MOUs) between and among the partners. These, as we have said earlier, are minicontracts, specifying what each partner will have as its responsibility and will receive from the other partners. MOUs that are required for certain government grant proposals are almost always studied by the applicants' lawyers to make sure the promises included are reasonable . . . and legal. If a city police department or mental health department signs an MOU saying that it will "provide services in a community in the manner described below," you can bet that the legal departments have looked it over once, twice, and even three times. Don't put an MOU into a proposal unless you fully understand all the ramifications. In addition to MOUs, minutes of partners' meetings often are required as proof that the partnership is real and ongoing, and not just a paper collaboration.

- *Letters from Elected Officials.* Foundations don't care at all about political support for your project, and a letter from an elected official may actually offend some. But it's sometimes a little different for government agencies. Although a support letter from your city council member, state senator, or member of Congress is not enough to get a proposal funded, it won't be seen as inappropriate pressure, and it could give you just the tiniest push if other applicants with equal scores don't have such letters. And staff of elected officials may, when it's appropriate, follow up with a phone call on your behalf if they have sent such a letter. At least a week before the proposal is due (longer if possible), send an abstract/executive summary of the proposal to the official's office, with some indication of the comments that would be most useful (some staff like to see a draft or a sample letter). The office may write directly to the commissioner or secretary of the agency receiving the proposal, or may send the letter to you for inclusion in the proposal package.

- *Resources in the Community and What Services These Resources Are Providing (Resource Mapping).* Government grantmakers are interested in knowing exactly what is going on in a target community so they can see precisely where the proposed project will fit in. As they see what is going on, they look for gaps in services that the grant, if funded, will fill.

- *Résumés for "Typical" Staff for Proposed Project.* Understanding that job announcements for important grant-funded positions may have to be widely posted in a fair and impartial manner once funding is approved, government grantmakers often are willing to look at a typical résumé of a well-qualified project director, for instance, rather than the résumé of the person who will be hired. Showing that you've given a lot of thought to the qualifications of project staff is reassuring to funders!

- *Job Descriptions of All Full- and Part-Time Grant-Funded Staff.* Include the duties and responsibilities of each staff member, how much time he or she will put into the project, and, if possible, to whom each will report in the organization's structure. Also, describe the duties of staff members who will work on the project as an in-kind contribution of the applicant—people who will participate in project activities but whose salaries are not paid for by the grant.

Pop Quiz

True or False?

1. The project cost should never appear in the abstract of a grant proposal.
2. A table of contents should only be included in a grant proposal if it is mentioned in the application.
3. The average length of a comprehensive abstract is five pages.
4. If you get letters of support from elected officials, you should make sure they are presented at the very front of your proposal.
5. Foundations never expect to see information about a not-for-profit organization's board of directors in the attachments.
6. A good rule of thumb for your abstract: Use as many words as you need as long as you're completely clear.

7. Government grant applications usually don't specify how many pages the appendix should be.

8. All grantmakers expect at least some attachments or appendix material included in the grant proposal.

9. Another word for "appendix" is "attachment."

Essay Question

1. Write a sample cover letter to a foundation to accompany a proposal.

FUNDERS' ROUNDTABLE II

Well, it's taken quite a while to get to this roundtable—after discussing (in painstaking detail) each element of a standard grant proposal. Before addressing these components with our panelists, we asked the funders to respond as holistically as possible to the grant proposal itself. We asked what three things a proposal writer could do to get their attention and make them want to give the grant (and we asked which single thing was most important). Then we asked about pet peeves. Their responses are scattered throughout the roundtables. But before we go on, we'd like to summarize these responses here.

What did the grantmakers really like?

The roundtable for Part I should have given you a good idea of the panelists' likes. Nearly every grantmaker said that what they like to see is that you've done your homework, read the guidelines, and understand the foundation or government program priorities. Almost all of them said they looked for a good idea, a good program, and clarity—and brevity—in the expression of the idea. Government funders were more concerned than most foundations about a formal statement of objectives and outcome measurement, but panelists from both types of institution wanted to see that applicants had thought about what they wanted to accomplish through the grant and how they would know if they had succeeded.

And what were their pet peeves?

Perhaps you can guess what the most common pet peeve was. As should be clear from the first roundtable, nearly every grantmaker talked about applicants who didn't do their homework. Foundation representatives were annoyed by applicants who didn't know what the foundation did, hadn't read the guidelines, and didn't even know who the current program officer or foundation director was. "Scattershot," "shotgun," and "over the transom" were some of the disparaging terms they used about proposals that apparently had been sent out at random and with no thought.

"I sometimes read a proposal and can't see

where it's going."

The other major complaint was about proposals in which the applicants hadn't made it clear what they wanted to do, how they were going to do it, or how the budget had been arrived at. "I sometimes read a proposal and can't see where it's going," was an annoyance expressed by one grantmaker, who could have been speaking for all of her colleagues. "If a proposal is a real mess, it's a reflection of a lack of coherence in the program." But the panelists were less hard on some aspects of the proposal that we thought might be poorly received. Spelling errors, poor writing (as long as the concepts are clear), and other stylistic problems are not necessarily held against the applicant—but they are noticed. We thought maybe we shouldn't even mention this fact to you, though. In more recent interviews, funders were clear that they could not take poorly written proposals to their boards and did not have time to help with rewrites as some might have done in the past for small, grassroots organizations or new immigrant groups who were just learning the grants process. So, unless you know the specific person who will review your proposal and that person's likes and dislikes, you just can't risk submitting a sloppily written proposal.

Are there "intangibles" that nobody thinks to tell grant seekers?

There are a number of things nobody ever really talks about—things that grantmakers and experienced grant seekers do or say almost instinctively. Before we left the preparation phase of the grants process, we asked our panelists to think about some intangibles—things that aren't mentioned (or even hinted at) in grant application packages or in any guidelines—that might help you get ready to develop and write your proposals.

Several panelists talked about their interest in improving the field, or making an impact on communities through their grants. For this reason they expected applicants to be aware of bigger issues, though they rarely said so in application guidelines. For example, one funder suggested that proposal writers put their programs in a "current political, economic, and environmental context." She wants to make sure that applicants "know exactly what the city is doing" when their program relates to urban issues. Another agreed: "Groups need to have a big picture about trends. Living for the day is good, but be strategic. And know the field—because the funders certainly do."

"Groups need to have a big picture about trends.
Know the field—because the funders certainly do."

Remember that although application packages do not generally say anything about "knowing the field," often you must demonstrate exactly that—especially for larger grants. Your organization really needs to make sure that it is up-to-date not only about the kinds of programs that have been shown to work successfully, but about local and state policies as well. The grant application must reflect this wisdom. (We talked about how to do that in Lesson 8.)

A government panelist suggested, "Large cities need to make their structure clear. Reviewers see New York, for example, as a monolith, and don't realize it's a bunch of little cities." She suggested that you try to use the language in your proposal to help the grantmakers visualize the neighborhoods. "Show funders around, take them to the neighborhoods, show them that the city and the nonprofits all sit at the same tables."

Some funders had specific, personal advice for proposal writers, sometimes not so complimentary to those of us who are not program staff: "I see development people—grant writers—as 'guns for hire.' I think of them as 'turnstile people'—this week they're writing grants for a youth organization, next week they've moved on to the arts, then to AIDS. Their proposals have a mechanical feel. They lack passion. The grant writer should convey a sense of commitment rather than a sense that a person is moving up a career ladder." Ouch! But the point is extremely important. If the person writing the proposal is not a staff member who is passionate about the program to be funded, he or she should be working closely with someone who is. It shows.

And although the proposal should be presentable in terms of format, spelling, grammar, and, above all, clarity, don't feel you have to spend money packaging it or put on a show with it. A funder said, "Make it easier to use, with headings, bullets, and so on; visuals put the reader in a good frame of mind . . . But at the other extreme, sometimes proposals can be so glossy you feel the applicants are spending too much money and fitting you into their pattern. This happens with the big organizations like think tanks." In other words, your proposal shouldn't look like a corporate marketing package that's been attached to a few pages in which you respond to the request for proposals.

"Make it easier to use, with headings, bullets, and so on . . ."

Another funder suggested that proposal writers should "spend time learning about the variety of financial mechanisms available in making a grant—charitable trusts, private banking, etc. Take classes! Establish relationships in private banking and estate planning" because it's the bankers, rather than lawyers, who increasingly advise their clients about setting up charitable trusts and making large donations.

How should the need be shown in the proposal, and how important is it really?

"Beginning grant writers tend to base their proposals on their ideas rather than on a real need," said a funder. "To show need is very important . . . yet there's an amazing lack of statistics included in proposals—and when they are included, they are often dated and out of context."

"There's an amazing lack of statistics included in proposals —and when they are included, they are often dated and out of context . . ."

Another funder suggested that "you use a commonsense approach to identifying need." Unlike her colleague, she doesn't want to see a lot of data because she is fully aware of which communities have the greatest need in the geographical area funded by her foundation. But do tell her about new needs in your community that require attention. "We know the territory pretty well," agreed a panelist. "We don't want to see proposals overladen with demographic proof. Be smart. More is not necessarily better."

You see—more is better when it comes to reading and studying guidelines, but it is not better if you haphazardly adorn your grant proposal with statistics that are overwhelming and irrelevant. Clearly you have to find a balance between failing to describe a problem and throwing in the statistical kitchen sink. One way to deal with this may be to include (brief) compelling stories that demonstrate the need. "I like to see some anecdotal data about how a program touched the lives of people, along with some relevant hard data and statistics," said a government funder. "I prefer a bigger picture view showing the organization's understanding of its role in making positive things happen," explained a foundation grantmaker, "rather than, 'our community has the worst so-and-so.'"

"I like to see some anecdotal data about how a program
touched the lives of people, along with some relevant
hard data and statistics."

"Applicants usually understand their needs," said a government grant-maker, "But being clear about them is another story." In other words, whatever information you include to make the case for a need, be sure you organize it well, state it clearly, and show how it is relevant to the program you want to implement.

Do grants always go to the communities with the greatest need?

The answer to this question surprised us a bit. Communities with the direst need aren't always the ones that get the grant. Most funders want to be sure the money will be well spent, so they look for strong organizations doing important things, wherever they are located. When pressed on the subject of need, they admitted that, as much as they may want to, it is very difficult to give grants to organizations that aren't likely to be able to implement and sustain the program, no matter how compelling the problem and how underserved the community.

"We fund underserved communities first and foremost," said one foundation panelist. But, another explained, "We don't give money just to spur community involvement—even if it is a very low-income community. We only give money to a community that can already demonstrate a commitment to making things better."

Another funder said that her foundation gets an idea about something that it thinks should happen—and then searches for a "fertile community where it is likely to happen—meaning one with key leadership in place, a track record, and a desire to extend good work that is already going on." Still another said, "We give money to the strongest people and the strongest program—not necessarily the one that is in the lowest-income area."

On the other hand, "If we fund in 'good' neighborhoods, the amount of money we give is far more modest . . . in fact, we'll generally use a challenge grant approach (which requires the grantees to find additional funders)," another of our panelists explained. One funder offered this hint: "If you are in a wealthy neighborhood or community asking for a grant, be modest. But geography doesn't automatically knock you out of the box."

Does the nonprofit status of a group matter?

The nonprofit status of an applicant matters, even if it has a wonderful program in a very needy community. "Sometimes a group will come to us and say, 'We don't have a 501(c)(3), but we feed hundreds of hungry people every night,'" a foundation grantmaker said. "It's frustrating because some groups have access—they know how to get help with that sort of thing—and other groups—like this one—can't manage it." Foundations usually can't give grants to organizations that don't have their paperwork in place, no matter how great their need is and how many people they serve, so it is easy to see why this funder may be frustrated.

Grantmaking panelists suggest that your needs statement will be different if your proposal is being sent to your local bank (which knows the neighborhood as well as you do), a small foundation in your community (which also knows the terrain), or to a large national foundation or federal government agency (both of which may be unfamiliar with your neighborhood or community). As one of our panelists said, "Be smart about it (which is always easier said than done). And be clear (which is also easier said than done)."

And now for those measurable objectives . . .
do we really need them?

Generally, the need or problem section of a proposal is followed by the objectives you hope to achieve in order to solve the problem you laid out. Because every program planner and proposal writer tends to have a difficult time arriving at suitable objectives, we asked our panel of grant-makers about the importance of objectives, and for suggestions about how to develop them.

"Measurable objectives—very important," said one funder, "I need to see benchmarks so I can sell the proposal to the board and senior staff." A government funder explained that the most important thing an applicant can do is "be results oriented," which is what objectives are all about. "What do you want to do—what are the gaps—and what services will you provide to fill in the gaps? This is important," said another funder. "There is a lot of research out there that can help you. Be realistic. Don't say you'll increase reading scores by three grade levels through a summer recreation program for children!"

"Frankly, I don't care how many widgets you made,
I only care if the widgets made a difference—
and how they made a difference."

"Frankly, I don't care how many widgets you made, I only care if the widgets made a difference . . . and how they made a difference," warned another government funder; this grantmaker is not quite as interested in how many people you served as how well the program worked. "Objectives weren't important to us until [recently]," said a panelist. "Our board didn't require them. But now, we don't just fund from our heart—we need to support groups that will make an impact."

"If you're having a problem setting up appropriate measurable objectives, suggested a grantmaker, "work with your program officer . . . or someone who can help you."

We understand that measurable objectives are important. But what if we don't achieve them? Will we have to give the money back?

"Once in a blue moon, if you've aimed too high, the foundation will ask for the money we gave you back," admitted one of our panelists. But this probably would happen only if the organization hasn't seriously worked at reaching the outcomes. "If you've engaged the community and really made an effort, we probably won't ask you to return the funds." Another said, "We want organizations to succeed. We don't want to take money back. If grantees keep the foundation informed about what's going on . . . we can help you," said a panelist.

Keeping the funder informed may be the key to what happens if the program isn't successful. "I like to see how grantees deal with challenges. Tell me, 'We thought this would happen, but then this happened. Luckily, we had a Plan B, a Plan C, and help from friends and supporters,'" explained a grantmaker.

"I like to see how grantees deal with challenges."

One funder suggested, "Large foundations can be understanding if you weren't successful doing what you said you'd do. Smaller foundations can't afford to be as flexible."

Organizations often can rely on help from funders in figuring out how to restate the objectives to be more realistic, how to achieve the desired outcomes, and why things went wrong. A government grantmaker said, "It's a new ballgame once you get a grant. The highest scores on the proposal are not necessarily the highest performers. The extent to which an applicant overstated its objectives might be revisited once the grant is actually being implemented."

To summarize: Of course funders are more concerned when you don't even try to achieve your objectives than when you try hard and fail to achieve the results you hoped you would. And they all want to see evidence that you've learned something when you haven't quite succeeded. Oh, and they like to be kept in the loop as you're attempting—or even struggling—to achieve your objectives. No one—not you, not us, certainly not grantmakers—likes surprises. If you're having trouble with your grant-funded program, make sure you talk to the funder. Not only can you get moral support, you can also get valuable help.

The program is the key, right? So what do grantmakers really look for in the program description?

First of all, you need to keep in mind that program officers can recommend grants, but generally don't have the final say about whether a proposal succeeds. Provide enough information so that they can make your case: "I need a very detailed program description because that's what I'm selling to my board. Your program description gives the program officer the power to make your case by using your words." A government grantmaker described a conversation with an applicant who had gotten a mediocre score on a proposal—and no grant—and was upset, because she had received grants for the same program before. "I sat down with the criteria and her application, and called her back and said, 'This is not a good application.' She hadn't clearly and cleanly explained what they wanted to do."

"I need a very detailed program description
because that's what I'm selling to my board."

Concerning the program's importance, the grantmakers also said, "The first thing we look at is your program—whether it reflects best practices, sustainability, and measurable outcomes." "The program should be a blueprint for everything." "A good program is the key: What is it you plan to do?"

And what do the grantmakers look for in a proposal that convinces them that it's a good program?

"The fewer questions I have about a program as I'm reading a proposal, the better the program is explained," one panelist said. Others noted, "I look at what and who: What is the program and who is the leadership?" "We want to see an explicit theory of action." "Be clear and concise. Build your case: Why is the program excellent, and why is it likely to accomplish what you hope it will?" "Make a good case that the proposed program is consistent with your organization's line of business. 'Stick to your knitting,' which means focus on your core line of work." "The project design should be clear and concise: We are going to implement this and this. We are going to manage it this way and that way." And watch your language. Funders told us, "Program staff are committed to doing a great job running their program . . . But they don't learn to sell their program. They learn jargon instead." "I hate pseudoscience babble," one panelist said. "I hate phrases like 'myriad approaches.' Just tell me what you're going to do."

"I hate pseudoscience babble . . .
Just tell me what you're going to do."

Above all, one grantmaker said, "Be reasonable. Doable. Implementable. In line with your organization's vision."

And how important is collaboration? If I collaborate, am I more likely to get a grant?

Grantmakers talk about collaboration, but grant seekers argue about it, What is it exactly? It's more trouble than it's worth. It's easy for you to like it—you don't have to do it. So we asked the panelists what they thought.

One funder said, "Collaboration is not necessarily a means to an end." But others disagreed. One said, "We've been encouraging collaborations at times when resources aren't abundant." "We fund community development, which works much better with collaboration. We give preference—for financial and policy reasons—to collaborative approaches. They're critical," she added. Her colleague agreed: "Collaboration is essential. Sometimes it isn't about collaboration, but mostly it is. Get together and talk!" Another panelist said, "We actually ask applicants who they are coordinating with . . . we want to make sure they're connecting with other groups to provide the highest-quality services."

Whether they preferred to see collaborations or not, grantmakers agreed that it's very difficult. As one said, "We like collaboration, but from personal experience, it takes a lot of work." "Sometimes collaboration makes sense . . . but it is difficult—especially when you're bringing together groups that have different cultures. It's messy," said another.

> *"Sometimes collaboration makes sense . . . but it is difficult—especially when you're bringing together groups that have different cultures. It's messy."*

In fact, the grantmakers recognized that collaboration should emerge from the community itself, rather than being required by the funder. "It's nice when two or three groups get together and approach you rather than your telling them to collaborate," said one. "Collaboration is beneficial but it shouldn't be funder driven—and it's awfully hard work," said a foundation grantmaker. "We help people collaborate . . . but we don't expect them to do so. We actually fund people to work on collaborations—funders need to be sensitive to the difficulty." "We don't force it but we're interested in collaboration," said a funder. "We've seen groups forced to work together who don't like each other."

"We haven't seen much collaboration," said another funder. "But our board would probably appreciate it. We'd be willing to give more money if the groups explained that they were asking for the extra money so they could actually collaborate."

Government grantmakers were even more committed to the concept of collaboration. One government funder said, "It's the best way to get things done. No single entity can do it all. Individuals we're concerned with have very complex needs—housing, primary health care, mental health care, child care, transportation, rehabilitation programs. The very stable, very creative and sophisticated agencies have multiple funding streams and established relationships, sharing information and working together. There's not enough money or expertise to make it happen any other way."

Government agencies are finding ways to collaborate with one another and with community-based organizations within the limits of their procurement regulations. A city government official told us, "Three non-profits got in touch with us about applying for a federal grant that required collaboration between the city and nonprofits. We . . . did a quick mini-RFP and sent it out to those three organizations and seven others we knew were working in the field. We lifted questions straight from the federal grant application and asked the nonprofits to respond. We got proposals back and had them reviewed just as we would any other. The review team unanimously selected one group, and we put that organization into our grant." This meant that once the city agency won the grant, it could start the program immediately without having to go through another protracted contracting process. This panelist also told us that more agencies within city government are collaborating, including agencies that are not directly under the mayor's control, like district attorneys' offices and others. And most important, "Forward-thinking commissioners and agencies are just interested in getting the money into the city. They understand that they don't have to be the grantee, and that they can work with whoever is the best applicant."

"Forward-thinking commissioners and agencies are just interested in getting the money into the city. They understand that they don't have to be the grantee."

Another government funder advised us that "collaboration is becoming more intense. To have a comprehensive impact on communities, you need a coordinated effort. It used to be acceptable to have a bunch of letters of support with different executive directors' signatures. Now there's been a paradigm shift: Create partnerships at the beginning of the project, not right before you're mailing out the grant proposal!"

How should collaboration work? A government panelist reminded us that "collaboration has the word 'labor' in it. 'I've got the costumes, you've got the stage—let's put on a show.' That's collaboration!" His colleague commented, "I see project staff as the key to building collaboration . . . an entrepreneurial person is needed." And a foundation panelist noted, "To do it well, someone must be in charge to nurture the collaboration . . . for the care and feeding of the partners . . . to facilitate the partnership."

"'I've got the costumes, you've got the stage—
let's put on a show.' That's collaboration."

One government panelist spoke of foundations as well as nonprofits when discussing collaboration. "There is a lot that foundations can offer without writing a check. They have information on best practices, research they've funded, a perspective outside the specific geographic location. They can donate space for meetings, sit on advisory boards, provide personal contacts. It rounds out the process."

In some ways, collaboration is still in its infancy. But most funders seem to agree that working together to solve a problem, help clients, and conduct a comprehensive, effective program is better than working in isolation. But doing it—and doing it well—is another matter altogether. It's probably safe to say that collaboration is a goal, but we haven't reached it yet. Clearly it is on the minds of grantmakers, though. A funder's last words on the subject: "Generally, like it or not, collaboration is not going away anytime soon."

The program is great, but how can I prove my organization is capable of implementing it?

As grantmakers are deciding whether to fund your project, they wonder about your organization's ability to do what you say you're going to do. It is one thing to talk the talk (and write up the write-up), and another thing to walk the walk. We asked our panelists to address "the Big Three"—capacity to implement the program, capacity to sustain the program once the funding cycle is over, and the adequacy of your budget to conduct the activities efficiently.

"For us, leadership is everything."

Leadership was a key to grantmakers' decisions. "I don't necessarily need to know the person in charge of an organization personally, but I want evidence of a track record . . . Who supports it, who funds it?" "For us, leadership is everything. Does the leader have the vision and capability to run the organization?" "We look for the proof that you have the ability to deliver what you say you will: staff and track record."

Collaboration, or at least the organization's solid place in the community or its relationships within its program area, is another indication of potential success. "If the organization is plugged into a network of other groups we fund, there is at least a context that helps us believe that the organization will do what it says it is going to do." "I want to know who will help the organization if things go wrong." "The size and length of time an organization has been around is not important. What is important is the ability to do what it says it will do—which is why we encourage applicants to form partnerships to build up their capacity." "Show that you've reached out to all the stakeholders the program is expected to impact."

A few grantmakers are willing to help by giving grants that can strengthen the organization: "My foundation gives capacity-building grants." Others look for a signal that the group is not overreaching: "We believe in an agency that knows what its niche is."

Sustainability is another story. How can I prove the program will live on when I'm not even sure myself?

Convincing grantmakers that you will sustain the program when there are no more grant funds is a monumental challenge. More than a monumental challenge. We asked our panel how important it is to show you'll sustain the program when the grant runs out, and how applicants can believably and convincingly address the issue of sustainability in their proposals.

"I like to fund programs that are transformative," explained a foundation funder, "but they don't necessarily need to lead to self-sufficiency. I like to see a certain level of democracy, where the beneficiaries of grants turn around and help other organizations."

Several panelists commented on the diversity of funding sources as one way to ensure sustainability. One grantmaker explained, "I am willing to understand that sustainability is a long-term process [rather than a program-by-program effort]—but some organizations don't have diversified funding sources and a healthy individual donor base." "No matter what kind of group you are, diversify your funding," warned a funder. Another said, "We need a sense of the organization. Is it planning for future financial stability? We like to see an economic plan for the future, although we know it's complicated. It gets back to leadership and vision."

"No matter what kind of group you
are, diversify your funding."

"Build a development staff," a member of our panel suggested, "and align programs of the organization in an orderly way to secure additional, diverse funding." "I like to fund systemic change," added another. "No pockets are deep enough to fund isolated programs." And another foundation funder said, "Look at other donors, earned income, show that you're thinking about sustaining the program, and that you have some understanding about sustainability."

Panelists offered these words of advice: "Be creative about sustainability. Do board development. If 10 of your board members raise $1,000 each, it's a lot easier than getting a $10,000 grant." "Look at grants as building blocks for financial sustainability—but not as the only building block." "Don't be dependent on only one sector for funding. If you are, foundations—or, at least, my foundation—will be concerned."

"Look at grants as building blocks for financial sustainability—but not as the only building block."

Perhaps we should not have been surprised at the reversal of a long-held assumption in philanthropy that foundations stimulate new programs and government sources take over to support those that are demonstrated to work well. A federal government grantmaker said, "Everyone in Washington expects grantees to have everything figured out once the federal investment runs out. Even if a grant doesn't require it, show that you've thought about sustaining the program or project. Remember: Programs are no longer funded into perpetuity . . . there is diminished entitlement." Another government funder is willing to give seed money to get a project started—but he wants to know, "What are your plans to sustain?"

"When there is a large community buy-in, there is likely to be sustainability because the community partners [i.e., local government] will take the project over," a federal government panelist said. "We expect programs to be institutionalized by the end of five years. We might reduce funding in the third and fourth year."

"The best way to ensure sustainability is to build relationships," a funder said. "Many cities are 'smokestacked.' No one talks to anyone. The schools don't talk to the police who don't talk to . . ." "Leverage resources—build public-private partnerships," suggested another grantmaker.

Which leads us to the budget: What do grantmakers look for?

"Too often grant writers obviously don't understand the financials of their organizations," said a foundation funder. "Trustees of foundations tend to be businesspeople, so the financial aspects of a proposal are really important to them. They'll ask, 'Why are consulting fees so high?' They'll ask questions about overhead costs." "It's funny," another panelist said, "Newer, less experienced groups don't build in overhead—and they undercut themselves. Larger groups, on the other hand, exaggerate their overhead costs. And everyone tends to underestimate in-kind contributions in their proposals." (See a discussion of in-kind contributions in Lesson 11.)

"A pet peeve of mine is when the budget isn't transparent. People like to bundle things together to leave themselves some room," explained a government grantmaker. "In one proposal I read, the applicant used the word 'modalities' in the budget (with no explanation)—and spent two-thirds of the grant to pay for this thing called 'modalities.'" "I also don't like to see a disproportionately small number of staff included in the budget—it makes me think that someone is trying to pull the wool over my eyes," he added.

"I hate it when budgets make no sense. And I loathe the
'blah-blah-blah syndrome' . . . when grant writers sort of go
blah, blah, blah instead of just telling us directly what
they plan to do with the money."

Another funder complains, "I hate it when budgets make no sense. And I loathe the 'blah-blah-blah syndrome'—when grant writers sort of go blah, blah, blah instead of just telling us directly what they plan to do with the money. Keep the budget simple." As a government panelist advised, "It all goes back to writing a clear proposal. Our application format has a proposal narrative and a budget narrative, and the two have to 'crosswalk.'"

And the funders can't think of any reason you shouldn't have a realistic, straightforward budget. "Spreadsheets and other software packages have allowed people to be more on top of things as far as crafting their budget is concerned."

Other elements of the budget are important to some funders. For example, "I like to see what I think of as 'added value' in the budget," said a grantmaker. "Things like in-kind contributions that show how resources are leveraged." "We're always looking at the reasoning behind your budget—your assumptions need to be clear." "Who are the other funders—name them in the budget." This approach also provides references: "Our grants are only for about $25,000 a year—so we hope that the organizations we're funding are stable. Who funded them last year? We call other funders—if we know them—to check the groups out."

As still another reminder about reading the guidelines, another funder said, "Don't slip something into the budget that we say we won't fund (rent, for example). Some grantmakers will stop reading proposals that do that." "I saw a funny one last year," added a government grantmaker. "Our announcement included a small amount of renovation if it was necessary to provide the services supported in the grant. We got an application asking for the entire amount of the grant for renovation! People don't understand: Leasing, car rental, renovation have to be tied to the services!"

"Don't slip something into the budget that we say
we won't fund (rent, for example). Some grantmakers
will stop reading proposals that do that."

"Be realistic about what it costs to run a program . . . don't short-change yourself," insisted a panel member. "Put it in front of the foundation's eyes—right smack in the middle of the proposal—that it costs money to do all the things you want to do. Don't say, 'We only need $45,000 to pay the salary of a staff member,' when it costs a hell of a lot more than $45,000 to run the program." Another panelist commented, "We don't want to be the sole support of someone's salary because, let's face it, when the grant runs out, there's a good chance the person will get fired. We don't mind paying a part of a salary, or we might be willing to pay the whole amount for a development staff member who will turn around and raise money for the organization." Even if you're just asking the foundation to support that salary, or part of it, show how it fits into the larger program budget.

Realistic. Reasonable. Appropriate. Grantmakers do want your staff to be paid adequately: "We want to see reasonable salaries." "I believe in reasonable salaries and benefits for not-for-profit staff. I hate to see high-priced consultants mentioned in budgets. They get paid an awful lot of money—and then they disappear."

Another foundation grantmaker expanded on the need to be realistic. "It's unrealistic, for instance, if you have an all-volunteer staff and suddenly you want to jump to 10 paid staffers. Jump gradually if you expect to get funded." Similarly, "It's silly for a group that we never funded before—never heard of, never dealt with—to ask for $100,000 for general support," warned a funder. "People ask for a larger amount of money than we can give them," said a grantmaker. "We need to see a realistic assessment of how you'll do what you said you'd do using a smaller amount of money." One funder said, "We look at the budget of the proposed project in the context of the organization's entire budget to make sure it fits and makes sense. The budget and the proposal narrative should be completely linked." And, "We don't nitpick about salaries—but we like to fund groups that have done everything possible to be fiscally smart. Are you getting donated space and services? What else are people contributing?"

One last thing on the topic of budget. A funder warned, "I have a dialogue with grant seekers and ask why certain items appear in the budget. I look at the program ideas first and the financials second. But I have to warn you—other grantmakers do it in the reverse. They look at costs first . . . and only after they've analyzed your budget do they look at the elements of your program."

What do grantmakers say about evaluation?
(Please say, "It's not very important!")

Sorry, but most grantmakers say evaluation *is* important. "Anyone can design a good program . . . but will it get good results? The world is littered with good programs. I want to focus on results," said a grantmaker. "Very few program staff actually care about evaluation—but they should use evaluation techniques to help them make changes in the program. No one ever says, 'We haven't succeeded.'"

"The world is littered with good programs.
I want to focus on results."

Although the ability to know if a program is working is important to almost all funders, foundation grantmakers are more sympathetic about the difficulties of program evaluation than are government grantmakers—probably because the latter are willing to pay for evaluation when it's important to them. "So few funders pay for evaluations that it seems cruel to ask grant writers to include them in proposals," said a foundation grantmaker. But "evaluations allow you to retool constantly to improve your program," another funder pointed out. "We'll help people work on their evaluation plans." Perhaps most reassuring to organizations that really don't know how to do evaluation, "We work with less sophisticated groups and are comfortable with simple deliverables. We just want to see that they have some ideas for evaluation."

A government funder offered a very practical warning: "Don't tack on the evaluation at the end. Front-load it—build in the evaluation component at the beginning. Explain what tests and other measures you're going to use to decide if you've achieved your objectives as you write your objectives. Use the evaluation section of the proposal to go into some detail about how you will use and analyze the measurements." And when you work with an outside evaluator, as required by many government grants, be sure the evaluator understands how important it is to integrate evaluation into the whole program—and the whole proposal. "Sometimes we see evaluations that don't fit in with the rest of the proposal—we suspect that high-priced consultants were probably used," another government grantmaker complained. "Garbage in, garbage out."

We were reassured to hear that grantmakers want to hear about failures too. "We're lenient if you say that your program didn't have an impact, as long as you try to figure out why it didn't work," said another panelist. "Tell us what lessons you learned. What you'd do differently. Say something like, 'We didn't realize the community wouldn't care about such-and-such. Next time we'd approach folks differently.' We love it when you say, 'We bombed this year . . . but we'll do better next time.'"

"Tell us what lessons you learned. We love it when
you say, 'We bombed this year . . . but
we'll do better next time.'"

Our conversations made it seem that foundation grantmakers are only now dipping into the evaluation waters—meaning that in the past they focused almost solely on the program design and implementation, not the results that were achieved. Grant seekers can help themselves if they recognize the importance of program evaluation, whether it is specifically addressed in the application or not. You don't have to conduct fancy "two-sample t-tests" or "analyses of variance." Try giving brief pre- and post-tests or attitude surveys to participants in your program. Conduct and document interviews and focus groups. And do so on a regular basis so you will know—and be able to tell grantmakers—if your program is working.

Whether it's called "appendix" or "attachment," what should I include?

Sometimes the guidelines or application specify what additional material should be sent; at other times, there is no mention of any supplementary information that funders want to see. We asked the grantmakers a question about what appendix material or attachments should or should not be included in a grant proposal if there's no guideline about this.

"In my opinion," said a government funder, "appendix material should be connected to the collaboration in some way. I like 'resource mapping.' I also like to see articles about past successes, past evaluations of the group's efforts, examples of the organization's track record. 'Soft stuff' [such as anecdotal information] is good too, if it is allowed. Also a brief résumé of the project director—I'm interested in human capital. Do you have the right leader?" Another government panelist pointed out that when grantees receive the grant, "All of a sudden they have to start implementing the project . . . all of a sudden the rubber must meet the road. I like to see letters of commitment and memoranda of understanding that define how often and how much. They really explain how things will get going." And yet another government member of our panel likes the appendix to include "minutes of partnership meetings—proving the partnership is real. Sometimes applicants go way overboard on the support letters," she said. "And they all have the same wording on different organizations' letterheads."

"Send what the foundation asks for."

But keep in mind that, especially for foundations, "when there is too much appendix material, there is a temptation to leaf through it and not read anything carefully." "Send what the foundation asks for—and this is like pulling teeth," explained a funder. "We expect to see an audit (our treasurer goes through this line by line)." "Don't send videos—they usually end up in the trash. And just don't send tons of stuff," said another grantmaker.

Before we move on, let's go back to those pet peeves.

You've heard what the panelists said about preparing for a proposal, finding the right funder, designing the best program, being clear about what you want to do and how you will do it, and making sure each part of the proposal reflects that design. You've followed their advice and created a great proposal. You're ready to go. Almost. Before you send out that proposal, let's focus for just a minute more on some of the more concrete, less holistic likes and dislikes of the grantmakers. Then comb through the proposal to be sure you haven't hit any sore spots. As with everything else the panelists have talked about, there are some differences of opinion along the way. But here goes.

Only one or two of the panelists were unconcerned about the proposal's presentation and formatting. Rather, panelists said things like, "I'm not the page police, but don't go over the page limit and get all wordy." "[I hate] proposals that don't reflect a clearly defined vision." "[I hate] when applicants don't stick to page limits and font-size limits. You're not considered serious. When people try to get around these limits it drives reviewers nuts. If you want to get on a reviewer's bad side, ignore these limits." "[I hate] incredibly long proposals. If we say two to three pages, don't send us 20 pages." "[I hate] jargon. I hate when things get overintellectualized as opposed to a clear, direct description of the organization's mission and the purpose of the grant." "[I hate] jargon and hyperbole. A woman actually said to me that the target audience for her program was 'potentially every child in the world.'" "[I hate] proposals that aren't precise, concise, and sharp."

"Our reviewers go off when there are
a lot of spelling errors."

"Our reviewers go off when there are a lot of spelling errors. 'Don't they know what spell-check is?' they say." "Because of spelling errors, ideas can be unclear and points are deducted from your score." "Lack of proofreading makes me crazy. From a small grassroots organization—that's one thing. But from a large organization—it's unacceptable. Even with computers, terrible errors can occur!" There's an echo in here: "Bad grammar drives me crazy. We're community oriented and know that English often isn't the first language of the writer. I try to understand but it's hard; bad grammar breaks the flow and it's jarring . . . It's less important with grassroots organizations, but I just finished reading proposals from groups that are teaching people to write proposals. That's different."

A few pet peeves were more personal or perhaps idiosyncratic, but they give a good idea of why you have to be so attentive. "[I hate] namedropping: When someone calls and says, 'Oh, So-and-So said your foundation would fund our project.'" "I hate it when someone says, 'We're the only one doing this program in the entire city, state, country, world, planet' (but I have to laugh)." "I don't like 'menus' of requests: 'We need support for this, this, this, and this. Do any of these things appeal to you?' Make up your mind about what's important to you!" "[I hate] budget costs that are obviously unrealistic—giving someone too much work to do for too little money and in too little time, for instance."

And we recommend that even if you're ready to put that proposal in the mail, you should go back to read the guidelines one more time. Listen:

"It makes me nuts when you don't read the guidelines. And you don't proofread. They're my grant guidelines. I wrote them and rewrote them—then my boss edited them some more and I rewrote them again. Then a consultant reviewed them. And you turn in an error-filled proposal that is obviously a first draft!" "When I was writing proposals I figured that if a question wasn't clear or wasn't to the point of what I was writing, I could finesse it. But when you're reviewing proposals it's clear in an answer that the proposer didn't like the question, didn't think it was important, or didn't get it. My agency spent months putting the proposal together. You can't finesse it."

And, "We don't accept the common application form—we ask for a letter of intent—yet people keep sending the application." "We include a checklist of things that should be part of a proposal. Only a minority of applicants come close to following the checklist. We go back and ask them to send things they excluded—and they still sometimes don't send them—but other funders don't necessarily have the time and inclination to do this."

"[I hate] proposals that have no business being sent to us."

One last question: What do I do if a foundation doesn't have application guidelines?

Sometimes the answer is a letter of inquiry. As we said earlier, there are thousands of small to middle-size foundations across the country that have no staff or a very small staff, maybe just a part-time person. They don't want lengthy applications or proposals. For example, "We're open to a broad range of presentations," a grantmaker said. "We're looking for something wonderful. Our program officers can ask you to rewrite if need be."

Another grantmaker whose foundation doesn't have a required application said, "I hate long, beautifully written proposals. I don't want to see more than five pages . . . and don't send everything you've got right away.

Remember, we're just dating. We're at the beginning stages. I don't want to meet your parents yet." (This is why it's a very good idea to call and check with a foundation before deciding what to send: Do you want a short letter of inquiry, a full-blown proposal, a miniproposal, a paragraph, attachments, no attachments? . . . You don't even have to bother the program officer—the receptionist probably has fielded this question many times before.)

"I like to see a one-page executive summary—even though we don't have an application—followed by a brief proposal," said one funder. "My board is persnickety about putting restraints on applicants, which is why they would never think of asking for an actual application," she explained. "They're afraid they'd miss the discovery of the Matterhorn or something if they reined applicants into submitting a form application, so they really look hard at the executive summary. It is the executive summary that is given to the board no matter what proposal an organization submits."

Many funders said that their process begins with a fairly short letter of inquiry (LOI), which is either accepted or rejected by the foundation. If it is accepted, applicants are asked to send a completed proposal. Sometimes site visits are arranged as well.

"I like a letter of inquiry to start with a 'grabber' —a startling fact, a compelling story."

"I like a letter of inquiry to start with a 'grabber'—a startling fact, a compelling story, and a program or strategy that deals with the issue," explained one funder. Another grantmaker said that her foundation expects a letter of inquiry after the applicant has carefully researched what the foundation is doing and invited the foundation to see the program. And, "I like applicants to mention in the LOI which other groups are funding them."

If you are asked to send a letter of inquiry, here's some useful advice from a funder: "The LOI should be a brief description of who you are and why you want a grant. It should be simple and show clarity of purpose—and reflect the foundation's guidelines. And don't forget to mention any telephone conversations you may have had with us."

PART III:
AND AFTER THE PROPOSAL . . .

YOU'RE NOT FINISHED YET. After you send off a proposal you may have one more step to go through in the grantmaking process. Many, though certainly not all, foundation grantmakers (and some government funders) try to make a site visit before they make any decision on a proposal. Lesson 17 gives a few pointers on how to prepare for the site visit.

Whether it's your first grant or your hundredth, you always feel a bit like a high school senior hefting that response letter from the grantmaker in your hand. Whether it's a one-time grant for a small but special project, or a multiyear grant that will support a large, important program for your agency and your community, that moment before you open the envelope is always difficult and exciting. Win or lose, there are things that you, the proposal writer, must do once you get the grantmaker's answer. If you don't get the grant, there are ways you need to follow up. If you do get it, before you plunge into implementing it or turn it over to program staff, you also have a few tasks to complete. Lesson 18 tells you what to do next, and how. Our final funders roundtable closes Part III and the book.

LESSON 17:
The Site Visit—Playing Host

OPENING REMARKS

Most site visits involve a program officer from a local foundation spending an hour or two at your office, meeting staff, chatting with the executive director, asking some quesions, observing the programs, and visiting with clients.

But when the federal government or a large national foundation makes a site visit you can bet there's a lot of money at stake (often grants for many millions of dollars), and the funders come with a posse and an agenda. They expect to see certain things and talk with certain people, often including the mayor. Getting ready for one of these site visits almost calls for an event planner—maybe the kind of talented, organized person who plans the Olympics for a host city or a political convention to choose the party's nominee for president.

Of course no such person is brought on board. Unfortunately! —EK

LEADING QUESTIONS
Once I Send in the Proposal I Can Relax, Right?

Sure, for most foundation and government grants, you can relax until the time comes for you to hear the outcome of the proposal. But a growing number of foundations (very rarely a government agency) aren't comfortable just with paper. They recognize that excellent proposals can come from organizations that may not be able to manage a grant, especially a large one. They want to see for themselves what your physical space is like, they want to meet the leadership, they want to see programs in operation, they want to meet the partners. And if they have given you a grant before, they want to see what's new, what's different now. There are a few prospective grantees who see this visit as the equivalent of a barracks inspection or testifying before the grand jury or the oral examination for a master's or doctoral degree, but this is absolutely the wrong way to look at it.

We know an organization that went through six site visits in six weeks— and the executive director was thrilled because a site visit is in fact a very good sign. If a grantmaker wants to visit your agency, it's because there is something in the proposal that appeals to her or him. Although a site visit is never a guarantee of a grant, because so many other factors affect the final decision by the foundation's board, it means that the funder is thinking seriously about giving one. And the site visit gives you an opportunity to strengthen that inclination.

How Do I Get Ready for a Site Visit?

Most preparation for a site visit is little more than common sense, but we'll go ahead and run through our suggestions just to be sure you touch all the bases.

Start with Scheduling—Programs and People. In the phone call when a site visit is requested, find out exactly what the funder wants to see and how long she or he plans to stay. Part of the visit will be a discussion with the executive director or agency head about the agency, the proposal, and any questions the program officer has about any of these things. But she or he undoubtedly will expect to be shown around the place and observe what's going on. Find out exactly what would be of interest, and schedule accordingly.

If the proposal is in support of an existing program, seeing that program is obviously one major purpose of the visit. But there may be other activities of interest, especially if the grant is for a new program. If the grant is for a program at a senior center, does the funder want to see the exercise program, the nutrition class, or other health-related activities? The painting or music class? Intergenerational programs? Your Alzheimer's group? Clearly, you should set up a day and time when those activities are in progress. And at a senior center the funder might prefer a late-morning visit, around lunchtime, usually the busiest time, to get a sense of how many people you serve. In contrast, a late-day or evening visit would give a grantmaker a better idea of your programs for children and teenagers.

If the request is for a general operating grant in a multiservice agency, the funder may hope to see a sample of everything that's going on in the organization. This is hard to schedule if you run senior programs, which normally end by midafternoon, and youth programs, which normally don't start until then. Find out how long the grantmaker would like to stay, to see if it's possible to offer a taste of everything, and ask which would be most important if it's not.

Just as important as when is the question of who. The funder will want to meet the executive director and other key managers, and especially the person who will be responsible for operating the program for which a grant is requested. Be sure you arrange a time when all or most of those key staff are available, and be sure they're prepared. The grantmaker also may like to meet some of the participants in your programs.

Bring in Other Players. Although you won't normally schedule the site visit around the availability of everyone who might be involved, if the proposal is for a collaborative effort, ask if the grantmaker would like to meet some of the partners. Invite a few of the key players who are available, at least for part of the visit. Of course, if a grant is of the magnitude mentioned in the opening remarks, you will schedule the visit around the availability of all partners, or at least as many as possible. (We'll talk a bit in a later section about what the big funders are looking for.) Select a location that makes it easy for partners to attend and at the same time gives the funder the best possible picture of the partnership.

Brush Up. It would be very surprising if the grantmaker did not arrive at a site visit with a lot of questions about the agency and the proposed program. Read the proposal again before the visit. Discuss it with everyone who may meet the funder. Be sure you all know exactly how the program will work, who will do what, and what the budget will support.

Know how the program will fit into the overall agency mission and operations. Know who the other funders of the program are, and how you will
sustain it when the grant ends.

But the Place Looks So Dingy.
Do I Have to Paint the Meeting Room?

You don't have to do anything extraordinary for foundation or government visitors. You may be sure they've seen plenty of dingy meeting
rooms, shabby offices, and old furniture. If your agency is large, airy, and
modern, you're among the lucky few. Grantmakers know that, beyond
keeping the place clean, your money goes into programs, not beautification. Just be sure that the Meals-on-Wheels lunch of beef stew, peas,
and mashed potatoes, which was accidentally dropped in the hallway
when it was being carried out to the car, is cleaned up quickly so nobody
slips. And let all staff know there will be a visitor that day so *they* won't
look dingy.

What If the Site Visit Is by a *Very Important* Funder?

All funders are important, and the preparation is the same whether the
site visit is being conducted by one program officer whose foundation is
deciding whether to give your organization a $10,000 grant or a team of
visitors from the federal government whose agency is deciding whether to
give your city a $48 million grant. But some elements are slightly differ-
ent when a very large grant is at stake.

When the big funders come to town, it's usually for a grant that involves one or more local government agencies and may include a few (or
a lot of) not-for-profits. They are looking for assurances that your city
or town not only will be able to manage a very sizable grant but will do
exactly what the proposal describes. Will partners who are from different
political parties—say, a mayor and a governor—work together to support
costly grant-funded projects? Will government red tape and turf issues

among different groups in the city keep the program from running smoothly and being successful? Is there real buy-in—is the program described in the proposal generated from the top down or the bottom up? Were there town hall meetings where community members actually had significant input in the design of the program, or did municipal government officials create the program without any real collaboration?

The site visit is a chance for those funders who are offering whopping grants to see if the written word and the spoken word are consistent, to see if no stone really was left unturned, as the proposal implied. Is there a unified vision? Has space been identified and reserved for grant-funded activities? Is a contracting procedure in place to make sure the program will hum?

Be sure to hold as many preparatory meetings of the collaborating groups as necessary so that everyone is fully prepared and will be able to speak (as much as any large, diverse partnership can) with one voice. And we were only partly kidding about the event planner!

Anything Else I Need to Know?

We think that the most important element in a site visit could be the enthusiasm of the agency's leadership about the organization and the programs it operates. If you usually enjoy showing people around, if you enjoy talking to people about the wonderful things the organization does and the wonderful people it serves, you will enjoy doing this with the grantmakers. And your guests will enjoy it too.

You also need to remember that whether it's a small foundation giving a small grant, or big funders coming to town for a visit to determine the outcome of an enormous grant proposal, it's just one of the (many) steps along the way to winning a grant. Being chosen for a site visit doesn't mean that you'll get the grant—not by any means. But proving your capacity to carry out the project and demonstrating your enthusiasm and your commitment certainly increase your chances.

Pop Quiz

Essay Question

1. You've applied for $75,000 from the WW Love Foundation to pay for components of an after-school tutoring program for at-risk teenagers in your community. Out of the clear blue, you get a call saying that a program officer from the foundation would like to pay a visit in three or four days. What is the very first thing you would do (after saying, "Sure, we're looking forward to meeting you")? What is the second thing you'd do? The third?

LESSON 18:
So Now You Know—What Next?

OPENING REMARKS

A community-based nonprofit organization we know applied for a federal substance abuse grant to offer programs for at-risk teenagers. The federal proposal was complex and the instructions sometimes difficult to comprehend. By the time the group submitted the proposal, it had stated the need clearly, set up measurable objectives, and demonstrated a strong, well-thought-out program with an excellent evaluation plan. But it didn't win the grant. In fact, more than 80 percent of the organizations that applied for this grant didn't win.—ASF

LEADING QUESTIONS
We Did Everything Right . . . and Our Grant Still Was Turned Down. Why? And What Do We Do About It?

Who wins every grant? What not-for-profit organization, local or state agency, school district, college, or individual artist ever gets every penny for which it (or he or she) applies? The answer is, of course, not one. We've said before (and the grantmakers support this), if you win one out of every 10 grants you apply for, you are in the Grant Seeker's Hall of Fame. Most foundation and government funders report that they can fund only 10 to 20 percent of the applications they receive, and the reason is not always because of poor proposals or programs.

Throughout the book, we've referred to getting turned down for grant funding—but we've generally "blamed the victim." You know—you must really, really have done something wrong, not followed directions, not studied the funder's guidelines, not answered all the questions, not submitted the grant on time, not gathered the required partners, not, not, not . . .

But what if you have done everything right and still get turned down? What if you have identified a compelling need and made a strong case for the program designed to address the need? What if you have demonstrated the capacity to implement the grant and even have strongly suggested how the program . . . gulp . . . would be sustained once the grant period was over? With all the right intentions, all the right moves, all the right homework, the program is not funded. Are you going to throw your hands up in defeat (and lapse into a deep depression)? Are you going to call the grantmaker and complain? Write a letter explaining why you should have won? The mistake is not that you lost the grant; it's failing to follow up in appropriate ways to help your chances of winning the same grant next time. Savvy proposal writers look at rejection as a challenge. (Savvy proposal writers must like challenges or they would be selling refrigerators or racing cars or tending bar or trying cases—anything but writing grant proposals!)

Wait a Minute: How Do I Find Out If My Program Will Receive Funding?

In the case of grant proposals, the old adage "No news is good news" does not apply. "No news" can sometimes be the worst news possible. It takes longer to hear that you didn't get a grant than to hear that you did—if the funder bothers to send a rejection letter at all. If you are waiting to hear if you received funding for a federal grant application and you still haven't heard by the time you were told the announcements would be made, it's possible that the agency hasn't made the decision yet—but it's also possible that the winners have been notified and you aren't among them. The same thing is true for foundations. If you know that the foundation board was going to meet on a certain date but you haven't heard anything by the end of the following week or two, you probably were not successful in this application.

But you want to be sure. Sometimes a government agency website will publish the list of programs that have been funded. Sometimes if you call the program officer, he or she may tell you the status of the grant-reviewing process (e.g., that the decisions haven't been made or, that the congressional representatives have to be notified first about grants in their districts)—but probably will not tell you whether your project will be funded. If you win a federal or state grant, the contact person listed on the application may receive a very exciting telephone call or letter from the funding agency or an elected official's office, telling you the good news. If you do not win, you will eventually receive a very unexciting letter from the agency, telling you how stiff the competition was and how sorry the agency is that your application didn't make it.

Foundations usually notify you by mail. Some actually enclose the check with the award letter; others ask you to fill out a form or sign a letter accepting the terms of the grant and acknowledging formally that you're still eligible for the grant under the foundation's guidelines. Although government agencies and most foundations eventually get around to letting you know you didn't get the grant, some foundations—usually the smaller ones with limited staff—only notify groups that are awarded a grant. Some say so in their publications, others do not. If you're not sure, you should call after a reasonable period has elapsed. But read through the rest of this chapter and the funders' roundtable before you call.

Reality Check: Did I Actually Do Everything Right?

The first thing you should do when you find out that your program wasn't funded is to drag out the proposal that you submitted, along with the request for proposals or guidelines, and take a cold, hard look at the whole package. The passage of a good deal of time since you wrote the proposal often makes it interesting—and sometimes upsetting—to read it again. It is smart to try to recognize and acknowledge flaws that you find in your proposal even before soliciting reviewers' comments or discussing your proposal with foundation program officers. But give yourself a little time to get over the shock, sadness, rejection, and, often, embarrassment (yep . . . those are the feelings when major proposals that you worked hard on for a long time don't get funded) and then ask yourself the following hard questions:

- Does the proposal look as if it was done in a big hurry (which it was)?
- Is the description of the project clear and believable?
- Did I make a good case for my program?
- Did I follow the guidelines and answer every single question?
- Is there anything I left out or didn't do because I ran out of time?
- Can I make sense out of the budget now, after not looking at it for a few months?
- Did I make any confusing computational errors in the budget?
- Is the proposal poorly written, or filled with spelling errors and grammatical mistakes that make it hard to understand?
- Are charts that I included clear and helpful or fuzzy and confusing?
- Is the appendix organized and relevant—or did I use it as a dumping ground for any piece of minutiae that I could find?
- Did I correctly spell the name of the person receiving the grant?

What Kinds of Information Can I Get About My Rejected Proposal?

After reading your proposal over with great resolve and a strong stomach, it is time to find out what the reviewers thought about your work. There isn't much that is standard about the procedures that foundations and government funding agencies use to let you know your scores (if there are scores) or to give you written or oral comments (whether there are numerical scores or not). The key thing is to get as much information about the reasons your proposal was rejected as the funder is willing to give. Politely. And without defensiveness or hostility.

It is possible that the things you now think are wrong with the proposal didn't bother the reviewers in the least. You may feel, after consideration, that your evaluation plan was weak; they might have found nothing wrong with it but thought your staffing seemed haphazard. That doesn't mean that you had a strong evaluation plan, so don't get excited; only that your reviewers were distracted by other flaws that they saw as more significant. Their feedback will help you when you return to this grantmaker and when you apply to others.

Reviewers' Comments: Government Agencies. Government program officers usually will not discuss a particular proposal with you, although you will find some who are willing to provide this kind of technical assistance for a variety of reasons ranging from personal style—he's a nice guy whose agency does not prohibit him from talking with you—to policy— the agency operates on a mandate to make technical assistance available as broadly as possible. Most, however, will refer you to the review process.

Most federal agencies and many state and local agencies employ outside reviewers, experts in the field, to read and score all competitive proposals. Some federal agencies send you a packet that includes your proposal's scores and reviewers' comments on its strengths and weaknesses, with re-viewers' names and other identification removed. Others do not, espe-cially if factors other than scores are involved in the awards. The cabinet secretary of each federal agency has discretion in awarding most grants (unless the underlying legislation specifies conditions in detail). For exam-ple, it is perfectly legitimate for the secretary to reject two high-scoring applications from one city because an even higher-scoring application from that city did get funded.

Geographical distribution and other fairness issues can play a part in everything from college admissions to grants. This can make it difficult and time-consuming to write to each applicant about the exact circum-stances that affected the decision on that proposal. For this reason, some agencies prefer to give you a summary of the comments on the telephone.

However the assessment is given, whether it is written or oral, you should always seek information about how you could improve a proposal the next time. Write a simple letter to the program officer, requesting the reviewers' comments. Make sure you give all the identifying information about your proposal so that the program officer knows exactly who you are, including a confirmation number that you may have received after submitting the proposal. If appropriate, follow up with a call. If comments are given over the phone, take careful notes.

Reviewers' Comments: Foundations. As in everything else, foundations differ widely on how they handle rejections. (As noted, some don't handle this at all; you never hear from them again.) Most foundation program officers routinely reject proposals outside their guidelines; these rejection letters normally are very brief, sometimes stating that they don't fund the kind of program in the proposal, and sometimes simply saying politely that the foundation has made other awards. In most other cases the letter will be similarly polite, saying that there were "many interesting proposals" but that the foundation couldn't fund them all, and wishing you luck in your fundraising. In a few cases you may be invited to apply at a later time. Very rarely, usually when you have a long-standing relationship with a foundation or have been invited to submit a proposal, you may be asked to provide additional information or to revise the proposal before the program officer takes it to the foundation's board.

So—What Do I Ask?

If the program officer of either a foundation or a government agency has your proposal sitting on his or her desk while you speak, that would be the most helpful to you—but this is rare. It may be useful to set up an appointment for a convenient time to talk to the program officer; you will explain that you'd like to have a few minutes to find out how you could improve the program or the proposal. (Don't be surprised if the individual is willing just to give you a few moments when you first call. Be ready to ask your questions right then.)

Plan for this conversation by having a carefully thought-out (short) list of questions and follow-up questions to ask. The program officer probably will make some preliminary comments. Don't interrupt as the comments are being delivered—just jot down notes that you can address later. The key is to remain calm and cheerful. If you get defensive and argumentative because you feel the person has it all wrong, the conversation will end quickly and will not be very satisfying to you. You also need to be alert to the individuals' responses, check periodically to be sure they're comfortable with the time it's taking, and be prepared to cut the call short if they seem impatient. This means you should ask your most critical questions first and know which ones you can omit. These are the types of questions you want answered:

- Can you tell me if there was a problem with the program or with the proposal itself, or if you just couldn't fund it at this time? (If there was a problem with the program or proposal, politely request some suggestions on how to improve it.)
- Did you think the proposal clearly addressed your guidelines, or should we have made that case more strongly? (Make notes!)
- Would you suggest that we apply again? (This is the most important question you need answered!) Is there a time frame for doing this? (If the funder doesn't assure you that you should apply again, ask if there are any other foundations she or he thinks might be interested in the program.)
- Do you have any other suggestions about how we could strengthen either our program or our proposal?

WHAT SHOULD I DO WITH THE INFORMATION I GET ABOUT MY PROPOSAL?

The more feedback you get about your proposal, the easier it will be for you to make an informed decision about how to proceed. If you are seeking support for a new program, but the grantmakers feel it's not strong or compelling, you will have to decide whether to drop the project, at least for the time being, or keep going and continue to seek funding once you make certain revisions. If it's an ongoing project that you wanted to maintain or expand, you still may want to rethink it in light of the funders' comments, but you probably will decide to go back to step one, defining it more clearly and finding the right funder.

Why Would We Drop a Project We Think Is Important? Most of the time you will be hesitant about discarding a project simply because a source didn't fund it, or even because reviewers didn't like it. But once in a while a grantmaker's rejection will make you rethink the whole thing, and you may become convinced that it just isn't a good idea. It may be too expensive in terms of staff, space, or other costs. It may be a one-shot deal that will not have an impact on a wide enough audience for long enough. It may be too ambitious and unrealistic, especially if you can't sell it to the grantmakers. It is hard to part with a project that you believe in—but it can be a smart, time-saving, cost-saving move that impresses grantmakers in the long run.

What Might the Funder Say to Let Me Know I Should Just Keep Trying? If you get high marks and/or warm, positive comments from reviewers or program officers, your project and proposal are probably on the right track. Maybe this government agency was only able to fund the top 15 proposals and you were ranked eighteenth (out of 567 applicants). Maybe the foundation ran out of money for this round and wasn't able to fund your particular project. Maybe a grant was already committed to a similar project in your neighborhood or town. Maybe the reviewers gave you generally high marks but found your collaboration to be too new and unstable. Maybe the foundation program officer liked your project and proposal very much but knew that the trustees of her foundation wouldn't feel comfortable funding it. Not all of this information will come out in your follow-up calls, but enough will become clear that you'll have a sense that your project has merit and that your proposal is appealing (albeit not that appealing) to this grantmaker.

If the foundation program officer says you should resubmit the proposal with suggested changes, find out when the best time would be to do this, and what changes make the most sense.

If the foundation program officer does not think you should resubmit to his or her foundation (for whatever reasons), ask the program officer to suggest other foundations that might be suitable for the project. And, even more important, if it seems appropriate, ask if you can use the program officer's name when contacting the new foundation, and whether she or he would be willing to serve as a reference.

For federal, state, or city grants that achieve high scores but do not receive funding, it makes sense to reapply if the opportunity arises. Although you will probably have different reviewers in the next round, it can't hurt to say in your proposal that you applied previously, received high marks, and have responded to reviewers' comments by strengthening your needs section or by partnering with a local university to strengthen your project or your evaluation. It can't hurt to explain how committed your organization and community are to the project, which is why you are reapplying.

A Few More Words of Advice and Encouragement

We have one last bit of advice to give you: Mind your manners. Your mother always told you to write a thank-you note when you got a gift. We think that a grantmaker who spent time talking with you about your proposal has given you a very important gift that should be acknowledged in writing. Say thanks for her or his time. Say that you regret not receiving a grant at this time, but that you hope the advice the individual gave you will help you develop a better program or proposal in the future. Even if you didn't get to talk with the funder, it's usually a good idea to write a letter expressing regret and saying you hope you'll be able to present a better proposal in the future.

Grant writers agree that the horrific news that the important proposal they slaved over for weeks (and weeks and weeks) didn't get funded can

rank right up there with the most painful disappointments in their lives. But use the loss as an opportunity to follow that other bit of your mother's advice, "If at first you don't succeed . . . ."

One last thing: In your thank-you letter to a funder who was kind enough to give you helpful information about your proposal, invite her or him to visit your organization sometime. Also, consider sending news-letters and other material that you routinely distribute. Don't inundate the program officer with paper, but do keep the foundation in mind when you've got something good to show.

AND IF YOU GET THE GRANT . . .

Winning a grant is the exact opposite of rejection—it is acceptance, ap-preciation, love. So the first thing you must do when you win is bask in your glory. Congratulate yourself on doing your homework so well, on making heads and tails of the guidelines and application, on writing a clear, comprehensible proposal with a realistic and sane budget. You may be the only one who does this, because only other proposal writers can really appreciate the obstacles that have to be overcome in order to bring home the bacon—and everything else the grant is bringing home—to the organization. But once you've won a few grants, you'll need to cut back a bit on the basking and just keep writing, because there's an organization depending on you.

Once you've finished celebrating, you still have a few things to take care of. Again, mind your manners. (We may be stating the obvious here, but we think it sometimes gets lost in the excitement of winning a grant.) If you got a foundation grant, write a thank-you note to the foundation's director (or the person who signed the letter announcing the grant). If it's appropriate, mention any help the foundation's program officer gave you. For a government grant, call or write to your elected official to say thanks for his or her help if that's relevant, or just to keep his or her office informed. Notify any program partners and set up a meeting to talk about next steps.

Both government and foundation grant award letters normally will restate the conditions for which the grant is being made and will advise you of the nature and timing of any reports you must submit. As soon as you hear about a grant award, go back to the proposal and start planning your final report. With the program staff, review the action plan, timetable, budget, and other elements of the program to be sure they are still appropriate. If there are any problems, concerns, or questions about your ability to implement the grant according to the proposal, now is the time to raise them with the funder. And if you hit snags after you've started your program, again, get in touch with the grantmaker, with a plan for alternative actions that may be necessary. Don't wait until a report is due. And, by the way, congratulations on winning the grant—you must have done a terrific job and we tip our hats to you!

Pop Quiz

True or False?

1. Always reapply for a grant after a rejection. Your odds have to be better the second time.

2. Once you've been turned down by a foundation, don't bother the program officer by asking a bunch of questions. You'll be written off as a pest.

3. By law, you are not permitted to receive scores on your federal grant proposals.

4. Because the same person won't be reading your federal proposal the next year, don't bother making any changes based on suggestions from reviewers.

5. It is too pushy to ask a foundation grantmaker to suggest other foundations that might be interested in giving you a grant.

FUNDERS' ROUNDTABLE III

The process of reviewing grant proposals can be sensitive (reviewing or grading anyone or anything can be a little dicey), so for this last roundtable, we asked the grantmakers on our panel to shed some additional light on the way grants are reviewed within their organizations. They also talked about another sensitive topic—what grant seekers should do if they don't win the grant—and the much less sensitive, much happier prospect of what they should do if they do get one.

Reviewing Federal Grant Proposals
Is Usually a Pretty Rigid Process . . . Right?

In Roundtable II a federal grantmaker explained in painstaking detail the elements of the peer review process. He was making an important point about how fair, objective, and serious the process of scoring a federal grant is. His remarks were echoed by another federal funder, who explained that her agency uses a scoring system ranging from 100 (best) to 500 (worst), using "an algorithm so we get a distribution point spread." She noted that nothing but the technical requirements of the application package is ever considered by reviewers, and that every section has an allocated number of points. There are panels of 12 to 15 reviewers, each having primary responsibility for up to eight proposals. Each proposal is read by at least three reviewers. Each reviewer scores the sections of the proposal based on the application criteria, and final scores are assigned after discussion. "There are agencies that do it differently," she said, "groups that are not as stringent." But the purpose is the same: to ensure the fairest, most objective review possible.

*"The purpose is . . . to ensure the fairest, most
objective review possible."*

"If you make a visit," said a government panelist, "the visitors will be able to see if all those letters of support that clogged up the proposal's appendix were bogus or if the partners were really at the table!" Although a few government agencies do conduct site visits as part of their decision-making process, most can't because of the tremendous costs involved in traveling throughout the country to visit grant applicants. This means that the proposal is a make-or-break opportunity for the grant seeker to communicate everything the reviewers can't see in person.

But Can't Foundations Take Other Things into Account in Making Their Decisions?

Looking at the foundation proposal review process, one of our panelists explained her thinking as she winnowed 26 proposals that had made the first cut down to the 14 that would actually receive funding. "It wasn't all about the proposals. We had to turn a solid group down because we ran out of money . . . The job is a balancing act. The bottom line is, good groups that fit should get in 80 percent of the time, but there are reasons why not. Here's what I ask myself: Have I spoken to this group at all during the year? Have I turned them down before even though they have done a good job? Do the trustees know and like this organization, or not?" For this particular funder, "whether or not the proposal is well written is the least of it!"

"We're looking for genuineness in making funding decisions," explained a foundation colleague, "even if the proposal isn't well put together."

"The main thing we look for in making a decision is whether the organization has a good leader," said another foundation funder. "And this is something we can tell once we make a site visit." The site visit means a lot—but not everything—to many grantmakers. "If we're interested in your organization based on the material you sent us, we'll arrange a site visit," said a foundation funder. "It gives us a chance to look at the program in action, meet the program director, the head of the organization. But the site visit isn't the be-all and end-all—we check with other funders too."

A grantmaker offered this reminder: "We're not only judging your program, we're mainly judging the fit." There's that word again—fit—which is all about how well your organization matches up with a particular grantmaker and its guidelines.

> *"We're not only judging your program,*
> *we're mainly judging the fit."*

Foundations Can Even Overlook the "Warts"

"I just made a grant to an organization and then learned that the unified picture everyone presented in the proposal and during the site visit was false," said a frustrated funder. "People want to show their best face— they're afraid if they show 'warts and all,' they won't get funded. But that's not necessarily true. If you show your warts, you may get even more money to help you get rid of them!"

It's a hard call for grant applicants to decide just how candid to be— how many warts to point out—during the process of seeking funds. The temptation to hide problems is great, assuming that by the time a site visit is arranged or the grant is ready to be implemented, the problem or problems will be long solved. Our grantmaker who saw a false unified picture during a site visit found out later that the staff was disgruntled, to say the least. This dire staff problem did not bode well for the smooth implementation of the project. Other problems that you may feel nervous about sharing with potential funders could include fiscal questions, hiring and procurement issues, and recruitment difficulties, to name just a few. If these issues are likely to impede the implementation of a grant, you might be better off waiting to submit a proposal until you've got them worked out. And if it will take a grant to get them worked out, you'd better say so. We're pretty sure from what our panelists told us that they're willing to work with an organization that levels with them. They may not be so forgiving of an organization that deceives them, and the next grant may be much harder to get. In fact, one of the foundation funders told us that it could take a change of leadership before she'd give a grant to such a troubled organization. It is our suggestion that you be as honest as possible when applying for a grant.

Decision Making Isn't As Easy for Grantmakers As We Thought

In a way, government funders, with their elaborate review procedures and scoring systems, have it easier than foundations, with their greater flexibility. But both types of grantmakers experience their own challenges. The most difficult is the limited funding available. Even in federal programs, when millions of dollars are granted for specific purposes, the program officers know that the needs are much greater than they are able to meet. As a foundation funder put it, really speaking for all of the panelists, the challenge is that "people who make funding decisions must do so with minimal funds for maximum needs—and with extreme pressure from the board and ultimate responsibility to the community."

"People who make funding decisions must do so with minimal funds for maximum needs—and with extreme pressure from the board and ultimate responsibility to the community."

In other words, deciding which groups to fund and which ones not to fund . . . well, it isn't easy.

Let's Look at the Bad News First.
After the Gut-Wrenching Rejection, What Should I Do?

It's always hard to receive a rejection letter, even for a small grant. But it's sometimes even harder to try to find out what went wrong. Some grantmakers are reluctant to talk about the reasons for rejecting a proposal, but many grantmakers told us that they really don't understand why they don't get more calls asking how the applicant could do better next time. "A smart grant writer will call and find out why a project wasn't funded," suggested a panel member. "And sometimes we'll make a site visit anyway."

"A smart grant writer will call and find out
why a project wasn't funded."

"When you get turned down, get some feedback," said another funder. "Only about 15 to 20 percent of those who were rejected call us back, and many of the ones who call are groups we already know. No more than 10 percent of the other groups—the ones we don't know at all—actually call to see why they were turned down. Yet feedback enhances an organization's chances of being funded the next time." Another panelist agreed: "Very few groups call when they're not funded. I'm impressed when a group calls and asks, 'Can we do something different?' If they tell us their challenges—for instance, 'We're no longer as small as we were, but we're not really big enough to appeal to most funders; what can you suggest?'— they're educating us. We can then tell our board about the challenges inherent in growing." This grantmaker summed up by suggesting, "Tell us your dilemma; maybe we can advocate for you."

Despite these helpful attitudes, it's sometimes (but not always) easier to get information about why a government proposal was turned down than why a foundation proposal was rejected. Although there's no policy carved in stone about how government grantmakers deal with letting applicants know why they didn't get the grant, most of them provide the reviewers' comments. "We routinely send copies of reviewers' comments to the applicants—without the names of the reviewers, of course," explained a federal grantmaker. But, according to another government funder, "Dealing with reviewers' comments varies wildly. Some agencies may be skittish about sending reviewers' comments because they want wiggle room." It is always worth asking.

Foundations vary more than government agencies do in providing feedback, but most are reluctant to be too specific. "If the proposed project is out of our guidelines, we have a form letter saying, 'We don't fund public schools, or the performing arts, or individuals.' Otherwise we use a general letter of rejection," said one of our funders. "For letters of intent," explained a panelist, "we use a standard template for rejection— no specifics, just, 'Your letter was not as highly ranked as the ones we chose.'" Another foundation funder uses the same procedure. "For letters of intent, we send form rejections: 'You're doing great work, but . . .'"

"We don't give comments," said another.

But one grantmaker said, "We call every grant seeker to tell them why they weren't funded, to brainstorm about possible other funders, and to give them advice and technical assistance. After every docket, we call and offer technical assistance."

If We Don't Get "Formal" Comments—Either by Mail or Through a Telephone Call—What Should We Do?

"Cold calling is hard, but be persistent so you can find out why you were turned down. You need to know whether the answer is 'Sorry, you didn't fit our guidelines and never will' or 'We liked your project but ran out of money,'" said one funder. "When you apply the next time, show us you've gotten better."

"You need to know whether the answer is, 'Sorry, you didn't fit our guidelines and never will' or 'We liked your project but ran out of money.'"

"We don't think it's productive to have discussions about why a group didn't get funded," explained a panelist. "It's usually not about the proposal, it's about the program. We turn conversations back to the types of things we're likely to fund, rather than why this particular organization didn't receive funding. If you go into a lot of detail, it takes an awful lot of time. Also, this program that we didn't approve for funding is someone's baby."

This panelist added the following extremely useful suggestion: "A good thing for a grant seeker who has been turned down to say is, 'Were there any questions about the program that I need to address?' A question of this kind gives the program officer an opportunity to say, 'I didn't see so-and-so mentioned.' And this, in turn, gives the grant seeker a chance to ask if there is anyone doing this type of work who may be able to give me some suggestions or pointers." In other words, you can get the funder to help you improve by the next time you come calling.

From another grantmaker: "People call or write polite letters, saying, 'We hope we can reapply in the future.' When they do this, we tell them why their proposals didn't rank as high as some others did. It could make them uncomfortable, but if they're nice . . . we'll tell them. And if it was a close call, we'll encourage them to apply again in January."

"If you call, we can help you. But some call angrily—or, I should say, with thinly disguised anger—and ask why they weren't funded," another grantmaker noted.

Is it Smart—or Obnoxious—to Ask Funders Who Have Turned You Down to Recommend Other Grantmakers?

One funder we spoke to will refer grant seekers to another grantmaker if they call to find out why they weren't funded, but she doesn't do this unless she knows the groups and the funder she's calling pretty well. "I usually fall in love with a couple of new groups that I can't fund every year . . . and I'll call other foundations on their behalf or let them use my name when contacting other grantmakers," she said. Another panelist said, "I refer groups to other funders all the time, especially when a group is doing such a valuable thing but I can't fund it."

"We don't refer to other foundations—it's too much like passing the buck," explained another funder. "But we do suggest that applicants that have been turned down talk to not-for-profit organizations that are doing similar work."

Before we left this issue of what steps to follow after getting rejected, one panelist speculated on why so many grant seekers don't call to find out why funding was denied. "Maybe it's the power dynamics between those who want money and those who have money. It's similar to kids applying to college. No matter how brilliant and accomplished the student is, the colleges hold all the cards, all the power. And most kids never find out why they were rejected from their first, second, and third choices. They can only guess."

It's clear from talking to our panel of grantmakers that you need to snap out of it—even if it takes joining a support group for proposal writers—and start calling funders to find out why you were turned down, how you might increase your chances of getting a grant the next time, and what other funders might be able to help in the meantime. We understand that old insecurities die hard, but proposal writers and the organizations that count on them can't afford to be insecure.

"Grant writing should be one-half job interview
and one-half date."

As one of our panelists said, "Grant writing should be one-half job interview and one-half date. The job interview part requires you to be self-promoting and smart; the date part calls for you to be charming and appealing." Easier said than done. But you can do it.

Now for the Good News: What If We Do Get the Grant?

Most grantmakers understand that your proposal was an optimistic statement of what you want to do, how you want to do it, and how much it will cost. What may surprise you is that, now that you're on their team, many funders are ready to help you do it. For example, a federal grantmaker said, "It's a new ballgame when you get the grant. Not always do the highest scorers become the higher performers. But now we think about start-up issues, and realize that implementation goals might be readjusted."

"Do what you say you're going to do. Report
as required, look back at the proposal."

A foundation funder advised, "Do what you say you're going to do. Report as required, look back at the proposal." The most important thing is that you bring implementation problems to the funder, preferably with a solution. "Think about the reporting when you're writing the proposal, go over expectations with program officers while developing the proposal. It's very difficult to say what you're going to accomplish. If there are problems, keep people informed. Let us know right away. We don't want to take the money back, but if you wait until the grant is over and then have to say you couldn't do it, you probably won't get any new funding." Another panelist said, "We like to hear about internal problems directly . . . and not read embarrassing (or worse) news in the newspaper. We tend to hang in through good times and bad. Our groups are sometimes up and sometimes down. We'll help. But you have to be straight with us."

And there's sometimes some negotiating to do, some rethinking about what's realistic. As another federal funder said, "Then reality sets in . . . One of the problems: The person who writes the proposal leaves, maybe a new administration comes into office, plans don't always work out." He described the type of conversation he might have with the grantee:

"'We can't do everything in our grant.'

'What can you do?'

'X, Y, and Z.'

'Okay, that's a good start.'"

Our panelist says, "It doesn't hurt if they can't do it; it hurts if they're not trying."

CONCLUDING REMARKS

After countless hours of conversation with funders, it's not easy to sum up everything we learned. Much to our surprise, not all grantmakers agree on some of the things we thought were "nonnegotiable." For instance, one funder couldn't care less if the applicant spelled her name right. This same funder puts "how well written the proposal is" as her least important criterion for funding.

But no panelist was sympathetic to applicants who didn't follow directions.

Some of the intangibles that we thought might be important were important to some funders, but not to others. Our advice to grant seekers is not to throw your hands up in the air and scream, "I give up!" Because when you think about it, remember what we said about how different foundations are. Government agencies too differ from one another in their missions, budgets, policies, and politics. The same is true for their staffs and for the reviewers who are brought on board for specific grant competitions. Why would everyone think the same way and have the same pet peeves and responses? And although one funder doesn't give a hoot how her name is butchered by prospective grantees, many of our panelists were very put off that people hadn't bothered to check the correct spelling of their names.

Rules of thumb: Although not everyone cares about everything, read the guidelines, do your homework, and be polite if you call with questions. Write the best grant proposal you can, identifying your needs, presenting measurable objectives and activities to achieve the objectives, and creating a realistic budget. Write about your organization's ability to implement your program and how you will measure its success. You should never be greedy—not in flush economic times, not in woeful economic times. You should always think about how to sustain grant-funded projects and cultivate additional supporters. And no matter what's going on, you need to stay calm and focused. It's part of the job.

APPENDICES
Appendix 1: 50 Tips for Improving
Your Chances of Winning a Grant

1. *Take stock of your own organization.* Know what type of organization you work for and the type and size of grants it can manage. If you don't know who you are, the funders won't either.

2. *Incorporate as a tax-exempt organization.* If you want to get grants from most foundation or government sources, you need to become a 501(c)(3).

3. *If you're not a 501(c)(3), link up now*—with an organization that is! If incorporation is a process that's too costly, too demanding, or not appropriate (say, if you're an individual artist), find a tax-exempt organization that is willing to be your fiscal conduit—to accept and manage grants for your benefit, sometimes taking a small fee for this service. Check out the financial arrangement in advance!

4. *Find the Foundation Center Library.* With main libraries in five cities and more than 200 participating collections across the country, there is a Foundation Library near you. This is your first resource for identifying private funding sources that are right for you.

5. *Get online.* If you don't use the Internet now, you should. The Foundation Center is online, so are all federal, most state, and many local agencies—and so are many, many foundations. Some websites you can start with are shown in Appendix 6.

6. *Find the right funding opportunity.* Don't submit a scattershot proposal to all the grantmakers in your area. Do some research to be sure your program is what a particular grantmaker can fund. If the proposed program is not an

exact fit with a grantmaker's priorities, you'll only annoy the funder and risk your chances for the next time.

7. *Read the guidelines.* Be absolutely sure that a particular foundation or government grant is appropriate for you. Is your organization eligible? Has this source funded programs like yours? Does this source want to fund programs like yours? Does it want to fund in your community?

8. *Do your homework.* Get your hands on foundations' annual reports, their 990 tax forms, their application guidelines. See what organizations they've funded recently, and how much they gave.

9. *Read the instructions.* Answer every question or cover every topic. Grantmakers and reviewers say it is astonishing how often proposal writers do not adhere to the requirements set out in the funding announcement or guidelines. Applicants fail to meet the submission deadline, exceed the specified budget or page limits, present materials in the order they think is appropriate rather than the order requested in the application package, ignore some sections of the application or questions they are asked to address, ignore instructions about format, and make other errors that either lead to outright rejection of the proposal or significantly lower the score.

10. *Get organized . . . now.* At slow times in your workday, workweek, or workyear, prepare a file with all of the documents you will need when you get ready to submit a proposal. Items to include are listed in various lessons; basically, they represent information about your organization, your programs, your management and staff, your participants, and the community.

11. *Give yourself plenty of time to prepare the proposal, especially if it's for a government agency.* Rome wasn't built in a day, and successful proposals aren't written in two weeks. Remember that in one study the average time it took to prepare a federal proposal was nearly 80 person-hours—but for those proposals that received awards, the average preparation time was more than 150 hours. We haven't seen any similar figures for local government proposals, but experience suggests it's pretty close.

12. **Try to bring partners into your project early, even if collaboration is not required by the funder.**

13. **Speak with the program officer to determine if a particular funding opportunity is appropriate for your organization.** Do this only after you have read the application package carefully and still are not sure.

14. **Call for technical assistance during the preparation of a government proposal (e.g., to ask for clarification if application instructions seem contradictory).** But never put the program officer in an awkward position by pushing for information if the officer indicates that she or he can't answer a particular question.

15. **Don't use acronyms!** Don't use jargon, either. Both can be annoying and confusing.

16. **Watch your language.** Be careful to be sensitive (if not downright politically correct) to all individuals, groups, neighborhoods, and communities mentioned in your proposal.

17. **Use the grantmaker's language.** In order to make it clear that you're concerned about the grantmaker's own priorities, use the language in the guidelines or application package as much as possible (and, of course, when it's appropriate).

18. **Repeat yourself when you have to.** Although repetition should be kept to a minimum in a proposal, a certain amount of repetition is inevitable in response to an application's questions and requirements for each section. You cannot assume that the reader will remember that an important point has been made earlier.

19. **Give grant proposal reviewers a break: Don't write pages and pages and pages of narrative.** Use charts, tables, graphs, and other illustrative material whenever possible—but only if they are clear, to the point, and easy to read. No need to get fancy.

20. **Create a checklist.** At the beginning of the proposal process, lay out a list of everyone you need to speak with, every piece of information you need, every document that has to be collected or prepared, and every signature

that you will need. Review it at least once a day, every day—and once more before you submit the proposal.

21. *Be sure each section of the proposal is consistent with every other section.* If a statement of need shows a gap in services in the community, the objectives and program description should show how that gap will be filled. If a program activity calls for a certain type/number of staff, this should be explained in the program description, accounted for realistically in the budget and budget narrative, and described in the agency capability or staff expertise section (depending on the specific requirements of the application); job descriptions and/or résumés should be included as requested.

22. *Use the application package's topics as the headings in your own proposal.* This will make it easy for the reader to see that you've addressed all the issues the grantmaker considers important.

23. *When designing your program objectives, be realistic.* Aim high, but not too high.

24. *Know how you will recognize success.* For each measurable objective included in your grant proposal, explain how you will know whether or not it was achieved.

25. *Read the instructions!*

26. *Get free consulting for the evaluation section of your proposal.* Many academics and freelance consultants will willingly work with you on a major proposal to help frame objectives and research methods for the evaluation, understanding that if you get the grant they will be paid to do the evaluation. Get the evaluation consultant involved early. Working backward and forward among the objectives, the program description, and the evaluation makes for a stronger proposal.

27. *Make sure your budget is reasonable.* Funders know if you're asking for too much, or for too little to make the program work. Get the fiscal staff involved.

28. *Compute your budget figures carefully.* Carelessness (adding or dropping a zero here and there) doesn't make funders trust you with their money.

29. ***Think about sustainability.*** Tell the grantmaker what you hope to do to keep a program going once the grant runs out. Do this whether the application requires it or not.

30. ***Include a time line in your proposal.*** It will help the grantmaker understand what you plan to do and when you plan to do it. If there is absolutely no room in your proposal for one extra word, construct a time line anyway—for your own use. It will keep you organized and your proposal orderly—and will help you implement the project when you get the grant.

31. ***Write your abstract or executive summary two days before you submit the proposal—no sooner and no later.*** By then you will have a really good understanding of exactly what the program you are describing is all about and enough time to do it right. Remember: This is the first thing that the reviewer sees.

32. ***Don't stuff the appendix.*** You don't need to throw in every press clipping; grantmakers probably won't read them. Be thoughtful about what you think they must see.

33. ***For a government proposal, include a letter from your elected official.*** For a foundation proposal, don't.

34. ***When in doubt, ask the grantmakers questions before submitting the proposal!***

35. ***Think about the final report.*** Remember, if you get the grant, someone has to implement it; it pays to keep this in mind while you're writing the proposal.

36. ***Use spell-check and friends and colleagues for proofreading help.***

37. ***Use your own reviewers.*** Ask different people to edit and comment on the proposal at different points in the process. If the same people keep reading it over and over, many inconsistencies, as well as grammatical and spelling errors, will be missed. Even more important, ask a friend to read the budget and budget narrative, and explain to you exactly what the money is going to be spent on. Ask a different friend to read the abstract and explain to you exactly what your proposed project is all about.

38. *Save your most trusted, honest, courageous "reviewer" to read the final draft while there's still enough time to edit.* Let this person know you expect the brutal truth. Buy a really good bottle of champagne as a thank-you.

39. *Get involved with advocacy groups.* Find organizations in your community that are working on issues that are important to your clients or participants. Work with them to generate new funding sources to meet the needs.

40. *Get on mailing lists.* Make sure you hear about all the funding that may be available for your community.

41. *Clip newspaper and magazine articles.* Keep a file of materials describing what your city or town, state, and country are doing in the areas that pertain to your organization's work. Someone should do this every day so you don't miss a court case, an important speech, a new law that will be relevant to the next proposal.

42. *Get to know your elected officials, and let them get to know you.* Invite them to see your operation. Let them speak to your participants. Even before submitting a government proposal (whether you work for a not-for-profit organization or a public agency), invite elected officials to be part of your program planning process. Don't wait until you are ready to send the proposal out to ask them for a letter of support or simply to put in a good word for your group or organization.

43. *Don't ask government or foundation program officers to change their guidelines for you.* However complicated an application package or guidelines may look, a lot of thought and work have gone into developing them.

44. *Do discuss the unmet needs and potential new funding directions in your community or in a particular program area.* You can join with a group of other organizations with a track record in a particular field to meet with appropriate program officers to discuss needs and suggest types of funding that would help to address them. This is a long-term approach that can be helpful to program officers interested in new solutions in their areas of expertise. And it ultimately may create a new funding stream for the field.

45. *If you do get funded, go back to the proposal to be sure you can implement it.* If there are problems, call the funder immediately to discuss what you may need to do instead.

46. *If you get turned down for funding, find out why, and how you can do better next time.* Politely.

47. *Wait until next year.* If you can't develop and write a high-quality proposal in the allotted time, wait until next year or the next funding cycle.

48. *Keep the funders informed.* Send them newsletters and press clippings about your programs and events. But be selective about what you send and don't overwhelm them with paper.

49. *Get on the funders' radar.* Go to conferences. Speak at conferences. Write papers, articles, and letters to the editor. Become a recognized expert in your field. Network.

50. *Read the instructions.* (Have we said this yet?)

Appendix 2: Proposal Checklist

Before you send your proposal, review it against the following checklist to be sure you have addressed all the requirements. Note: As you should realize by now, if the application package includes a checklist, it takes priority. But use this one too, just to be sure.

✔   I have read and reread the entire application package or foundation guidelines, including all regulations and resources listed or referred to in the package. I would get a very high mark if someone gave me a test on the information included in the application.

✔   My grant proposal reflects the priority areas and requirements described by the grantmaker. I have not tried to sneak in any of my priorities except the ones that clearly mesh with the funder's.

✔   I have identified a compelling need for the grant, based on what I know about the community, the target population for the program, and the issues involved.

✔ I have brought to the table each and every partner and stakeholder, and anyone else who is concerned about the need that has been identified and who is likely to be helpful addressing it.

✔ I did not break any of the 12 Rules of Proposal Writing that I learned in Lesson 6.

✔ In spite of the fact that I don't like to write objectives, they are sharply defined, clearly relate to the compelling need I have demonstrated, are realistic, and are capable of being measured.

✔ There are well-conceived and specific programmatic activities for each objective—showing how and why the grant writer fully expects the objective to be achieved.

✔ The qualifications and relevant experience of staff expected to carry out the activities are explained, and résumés and/or job descriptions are attached if requested or allowed.

✔ I have demonstrated that my organization's leadership, fiscal controls, staff, partners, facilities, and other resources can implement the program.

✔ My evaluation plan clearly stipulates how, when, and by whom each objective will be measured.

✔ When appropriate, I have included a time line that shows we know how to structure the activities to get the job done.

✔ My budget is reasonable in relation to the objectives the project expects to achieve, including number of staff, salary levels, and other resources. I have not tried to sneak in anything—like a new car or a sofa—that is unrelated to the project.

✔ My budget is neither excessive nor underestimated.

✔ I have shown what resources such as space, staff time, and equipment will be available in kind (as a contribution of my organization to the project).

✔ I have intelligently addressed the really hard question of sustainability—how we will continue the project once the grant period is over.

✔   I have included everything in my proposal that was asked for—and I mean everything—even if I don't fully understand why the grantmaker wanted certain pieces of very strange information.

✔   I have organized the proposal—including my abstract, program narrative, budget, and appendix—exactly the way the grantmaker told me to. No one could ever say that my organization doesn't know how to follow directions.

✔   I did not go over the page limit and I did not cheat on margins or font. I'm sending the proposal on time to arrive by the grantmaker's deadline.

Appendix 3: Glossary

Abstract, Executive Summary. A brief (half a page to no more than two pages) summary of the entire proposal, including a sentence or two each on the applicant's history and capability to administer a grant, the need for the proposed program, the objectives, a description of the program and any partners, the expected outcomes, and methods of evaluating the program.

Administrative Overhead, Indirect Cost. A portion of a grant or contract that may be used for nonprogrammatic costs, usually set by a funder as a percentage of the total grant. (See also General Operating Funds.)

Advisory Committee/Advisory Board. A panel of representatives from all interested organizations and groups in the community who are concerned with a particular program and will help design, support, and oversee it.

Anecdotal Information. Informal reports that document or describe, without statistics, conditions that demonstrate a need or that demonstrate the impact of a program on clients. Anecdotal information usually includes compelling stories of individual program participants (e.g., an elderly person who has to choose between heating her home and the medication she needs; the low-income mother who loses her job because she has to stay home to take care of her children during school vacations; the formerly homeless family that now has a home; the child with dyslexia who is now thriving in school).

Annual Report. A report issued by an organization (including businesses, foundations, and not-for-profits) that provides a description of its activities during the year and a financial report of its income, expenses, and current status. For grant seekers, foundation annual reports may be a valuable source of information about a foundation's priorities and interests.

Appropriations Bill. Congressional legislation that approves spending for a particular federal agency or group of agencies.

Audit. A detailed financial analysis performed by an independent accountant at the end of an organization's fiscal year, or by a funding agency at the end of a major project grant, to assure the public (or the funder) that the organization has handled its money appropriately and in accordance with proper accounting procedures. For not-for-profit organizations, a program audit also assures the funder that the grantee has spent the money in the manner promised in the application.

Best Practices. Within a given field, the theories and activities that have been demonstrated to be successful in addressing problems and issues in that field. Programs that have been successfully tested and may be replicated elsewhere.

Bidders' Conference, Proposer's Conference, Technical Assistance Conference. A meeting (or series of meetings) convened by a grantmaker, usually but not only by a government agency or large national foundation, to discuss a particular funding opportunity and to provide prospective applicants with answers to questions. Normally, questions and answers are compiled and distributed to every prospective applicant, including those who are unable to attend. Increasingly, questions and answers are published on the agency's website. Some bidders' conferences are held by teleconference to allow a wider audience (and to save the costs of travel for the grantmaker's staff).

Block Grants. Funds distributed by the federal government to a state or city for broad purposes (e.g., community development block grant), allocated based on population.

Board of Directors. Every established not-for-profit organization has a board of
directors responsible for setting policy and ensuring fiscal stability. The list
of directors, their business affiliations, their home addresses, and any other
affiliations should be kept up-to-date for inclusion in most grant proposals.
Many funders expect that the board will reflect the community's population.
(See also Development, Board.)

Boilerplate Language. For grants purposes, boilerplate language refers to standard descriptions about an organization or a program that can be kept on file
and essentially pasted into a proposal with minimal adaptation for the new
purpose. Boilerplate may include, for example, a description of the agency's
history; descriptions of its ongoing programs and its key staff members; a description of awards and honors received by the organization or its key staff;
the equal opportunity statement and other personnel matters; and similar
topics that don't change significantly from proposal to proposal. Note the
phrase "minimal adaptation" above, and keep in mind that the boilerplate
often needs to be modified to address the interest of a particular funder, as
when the proposal writer deletes or significantly abbreviates descriptions of
programs for the elderly when preparing a proposal for youth services.

Budget. A fiscal plan for an entire organization (usually annual) or a specific
program that includes an itemized list of anticipated income (revenues) and
expenses. For proposals, the budget must reflect as closely as possible the activities and staffing described in the narrative.

Budget Line. An item (line) in a budget (e.g., one supervisor at a specified
salary; four teachers at a total hourly cost for a year; travel; books; software).

Budget Modification. A formal change in the way grant funds are scheduled to be
spent, occurring after the initial approval of the budget by the funding source,
with the approval of the funder. Primarily required for government grants.

Budget Narrative, Budget Justification. A verbal description of each line item
in the budget, describing how the amount was calculated and how the
item relates to the program. Almost all government grants require a budget
narrative. Most foundations do not require it but should be able to see

clearly, even without a separate narrative, exactly how the budget costs relate to the activities to be provided.

Capacity, Organizational. The organization's ability to manage a grant and ensure that the funded program is implemented successfully. Most grantmakers want to hear about the organization's management structure, the background of the managers and people who will run the program, and how the board of directors oversees the agency. The term also includes fiscal systems that are sophisticated enough to handle the large amounts of money in some government grants and the required financial reports that must be submitted. A description of capacity may also include resources like space, volunteers, equipment, supplies, and other assets that will be used in support of the proposed program.

Capital Funding. A grant or donation to assist in the construction or renovation of a building or space in a building, or the acquisition of equipment.

Catalog of Federal Domestic Assistance (CFDA). A resource listing all new, existing, and past federal programs. Each federal grant program has a CFDA number. You must know this number when you fill out Standard Form 424 (SF-424), the federal cover sheet for the proposal and budget.

Certificate of Incorporation. A document spelling out the organization's purposes and powers in accordance with the laws of a particular state, and filed with the designated office of the state (normally the secretary of state or department of state). When it is filed, the state issues a filing receipt confirming that the organization has legally come into existence. A copy of the certificate of incorporation usually must be submitted with proposals.

Challenge Grant. A grant offered by a funder to encourage other grantmakers or individuals to support a particular program or organization. Payable only if other funds are obtained in an amount specified by the donor. (See also Matching Grant.)

Collaboration. Two or more individuals and/or groups jointly working out an approach to a problem that is of mutual concern, and developing solutions that make the best use of the strengths of each partner.

Common Grant Application Form, Standard Application Form. A proposal format required or accepted by a group of grantmakers in a given area. Usually developed through a regional association of grantmakers. The common application form lays out the information, proposal format, and attachments that must be provided by a grant applicant to any of the participants.

Common Report Form. A reporting format required or accepted by a group of grantmakers in an area, usually developed through a regional association of grantmakers. It spells out the information required from an organization that is submitting an interim or final report on a grant.

Community-Based Organization (CBO). Any nonprofit organization that is located in and established to serve residents of a defined geographic area (in contrast to city- or countywide or national nonprofit organizations that provide services within a broad geographic area or in many smaller communities).

Community Foundation, Community Trust. A foundation established for the purpose of managing funds for the benefit of the community in which it functions. Community foundations are designated as public charities by the IRS because they raise money from the public each year. Support is provided by individuals, either during their lifetimes or after their deaths, who want to benefit their particular town, city, or region, but either cannot afford or prefer not to establish a separate foundation. Because donors can specify the areas in which they prefer that grants are to be made, community foundations usually have several diverse priorities for grants and are often a good place to start exploring funding opportunities. Community foundations differ from place to place, but they share several characteristics: a mission to enrich the quality of life in a defined geographic area and service to three constituencies—their donors, charitable organizations, and the community at large.

Competitive Grant. A grant awarded by a government or private funder through a competitive screening process such as a request for proposals or notice of funding availability, after proposals have been scored by independent reviewers.

Corporate Foundation, Company-Sponsored Foundation. A separate, independent foundation created by a large business with funds from the business itself.

In most cases the foundation functions like other foundations, receiving proposals and making grants, but giving may be somewhat more tied in to the corporation's own goals. For example, a drug company's foundation may give for medical research; a bank's foundation may give for community development.

Corporate Giving Program, Corporate Philanthropy. A grantmaking program established and administered within a business by its own staff and allocated from its own annual budget. Grants go directly to charitable organizations from the corporation. Such programs usually are funded with pretax income, and grants may be even more closely tied to business objectives than are grants from a corporate foundation.

Corporate Sponsorships. Direct giving from a corporation to a not-for-profit organization that brings publicity and recognition to the sponsor. Sponsorship can range from support of a Little League team that wears T-shirts with the corporate logo to support of public television with announcements of sponsorship that may be indistinguishable from commercial television advertising. It may include activities like the purchase of greetings in an organization's fundraising journal or of tables at a fundraising event, gifts in kind (like computers, food, or furniture), and other assistance.

Demographics. The description, usually numerical, of a population in terms of characteristics like age, sex, income, race and ethnicity, and national origin. In a proposal it usually is important to describe the demographics of the program's target population in order to provide the reader with an understanding of why the program is important.

Demonstration Project. A project designed (and funded) to determine the viability of new or promising programs or ideas.

Determination Letter. A letter from the IRS acknowledging that an organization is eligible for tax-exempt status.

Direct Costs. All budget items that directly support a program, including the salaries of staff and other-than-personnel costs like materials, supplies, travel, and equipment. (See also Administrative or Indirect Costs.)

Development. The term development is used for most fundraising activities, including foundation research, proposal writing, and all other strategies for bringing money into an organization. These may include, for example, annual and special appeal letters, events such as street fairs, gala dinners, and bazaars, benefit golf outings, alumni gatherings, and so on. In very small organizations any such strategies are implemented by an executive director, a board member or committee, or, perhaps, a single staff member devoted to fundraising. As organizations grow, their development departments also grow and become more specialized.

Development, Board. Board development is the formal or informal process of training board members in their role as overseers of the organization and their fundraising function. It may be done by experienced board members, the executive director, or an outside board development organization.

Discretionary Spending, Discretionary Grants. All resources that are available to support government functions, purchase goods and services, and issue grants to other entities after debt service and entitlement payments. At the federal level, discretionary spending includes the military, homeland security, education, the IRS, the FBI and CIA, and all other government agencies and programs and their grantees and contractors. Compare to formula grants, which are based on the number of individuals in an area eligible for a particular funding source (see also Entitlements).

DUNS Number. Dun & Bradstreet assigns a number (a "data universal numbering system" number) to every organization that applies. Required for all federal applications and increasingly requested by other government funders. Apply online (https://eupdate.dnb.com/requestoptions.html) or, if applying for a federal grant, at 866-705-5711.

Earmark. For grants purposes, the inclusion in a budget bill of a specific amount of funding for a project supported by an elected official. Also called pork.

Employer Identification Number (EIN). The EIN is the organizational version of an individual's Social Security number. The organization receives the EIN from the Internal Revenue Service. The EIN is required to open an organization's bank account and must be included in all government and many foundation applications.

Entitlements. Various federal laws specify benefits that must be paid to all individuals who fall into a certain class. Examples are Social Security, Medicare, and Medicaid. Entitlement benefits may be paid directly (Social Security) or through states and localities that receive formula grants for the purpose (Medicaid).

Evaluation. A detailed plan for measuring a program's effectiveness and its impact on program participants. The plan describes the kinds of data that will be gathered, the methods for gathering it, and the ways the data will be analyzed and reported.

Executive Summary. An overview of a document such as a report or proposal. Often longer than an abstract, it may be distributed in place of the primary document to the public or to specific interested parties.

Family Foundation. A family foundation is an independent foundation (see below) in which the trustees, directors, officers, or other decision makers are members of the family of the original donor, and may be donors themselves. Although some family foundations are very large, use outside trustees, and/or employ professional staff in addition to family members, most are fairly small and decisions about grants are made by members of the family.

Federal Register. The publication where federal NOFAs, RFAs, RFPs, SGAs, rules and regulations, and other notices can be found. Published daily by the Government Printing Office in paper copy and online in electronic format that is easily searched by keywords.

Federated Funds. Federated funds raise money each year to support nonprofit organizations. Examples include United Way, Federation of Protestant Welfare Agencies, Federation of Jewish Philanthropies, and local, state, and federal employee campaigns.

501(c)(3). 501(c) is the section of the Internal Revenue Code that authorizes and defines most tax-exempt organizations, which must be organized and operated for a public purpose. The 501(c)(3) is the most common type of not-for-profit designation. Contributions to a 501(c) organization are tax-deductible.

Fiscal Conduit. An established 501(c)(3) organization that administers a grant for an individual or an organization that is not incorporated or does not have tax-exempt status or for some other reason is not able to receive a foundation or government grant. The fiscal conduit is responsible for managing and reporting on the money and usually receives a small portion of the grant to cover administrative costs.

Fiscal Year. A 12-month period of operation of a given organization under its annual budget for that year. The fiscal year may or may not differ from the calendar year because an organization can establish its fiscal year for its own purposes. For example, the federal government's fiscal year begins on October 1 and runs through the following September 30. Nonprofit organizations that receive most of their funding from a federal agency may designate the same fiscal year as that entity. The fiscal year is designated by the year in which it ends. A fiscal year starting on July 1, 2009, is called Fiscal Year (or FY) 2010.

Focus Group. A group of individuals brought together to discuss an issue. This is a research method often used in marketing to determine a sales strategy. In preparing a proposal or reporting on a program, it is a method that is used to determine the needs and wishes of a target population for the program or to assess the effects of the program on that population.

Format. In grantsmanship, the physical presentation of a proposal, including layout, type size, line spacing, and so on. Whenever an application package or guidelines specifies elements of the proposal format, the instructions are to be followed precisely.

Formative Evaluation. See Process Evaluation.

Formula Grant. Federal government funding to states and major localities is based on formulas that account for the number of individuals who are entitled to that funding. They may be based strictly on total population, or they may be based on the number of individuals in specific categories: elderly, youth, people with disabilities, and so on. This kind of funding also is known as "entitlements."

Fringe Benefits. In a budget, personnel costs above the basic salary, such as vacation, health and dental benefits, unemployment insurance, the employer's share of Social Security contributions, and other benefits. Usually calculated as a percentage of the base personnel costs. Full-time and part-time staff may have different fringe-benefit levels, which should be shown in the budget and described in the budget narrative.

Funding Priorities. Funding priorities are activities that a government agency states in a Request for Proposals (RFP) that it intends to fund in a given year. If the RFP states an absolute priority, only proposals that address that priority will be funded. If the RFP describes a competitive priority, applicants addressing this priority may receive additional points during the review process, but it they are not required to address it. For invitational priorities, applicants are encouraged to address certain issues, but they do not receive preference over applicants that do not do so.

Funding Streams, Income Sources. Government income is generated from tax levy revenues, including property taxes, income taxes, and sales taxes. Funds for capital purposes such as buildings, roads, and mass transit generally are raised through bond issues. Funding from higher levels of government may come through block grants, program grants, or formula grants.

General Operating Support, General Operating Funds. Also called unrestricted funds, this refers to support for the organization as a whole, and for any purpose that furthers the organization's mission. In practical use, it pays for costs that can't be allocated to specific programs. Examples might include some portion or all of the costs of secretarial support, rent, building security and maintenance, development staff, a fiscal manager, insurance, and auditing costs. General operating funds may come from a line in the budget called administrative overhead, set at a percentage of the total budget by a grantmaker. Because the administrative percentages allowed often do not cover all overhead costs, general operating funds, or unrestricted funds usually must come from individual donations to the organization. A few foundations also provide grants for general operating support.

Goals. Goals are broad intentions, which may not be measurable and, in fact, may never be met. They are the desired, long-term purpose (e.g., ending hunger; improving education) of the program or the organization.

GPO, U.S. Government Printing Office. Publishes the *Federal Register*, the *Congressional Record*, congressional bills, *Economic Report of the President*, and many other reports and databases, which are available to the public in print and online.

Grant. An award of money or, more rarely, goods or services to accomplish a purpose defined by the grantmaker.

Grantmaker. Any entity that gives grants, including a government agency, foundation, federated fund, or not-for-profit organization (like federations) that receive grants and regrant them to smaller not-for-profits.

Grassroots Organization. Small, local groups like block and tenant associations, neighborhood-improvement groups, and merchants' associations. Usually led by one or more community residents without a formal organization structure. A grassroots organization usually raises money from dues or contributions given by neighborhood residents, or through group fundraising efforts such as raffles, bake sales, and so on. It also may receive contributions or in-kind goods from local businesses, or may win grant funding as part of a collaboration or through a larger organization that serves as its fiscal conduit.

Guidelines. Broad or detailed specifications published by grantmakers to describe eligible applicants and to alert prospective applicants about the programs and activities that the grantmakers will fund.

Independent Foundation, Private Foundation. A fund or endowment whose primary function is to make grants. Unlike federated funds and some community foundations, independent foundations normally do not raise funds or seek public financial support because their assets are in endowments. Unlike family foundations, independent foundations are not controlled by the original donor or the donor's family. Nevertheless, some of the largest independent foundations began as family foundations.

Indirect Costs. A percentage of total program costs allowable to pay for overhead costs like lighting, heat, wear and tear on equipment. (See Administrative Overhead.)

In-Kind Contribution. Goods and services that are donated to a particular organization for a grant program. Volunteer time is an in-kind contribution; so are food, equipment, space rental, and even staff or management time that is paid for by other programs or absorbed by general operating funds. All available in-kind contributions for a proposed program should be shown in the budget and described in the narrative.

Institutionalization. The permanent or long-term support for or absorption of a particular program by or into another entity in order to sustain it after the end of a grant period. A program may be institutionalized if its support is taken over by a larger nonprofit or local government organization, a business enterprise, a council of churches, or any another entity. (See also Sustainability.)

Job Description. Specification of the responsibilities of a particular staff position and the qualifications required for the job. Job descriptions should be created and updated for every current staff position and maintained in a file to facilitate both proposal preparation and advertising to fill the position when vacant.

Key Staff. Those managers and staff who are critical to an agency's functioning or the implementation of a particular program.

Letter of Commitment. See Memorandum of Understanding.

Letter of Inquiry. A letter to a foundation exploring the possibility that the foundation will consider a grant for a particular program. For some foundations this is the preferred initial approach; for others it is a way for unknown not-for-profits to introduce themselves. In some cases the foundation has published guidelines for a letter of inquiry. In all cases the letter should be treated as a miniproposal, with a brief statement of the need to be addressed, the objectives of a program to address the need, a capsule description of the program, the outcomes to be expected, and the cost.

Letter of Intent. A letter to a foundation or government agency indicating an intention to apply for a particular grant. Sometimes requested by a grant-maker specifically for the purpose of determining how many proposals will be received and therefore how many reviewers they will need to hire. Unless otherwise specified, a letter of intent is not a miniproposal; it is a short, to-the-point notification of an intent to apply for a grant.

Letter of Support. In the past, a letter from an individual or agency in a community that provided, in effect, a reference for a proposal applicant. It includes a broad and general statement of knowledge of and support for the organization. Most funders no longer accept or review support letters. Instead, they insist on linkage letters, letters of commitment, or memoranda of understanding (see below).

Linkages, Linkage Letters. Linkage is the term used to describe relationships between and among organizations working together within a community. Linkages tend to be routine and ongoing rather than project oriented, as when a hospital arranges for home care services for patients at discharge or when a school provides space and security for an after-school program run by a nonprofit organization. Partners may refer clients to one another, place staff from one agency at other agencies' sites to provide services that are not provided at those sites, offer training to staff of partner agencies, and work together to assist clients in other ways. For grants requiring collaboration, linkage letters spell out the arrangements in detail.

Local Education Agency (LEA). The government agency responsible for education in a given community. It may be a school board, a school district, a department of education, or, for some funding sources, a school.

Match. An amount or percentage of the total budget that a funder may require an applicant to commit to a program if it is funded. The match can be an in-kind contribution of goods and services, cash, or a combination of both. The funder makes the determination of what is acceptable.

Matching Grant. A grant that is made specifically to match or supplement funds provided by another donor, usually as a specified proportion of the total program cost. Often provided as a challenge grant, and paid on the condition that the other funds are obtained.

Memorandum of Understanding (MOU). A letter, signed by an authorized representative of each organization, from each partner in a collaborative project, specifying the activities and services that the partner will provide and the expectations the partner may have from the other partners and from the grant itself. This should be thought of as a brief contract that will take effect if a grant is awarded. Depending on the complexity of its contents, a MOU may need to be reviewed by a lawyer before you sign it.

Mission Statement. A brief, focused statement of an organization's reason for being; its overall purpose. The mission is the context in which all the organization's programs operate and for which the programs exist.

Needs Assessment. Qualitative and/or quantitative documentation or data organized to demonstrate issues, needs, or problems in a community. This may be as simple as a description of the waiting lists for services at an agency or as elaborate as a statistical analysis demonstrating that the target population experiences more of a particular problem (e.g., crime, drug use, the proportion of teenagers or the elderly with no place to go) than other communities.

Needs Statement, Problems Statement. The section of a proposal that lays out the issues, needs, or problems that a program will address. Normally proposals to government agencies require greater documentation of the problem (crime, substance use, lack of services for youth or the elderly) and demographics of the community (race, ethnicity, income and poverty level, etc.) than do proposals to foundations. Depending on the funder, the needs section also may include research from "the field" and may put your community's problem in the context of the town or city as a whole as well as your state (and sometimes country).

990, 990-PF. Federal tax form used by foundations and public charities (including nonprofit organizations). Available at www.GrantSmart.com, these forms usually include lists of the grants that have been made during the current tax year and sometimes indicate grants that have been committed for the following tax year.

NOFA. See Notice of Funding Availability.

Not-for-Profit Organization. An organization of any size that is incorporated under the laws of the state in which it operates and has been granted tax-exempt status, usually under Section 501(c)(3), by the U.S. Internal Revenue Service. It must have a board of directors, elected officers, and approved financial procedures for managing grants and reporting on expenditures. Known informally as a nonprofit organization.

Notice of Funding Availability (NOFA). A formal, published announcement by a grantmaking entity, usually a government agency but sometimes a large foundation, that it will accept applications or proposals for a specific purpose detailed in the announcement. (See also Request for Proposals, Request for Applications.)

Notice of Proposed Rulemaking. A notice published in the *Federal Register* that outlines proposed rules and priorities for certain programs or funding opportunities, and that invites the public to comment on them by a certain deadline.

Objectives. Clearly defined and measurable results (outcomes) that a program is intended to achieve.

Other than Personnel Services, Other than Personal Services (OTPS). All budgeted costs of a program that do not relate to staffing costs. This budget category may include items like rent, equipment purchase or lease, consultants, supplies, postage, utilities, and so on.

Organization Chart. A diagram of an organization's structure, showing its internal lines of responsibility and reporting relationships for all departments and programs. Large organizations also may maintain organization charts for individual departments or programs.

Outcome, Outcomes. The intended, measurable result or results of a program, usually spelled out in objectives.

Outcome Evaluation. A process of determining, usually through formal, quantitative research methods, whether and to what extent a program has achieved the results (outcomes) that it set out to achieve. Assesses what a program accomplishes. May require an external evaluator using sophisticated analytic approaches and control or comparison groups that do not experience the program. Also called summative evaluation.

Personnel Services, Personal Services (PS). The section of a budget relating to staffing costs. Each position is shown with the full-time or part-time base yearly or hourly salary for that staff member, and, depending on the application format, the number of hours and proportion of the cost allocated to the proposal request or to other sources. Includes fringe benefits, which are shown on a line separate from the base salaries.

Private Operating Foundation, Operating Foundation. This type of private foundation provides charitable services or runs research, social welfare, or other charitable programs of its own. Private operating foundations make few, if any, grants to outside organizations.

Process Evaluation. The application of (usually qualitative) research methods to determine whether a program is being implemented in the way in which it was intended to be implemented (e.g., whether it is using the activities it said it would use, deploying staff in the ways it intended to do, serving the number and type of participants in the way it intended) and providing feedback to program managers to take corrective action. Also called formative evaluation because it helps shape the program. Process evaluation provides a way to understand why outcomes are achieved or fail to be achieved.

Program Evaluation. Systematic documentation and analysis of indicators demonstrating that a program has achieved its objectives or intended outcomes. May include both outcome and process evaluation components but need not be complex or formal unless required by the funder.

Program Officer, Grants Officer. The staff member of a funding organization who receives grant proposals and processes applications for a government agency or board of trustees.

Project Period. The total time for which support of a project can be approved by a funder. A project period may last for one or more years. If there is a multiple-year project period, each year's renewal of the grant probably depends on program performance during the previous year.

Program Plan. Detailed description of the program's functioning, including activities time frames, staffing plan and job descriptions, and costs.

Public Foundations, Public Charities. Public foundations raise a significant portion of their resources from a broad cross-section of the public each year and redistribute it in grants to nonprofit organizations. (Public charity is the designation used by the IRS for an organization that raises funds from the public.) Community foundations normally are public foundations.

Regional Association of Grantmakers (RAGs). As the name indicates, most areas of the United States have a regional membership association that includes many (but usually not all) of the foundations and corporate grant-makers in the area. Some publish membership directories, common application forms, and other information about their members and are a good reference source for grant seekers.

Request for Proposals (RFP), Request for Applications (RFA), Solicitation of Grant Applications (SGA). A document issued by a public or private funding agency, inviting qualified organizations to submit a proposal for a specific funding opportunity. (See also Notice of Funding Availability.)

Reviewers, Readers. Most federal proposals and many submissions to state and local government agencies and national foundations are read and scored by outside professionals, called reviewers or readers, acting as outside consultants to the funding agency. Reviewers are selected for their background in the relevant field (e.g., educators or directors of youth programs for proposals affecting children and teenagers; health care professionals for proposals in that field). Normally reviewers will not read proposals from their home state or region.

Reviewers' Comments. Most federal agencies make available to an applicant (usually only on request) the scores for that proposal, which are provided to the funding agency by the outside readers. The reviewers' names are removed but all comments explaining the scores are shown.

Seed Grant, Seed Money. A grant that is made to start a program, with the intention of leveraging other support to sustain it.

SF-424, Standard Form 424. This serves as a cover sheet for a federal grant application. Information to be filled in on this form includes organization name and address, contact person, name of federal program, CFDA number, name of your project, total budget request, and other items. Sometimes a federal agency will substitute a designation such as ED (Department of Education) in place of the notation SF, but the form is the same.

Site Visit. A visit by a funding agency that is considering giving a grant to an applicant. It gives the funder a chance to assess the accuracy of descriptions in a proposal and to ask additional questions that may help determine whether the agency can manage the grant and accomplish its objectives.

Stakeholder. A term applied to any party with an interest in a particular program or who may be affected by the program. In a school program, stakeholders may include parents, faculty, the children themselves, the administration, nonprofit organizations, and local businesses.

Sustainability. The prospect that an organization will be able to keep a program going (sustain it) after the end of a particular grant. Increasingly a concern of grantmakers at all levels. Applicants should be able to show what resources they expect will be available to sustain the program or how they will work toward that end.

Summative Evaluation. See Outcome Evaluation.

Tax Levy Funds. Revenues raised through taxes of all sorts (income, sales, property, and other taxes) by government at the local, state, and federal levels to support ongoing operations of the government.

Technical Assistance. Services provided to organizations to teach or assist them with proposal writing and other fundraising, organization development and management, financial planning, legal issues, marketing, and other operational matters. May be provided by nonprofit or for-profit organizations, individual consultants, or grantmakers themselves. Some funders give grants specifically for technical assistance.

Time Line. A chart or narrative showing the month-by-month time frame for the beginning, implementation, and end of each program activity. Some time lines also show activities with the staff person responsible.

Trustee, Director. A foundation board member or officer who is responsible for the fiscal well-being of the foundation and for ensuring that the donor's wishes are carried out in the foundation's grantmaking activities. In larger foundations, trustees may depend on professional staff to recommend grants, but the trustees are the ultimate authority.

Unrestricted Funds. Money donated by individuals or businesses, or given in general operating grants, to further the mission of an organization. May be spent for any organizational priority or need.

Waiting Lists. Lists of potential users of a service who have requested the service but cannot be accommodated at a given time. In the grants world, waiting lists are one important way to document the need for a particular service.

Appendix 4:

Sample Grant Forms

WASHINGTON

Regional Association of

GRANTMAKERS

Common Grant Application Form

Formatting notes

- Proposals should be printed on white paper, using a 12-point font (Times or similar) and one-inch margins on all sides; pages should be numbered.
- Proposals should not be placed in binders or folders; one staple or paper clip in the upper-left hand corner, securing all pages, is sufficient.

I. Executive Summary (1–2 pages single spaced)

1. Application date
2. Organization's name and contact information (full address, including mailing address if different, telephone, fax, and Web address)
3. Organization's federal tax-exempt number
4. Contact person's name, title, and contact information (telephone, fax, e-mail)
5. Dollar amount of this funding request
6. Total program budget (if applicable)
7. Total current organizational budget and fiscal year
8. Period this funding request will cover
9. Purpose of this funding request, including target population, number of individuals, and geographic area(s) that will benefit from this proposal
10. Brief organizational history and brief description of previous year's accomplishments
11. Total support from this funder for the past three years: List year, amount, and purpose for all support
12. Signature of executive director

II. Narrative (no more than 8 double-spaced pages)

1. **For All Requests:** Information on Your Organization
   1. Describe, in one paragraph, the organization's history, mission, and goals.
   2. Describe current programs and activities, and recent organizational accomplishments.
   3. How will this request enable the organization to build its capacity, address current limitations, and/or improve its ability to meet program or organizational goals?
   4. Describe briefly the involvement of your target population(s) in implementing the work of the organization, if applicable.

The Common Grant Application is developed and produced by the Washington Regional Associaiton of Grantmakers, who give in the Washington, D.C., region.

PLEASE COMPLETE THE **ONE** SECTION BELOW WHICH IS RELEVANT TO THIS REQUEST. Be sure that the foundation to which you are applying supports the type of request you are making.

B. **For Program Requests** (including capacity building projects)
1. What is the issue/need to be addressed and evidence of that need?
2. For a **new** program: how was the program approach developed?
3. For an **ongoing** program: what measurable *outcomes (defined as concrete changes or impact)* have been achieved over the past year?
4. Does this program use best practices – i.e., is this program based on a program that has been shown to be effective in other settings, based on national standards, etc? If so, please describe.
5. What is the plan for implementation? (Narrative, table, or logic model format is acceptable.) What existing community resources (e.g., facilities, people) will be used? If applicable: what is the target population's involvement in *this program's* development and implementation?
6. Based on the implementation plan, what measurable outcomes will be achieved during this grant period? What are the measurable longer-term outcomes of this program? What methods/strategies will be used to gather data on the project? How will the program evaluation be used?
7. How does this program fit into the work of this organization?
8. How does this program relate to the work of other organizations in the same field and/or geographic area?
9. What resources (financial, personnel, partnerships, etc.) will be needed to sustain this effort over time? How will those resources be secured?

C. **For General Support Requests**
1. What are the issue(s) or need(s) to be addressed and the evidence of those issues or needs?
2. For a **new** organization: how and why was the organization formed?
3. For an **existing** organization: what measurable *outcomes (defined as concrete change or impact)* have been achieved over the past year?
4. Does the organization use best practices – i.e., are any programs or operations based on ones that have been shown to be effective in other settings, based on national standards, etc? If so, please describe.
5. What are the plans for the organization's major program activities? (Narrative or table format is acceptable.) What existing community resources (e.g., facilities, people) will be used?
6. Based on these activities, what measurable outcomes will be achieved during this grant period? What are the measurable longer-term outcomes of the organization's work? What methods/strategies will be used to gather data? How will the evaluation be used?
7. How does the work of this organization relate to the work of other organizations in the same field and/or geographic area?
8. What resources (financial, personnel, partnerships, etc.) will be needed to sustain the organization over time? How will those resources be secured?

2

D. **For Capital Campaign Requests**: Capital campaign requests are designated for the acquisition, construction, renovation, or improvement of a property. Include information on the following, as applicable to your organization's request.
1. Discuss the need, feasibility, and cost of the capital campaign, and its implications for the organization's ongoing operational expenses.
2. Specify contributions in hand as well as pending or prospective.
3. Specify loans, including amounts and terms.
4. Include the financial participation in the campaign of the board and the capital/leadership campaign committee (percent participating and total contributed).
5. Specify whether purchase agreements or purchase options are signed or imminent. Specify also whether regulatory approvals (e.g., Certificate of Need, zoning, historic preservation, environmental impact) in place or are imminent.
6. Indicate if timing is a factor, i.e., if a "window of opportunity" exists that affects the success of the campaign.

III. Finances (for all requests) – This information is not considered part of the narrative.

The following information must accompany all proposals, regardless of the size of the request. Not all categories may be applicable to your organization or request. You may submit this information in the format most convenient to you; it must, however, include as much of the following detail as possible. Footnotes may be used to explain budget items.

A. **For all requests**
1. Fiscal year
2. Financial statements:
   a. For previous fiscal year: organizational budget v. actual, for both revenue and expenses (using categories below)
   b. For current fiscal year:
      i. Organizational budget v. actual, for both revenue and expenses (using categories below)
      ii. Organization's year-to-date Statement of Financial Position (Balance Sheet) and year-to-date Statement of Activities (Income Statement)
   c. If this application is being made during the last quarter of the organization's fiscal year, provide the organization's projected/proposed/draft budget for the next fiscal year
3. If available: most recent audited financial statements (include auditor's letter and notes). If you do not have an audit, provide pages 1-6 of most recent IRS Form-990.

B. **For Program Requests** (including capacity building and capital campaign requests) - In addition to the information requested above:
1. Financial statements:
   a. For previous fiscal year: program budget v. actual, for both revenue and expenses (using categories below)
   b. For current fiscal year: program budget v. actual, for both revenue and expenses (using categories below)
   c. If this application is being made during the last quarter of the organization's fiscal year, provide the program's projected/proposed/draft budget for the next fiscal year

3

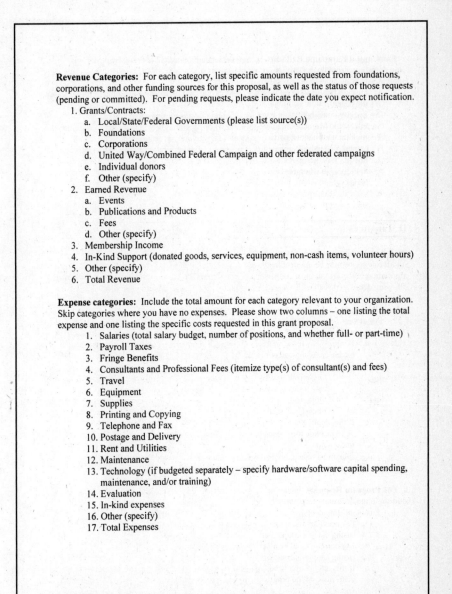

Revenue Categories: For each category, list specific amounts requested from foundations, corporations, and other funding sources for this proposal, as well as the status of those requests (pending or committed). For pending requests, please indicate the date you expect notification.
1. Grants/Contracts:
    a. Local/State/Federal Governments (please list source(s))
    b. Foundations
    c. Corporations
    d. United Way/Combined Federal Campaign and other federated campaigns
    e. Individual donors
    f. Other (specify)
2. Earned Revenue
    a. Events
    b. Publications and Products
    c. Fees
    d. Other (specify)
3. Membership Income
4. In-Kind Support (donated goods, services, equipment, non-cash items, volunteer hours)
5. Other (specify)
6. Total Revenue

Expense categories: Include the total amount for each category relevant to your organization. Skip categories where you have no expenses. Please show two columns – one listing the total expense and one listing the specific costs requested in this grant proposal.
1. Salaries (total salary budget, number of positions, and whether full- or part-time)
2. Payroll Taxes
3. Fringe Benefits
4. Consultants and Professional Fees (itemize type(s) of consultant(s) and fees)
5. Travel
6. Equipment
7. Supplies
8. Printing and Copying
9. Telephone and Fax
10. Postage and Delivery
11. Rent and Utilities
12. Maintenance
13. Technology (if budgeted separately – specify hardware/software capital spending, maintenance, and/or training)
14. Evaluation
15. In-kind expenses
16. Other (specify)
17. Total Expenses

IV. Required Attachments (for all requests) – This information is not considered part of the narrative.

4

1. A copy of your current IRS tax-exempt determination letter. If tax-exempt status is pending, provide an explanation of application status.
2. A one-page organizational chart.
3. Short biographies (no more than 1/2 page) of staff and volunteers essential to the success of this request.
4. List of board members with terms, occupations, and places of employment.
5. Current, dated Memoranda of Understanding or Memoranda of Agreement with other organizations for collaborative or cooperative activities, as appropriate.
6. For Capital Spending Projects: list of members of the capital campaign/leadership committee.
7. Annual report, if available.

5

Application for Federal
Education Assistance (ED 424)

U.S. Department of Education
Form Approved
OMB No. 1890-0017
Exp. 04/30/2008

Applicant Information

1. Name and Address
Legal Name: _____

Address: _____

_____

City _____ State ___ County ___ ZIP Code + 4 ___

Organizational Unit
[   ]

2. Applicant's D-U-N-S Number |__|__|__|__|__|__|__|__|__|

3. Applicant's T-I-N |__|__|-|__|__|__|__|__|__|__|

4. Catalog of Federal Domestic Assistance #: 84. |__|__|__|

Title: _____

_____

5. Project Director: _____

Address: _____

City _____ State ___ Zip code + 4 ___
Tel. #: (   ) _____-_____ Fax #: (   ) _____-_____

E-Mail Address: _____

6. Novice Applicant ___Yes ___No

7. Is the applicant delinquent on any Federal debt? ___Yes ___No
(If "Yes," attach an explanation.)

8. Type of Applicant *(Enter appropriate letter in the box.)* |__|

A - State   F - Independent School District
B - Local   G - Public College or University
C - Special District   H - Private, Non-profit College or University
D - Indian Tribe   I - Non-profit Organization
E - Individual   J - Private, Profit-Making Organization

K - Other *(Specify)*: _____

9. State Application Identifier _____

Application Information

10. Type of Submission:

-PreApplication   *-Application*
___ Construction   ___ Construction
___ Non-Construction   ___ Non-Construction

11. Is application subject to review by Executive Order 12372 process?
___ Yes *(Date made available to the Executive Order 12372 process for review):* ___/___/___

___ No *(If "No," check appropriate box below.)*
    ___ Program is not covered by E.O. 12372.
    ___ Program has not been selected by State for review.

12. Proposed Project Dates: ___/___/___   ___/___/___
                                Start Date: End Date:

13. Are any research activities involving human subjects planned at any time during the proposed project period?
___ Yes (Go to 13a.)   ___ No (Go to item 14.)

13a. Are all the research activities proposed designated to be exempt from the regulations?
___ Yes (Provide Exemption(s) #): _____

___ No (Provide Assurance #): _____

14. Descriptive Title of Applicant's Project:

_____

_____

Estimated Funding

15a. Federal	$ _____	. 00
b. Applicant	$ _____	. 00
c. State	$ _____	. 00
d. Local	$ _____	. 00
e. Other	$ _____	. 00
f. Program Income	$ _____	. 00
g. TOTAL	$ _____	. 00

Authorized Representative Information

16. To the best of my knowledge and belief, all data in this preapplication/application are true and correct. The document has been duly authorized by the governing body of the applicant and the applicant will comply with the attached assurances if the assistance is awarded.

a. Authorized Representative *(Please type or print name clearly.)*

_____

b. Title: _____

c. Tel. #: (   ) _____-_____ Fax #: (   ) _____-_____

d. E-Mail Address: _____

e. Signature of Authorized Representative

_____ Date: ___/___/___

228

Definitions for Form ED 424

Novice Applicant (See 34 CFR 75.225). For discretionary grant programs under which the Secretary gives special consideration to novice applications, a novice applicant means any applicant for a grant from ED that—

- Has never received a grant or subgrant under the program from which it seeks funding;

- Has never been a member of a group application, submitted in accordance with 34 CFR 75.127-75.129, that received a grant under the program from which it seeks funding; and

- Has not had an active discretionary grant from the Federal government in the five years before the deadline date for applications under the program. For the purposes of this requirement, a grant is active until the end of the grant's project or funding period, including any extensions of those periods that extend the grantee's authority to obligate funds.

In the case of a group application submitted in accordance with 34 CFR 75.127-75.129, a group includes only parties that meet the requirements listed above.

Type of Submission. "Construction" includes construction of new buildings and acquisition, expansion, remodeling, and alteration of existing buildings, and initial equipment of any such buildings, or any combination of such activities (including architects' fees and the cost of acquisition of land). "Construction" also includes remodeling to meet standards, remodeling designed to conserve energy, renovation or remodeling to accommodate new technologies, and the purchase of existing historic buildings for conversion to public libraries. For the purposes of this paragraph, the term "equipment" includes machinery, utilities, and built-in equipment and any necessary enclosures or structures to house them; and such term includes all other items necessary for the functioning of a particular facility as a facility for the provision of library services.

Executive Order 12372. The purpose of Executive Order 12372 is to foster an intergovernmental partnership and strengthen federalism by relying on State and local processes for the coordination and review of proposed Federal financial assistance and direct Federal development. The application notice, as published in the Federal Register, informs the applicant as to whether the program is subject to the requirements of E.O. 12372. In addition, the application package contains information on the State Single Point of Contact. An applicant is still eligible to apply for a grant or grants even if its respective State, Territory, Commonwealth, etc. does not have a State Single Point of Contact. For additional information on E.O. 12372 go to http://12.46.245.173/pls/portal30/catalog.REQ_FOR_12372.show

PROTECTION OF HUMAN SUBJECTS IN RESEARCH

I. Definitions and Exemptions

A. Definitions.

A research activity involves human subjects if the activity is research, as defined in the Department's regulations, and the research activity will involve use of human subjects, as defined in the regulations.

—Research

The ED Regulations for the Protection of Human Subjects, Title 34, Code of Federal Regulations, Part 97, define research as "a systematic investigation, including research development, testing and evaluation, designed to develop or contribute to generalizable knowledge." *If an activity follows a deliberate plan whose purpose is to develop or contribute to generalizable knowledge it is research.* Activities which meet this definition constitute research whether or not they are conducted or supported under a program which is considered research for other purposes. For example, some demonstration and service programs may include research activities.

—Human Subject

The regulations define human subject as "a living individual about whom an investigator (whether professional or student) conducting research obtains (1) data through intervention or interaction with the individual, or (2) identifiable private information." *(1) If an activity involves obtaining information about a living person by manipulating that person or that person's environment, as might occur when a new instructional technique is tested, or by communicating or interacting with the individual, as occurs with surveys and interviews, the definition of human subject is met. (2) If an activity involves obtaining private information about a living person in such a way that the information can be linked to that individual (the identity of the subject is or may be readily determined by the investigator or associated with the information), the definition of human subject is met.* [Private information includes information about behavior that occurs in a context in which an individual can reasonably expect that no observation or recording is taking place, and information which has been provided for specific purposes by an individual and which the individual can reasonably expect will not be made public (for example, a school health record).]

B. Exemptions.

Research activities in which the **only** involvement of human subjects will be in one or more of the following six categories of *exemptions* are not covered by the regulations:

(1) Research conducted in established or commonly accepted educational settings, involving normal educational practices, such as (a) research on regular and special education instructional strategies, or (b) research on the effectiveness of or the comparison among instructional techniques, curricula, or classroom management methods.

(2) Research involving the use of educational tests (cognitive, diagnostic, aptitude, achievement), survey procedures, interview procedures or observation of public behavior, unless: (a) information obtained is recorded in such a manner that human subjects can be identified, directly or through identifiers linked to the subjects; and (b) any disclosure of the human subjects' responses outside the research could

reasonably place the subjects at risk of criminal or civil liability or be damaging to the subjects' financial standing, employability, or reputation. *If the subjects are children, exemption 2 applies only to research involving educational tests and observations of public behavior when the investigator(s) do not participate in the activities being observed. Exemption 2 does not apply if children are surveyed or interviewed or if the research involves observation of public behavior and the investigator(s) participate in the activities being observed.* [Children are defined as persons who have not attained the legal age for consent to treatments or procedures involved in the research, under the applicable law or jurisdiction in which the research will be conducted.]

(3) Research involving the use of educational tests (cognitive, diagnostic, aptitude, achievement), survey procedures, interview procedures or observation of public behavior that is not exempt under section (2) above, if the human subjects are elected or appointed public officials or candidates for public office; or federal statute(s) require(s) without exception that the confidentiality of the personally identifiable information will be maintained throughout the research and thereafter.

(4) Research involving the collection or study of existing data, documents, records, pathological specimens, or diagnostic specimens, if these sources are publicly available or if the information is recorded by the investigator in a manner that subjects cannot be identified, directly or through identifiers linked to the subjects.

(5) Research and demonstration projects which are conducted by or subject to the approval of department or agency heads, and which are designed to study, evaluate, or otherwise examine: (a) public benefit or service programs; (b) procedures for obtaining benefits or services under those programs; (c) possible changes in or alternatives to those programs or procedures; or (d) possible changes in methods or levels of payment for benefits or services under those programs.

(6) Taste and food quality evaluation and consumer acceptance studies, (a) if wholesome foods without additives are consumed or (b) if a food is consumed that contains a food ingredient at or below the level and for a use found to be safe, or agricultural chemical or environmental contaminant at or below the level

found to be safe, by the Food and Drug Administration or approved by the Environmental Protection Agency or the Food Safety and Inspection Service of the U.S. Department of Agriculture.

II. Instructions for Exempt and Nonexempt Human Subjects Research Narratives

If the applicant marked "Yes" for Item 13 on the ED 424, the applicant must provide a human subjects "exempt research" or "nonexempt research" narrative and insert it immediately following the ED 424 face page.

A. Exempt Research Narrative.

If you marked "Yes" for item 13 a. and designated exemption numbers(s), provide the "exempt research" narrative. The narrative must contain sufficient information about the involvement of human subjects in the proposed research to allow a determination by ED that the designated exemption(s) are appropriate. The narrative must be succinct.

B. Nonexempt Research Narrative.

If you marked "No" for item 13 a. you must provide the "nonexempt research" narrative. The narrative must address the following seven points. Although no specific page limitation applies to this section of the application, be succinct.

(1) **Human Subjects Involvement and Characteristics**: Provide a detailed description of the proposed involvement of human subjects. Describe the characteristics of the subject population, including their anticipated number, age range, and health status. Identify the criteria for inclusion or exclusion of any subpopulation. Explain the rationale for the involvement of special classes of subjects, such as children, children with disabilities, adults with disabilities, persons with mental disabilities, pregnant women, prisoners, institutionalized individuals, or others who are likely to be vulnerable

(2) **Sources of Materials**: Identify the sources of research material obtained from individually identifiable living human subjects in the form of specimens, records, or data. Indicate whether the material or data will be obtained specifically for research purposes or whether use will be made of existing specimens, records, or data.

(3) **Recruitment and Informed Consent**: Describe plans for the recruitment of subjects and the consent procedures to be followed. Include the circumstances under which consent will be sought and obtained, who will seek it, the nature of the information to be provided to prospective subjects, and the method of documenting consent. State if the Institutional Review Board (IRB) has authorized a modification or waiver of the elements of consent or the requirement for documentation of consent.

(4) **Potential Risks**: Describe potential risks (physical, psychological, social, legal, or other) and assess their likelihood and seriousness. Where appropriate, describe alternative treatments and procedures that might be advantageous to the subjects.

(5) **Protection Against Risk**: Describe the procedures for protecting against or minimizing potential risks, including risks to confidentiality, and assess their likely effectiveness. Where appropriate, discuss provisions for ensuring necessary medical or professional intervention in the event of adverse effects to the subjects. Also, where appropriate, describe the provisions for monitoring the data collected to ensure the safety of the subjects.

(6) **Importance of the Knowledge to be Gained**: Discuss the importance of the knowledge gained or to be gained as a result of the proposed research. Discuss why the risks to subjects are reasonable in relation to the anticipated benefits to subjects and in relation to the importance of the knowledge that may reasonably be expected to result.

(7) **Collaborating Site(s)**: If research involving human subjects will take place at collaborating site(s) or other performance site(s), name the sites and briefly describe their involvement or role in the research.

Copies of the Department of Education's Regulations for the Protection of Human Subjects, 34 CFR Part 97 and other pertinent materials on the protection of human subjects in research are available from the Grants Policy and Oversight Staff, Office of the Chief Financial Officer, U.S. Department of Education, Washington, D.C. 20202-4250, telephone: (202) 245-6120, and on the U.S. Department of Education's Protection of Human Subjects in Research Web Site at http://www.ed.gov/about/offices/list/ocfo/humansub.html

SAMPLE COVER LETTER

Rosemont Youth Center

101 South Fourth Street

Rosemont, Newstate 11111-1111

[DATE]

Mr. Mark Rosenfeld, Executive Director

Rosemont Community Trust

574 East Main Street

Rosemont, Newstate 11111-2222

Dear Mr. Rosenfeld:

I am pleased to submit the enclosed proposal to the Rosemont Community Trust. We are requesting $6,000 to provide an after-school karate program for children from 10 to 13 years of age who are having disciplinary difficulties in school. As you probably are aware, karate engages high-energy children who need a physical outlet, and at the same time teaches respect and discipline.

We understand that in the last year you have given grants to assist several athletic programs for children at this age, and we hope that you will be able to assist us in the coming year.

Please visit our website, www.rosemontcenter.org or call me at (555) 666-7777 if you have any questions. If you'd like to visit, I'd be happy to show you around the Youth Center.

Sincerely,

Judy Morrison

Executive Director

SAMPLE LETTER OF INQUIRY (LOI)

Princeton Community College

67–12 Water Street, Second Floor

Princeton, Newstate 10000

[DATE]

Mr. Mark Rosenfeld, Executive Director

Rosemont Community Trust

574 East Main Street

Rosemont, Newstate 11111–2222

Dear Mr. Rosenfeld:

I am writing to ask whether the Rosemont Community Trust would be interested in receiving a proposal for an adult literacy program for Spanish-speaking immigrants.

As you may know, the town of Princeton has experienced a significant influx of immigrants from South and Central America over the last 10 years. The U.S. Census Bureau reports that the immigrant population from these countries has increased by 12 percent since the 2000 census, compared to 4 percent for Newstate as a whole. The Newstate Department of Employment indicates that lack of English language skills is the major barrier to employment in our area. The adult literacy program is intended to provide about 60 immigrants with English skills at a level that will allow them to find and keep employment. At the same time, participants will develop résumés and job-seeking skills and will learn about the cultural expectations of local employers.

Three teachers of English for speakers of other languages will offer two-hour computer-assisted ESOL classes at Princeton's computer lab twice a week for 40 weeks. Classes will be limited to 10 to 15 students. The project director, a skilled bilingual employment counselor, will assess students' abilities and interests and will work with each group for two hours on a third day each week, helping each student prepare for employment. All classes will emphasize job-related English conversation.

Students' English will be tested at the beginning of the program and periodically through the year. By the end of the school year, at least 70 percent of the students will have reached at least an intermediate level of English fluency, will be able to carry out instructions given in English and ask questions in response, will have created an appropriate résumé, and will be comfortable taking part in job interviews in English.

The total cost for this program is $107,000. If the Rosemont Community Trust were to accept a formal proposal, we would request $25,000 of this cost. We have received a commitment from the Barish Foundation for $25,000 and have begun to prepare a proposal to the Rosemont Department of Employment for the balance; we understand that a request for proposals will be issued in about a month and that grants are expected to be in the $50,000 to $60,000 range.

We are very excited about the benefits this program can provide to our new immigrant population. I hope you will consider helping us to develop it. Please visit our website, www.princetoncc.edu or call me at (555) 333-4444 if you have any questions. If you'd like to visit, I'd be happy to introduce you to our staff and show you our new computer lab. I look forward to hearing from you.

Sincerely,

Linda Lamb
Director

SAMPLE ABSTRACT

Throughout this book we've referred to the Safe Schools/Healthy Students grant application package. Below is a short example of an abstract that might lead off a proposal requesting the $3 million per year that three federal funding agencies are offering in this very competitive grant opportunity.

The Rosemont School District South, a high-need, culturally and ethnically diverse district (75 percent of the students are non-English speakers whose family incomes fall below the poverty level) on the south side of Rosemont, in collaboration with three city government agencies (the police, health, and youth departments), the Third Street YMCA, the Rosemont South Teen Center, the Community Day Care Collective, the Southside Methodist Church, the Rosemont South Hospital, Rosemont Junior College, the William T. Rosemont Family Foundation, and many other individuals and groups, has designed ROSEMONT ROCKS FOR SAFETY AND HEALTH!

This initiative will build on existing resources and coordinate new partnerships and linkages to create safe and drug-free schools and promote healthy child development for all of the 9,234 students (and their families and caregivers) in the target school district in the city of Rosemont.

To achieve its overall goal of safe and healthy students and ensure system-wide change in the target school district, ROSEMONT ROCKS FOR SAFETY AND HEALTH! will conduct the following activities that are designed to meet the program's objectives:

- Form a cross-disciplinary advisory board to publicize and support the initiative as well as to take the lead in raising additional funds to supplement and sustain project activities
- Hire five police officers to patrol the streets near the schools in the target district before, during, and after school hours
- Provide weekly professional development seminars for all school personnel, conducted by police officers, parole officers, mental health counselors, physicians, and others with expertise in the field of health and safety for children
- Provide training for parents of school children, conducted by school staff and outside experts
- Develop a referral protocol (a memorandum of understanding has been drawn up and signed) among the schools, not-for-profit organizations,

hospital, and health care providers to address mental and other health problems affecting students in the target district

- Expand the school day to include before- and after-school counseling, recreation, and academic programs, both in school buildings and at collaborating not-for-profit organizations for at-risk students
- Provide intensive preschool counseling and instruction to very young children in the community

Because the literature (e.g., Smith's 2008 landmark study on school violence) suggests that students in grades 6 and 7 are at the highest risk for violent activities, middle schools will serve as the hub for all project activities—with services radiating out to early childhood programs, elementary schools, high schools, and the community. It is expected that the $2,876,987 program will begin in January 2010.

Appendix 5: Representative List of Community Foundations

Community foundations are a good place to start searching for grants. If your organization or program doesn't fit their guidelines, their staff may be able to refer you to other foundations in the area. There are more than 600 community foundations and community trusts across the United States, so it is impractical to list them all here. They are as diverse in size and scope as other foundations are, and often were started by a single donor. The community foundations listed below are selected to show you how widely they are distributed (there's at least one for every state). We have deliberately chosen a few of the largest online urban community foundations, and some of the smallest, with only a mailing address. We've included one or two from each state (and some that are located in a nearby state but that serve part of your state) to give you a start, but we encourage you to look further to find the community foundation nearest you.

One quick way to do this is to search the Grantsmanship Center's website (www.tgci.com) and search on "community foundations." You'll come to a map that lets you select your state, and then click again on "community foundations" for a list. You can search for other types of foundation this way as well. This site includes links to many of the community foundations in each state, if they have websites. Be aware that there are more community foundations than are listed, although they don't all have online access! If you don't see a community foundation in your area, check with your local librarian—or the telephone book—to find the closest one. Be alert that email addresses may change if staff changes.

Alabama
Statewide
The Black Belt
Community Foundation, Inc.
PO Box 2020
Selma, AL 36702
384/874-1126
www.blackbeltfound.org

The Community Foundation
of Greater Birmingham
2100 First Avenue North, Suite 700
Birmingham, AL 35203
info@foundationbirmingham.org
www.foundationbirmingham.org/

The Community Foundation of
Southeast Alabama
www.cfsea.org

Community Foundation of
West Alabama
PO Box 3033
Tuscaloosa, AL 35403
205/366-0698
Fax: 205/366-0831
www.thecfwa.org

Alaska
Statewide
The Alaska Community Foundation
400 L Street, Suite 1000
Anchorage, AK 99501
907/334-6700
www.alaskacf.org

Alaska Conservation Foundation
441 West Fifth Avenue, Suite 402
Anchorage, AK 99501-2340
Phone 907/276-1917
Fax 907 /274-4145
www.akcf.org

Arizona
Statewide
Arizona Community
Foundation
2201 E. Camelback Road, Suite 202
Phoenix, AZ 85016
602/381-1400
Fax: 602/381-1575
grants@azfoundation.org
www.azfoundation.org

Community Foundation for
Southern Arizona
2250 E. Broadway Boulevard
Tuscon, AX 85179
520/770-0800
Fax: 520/770-1500
www.cfsoaz.org

Arkansas
Statewide
Arkansas Community
Foundation, Inc.
1400 W. Markham, Suite 206
Little Rock, AR 72201
501/372-1116
Fax: 501/372-1166
www.arcf.org

Northwest Arkansas Community
Foundation
800 Founders Park Drive East
Springdale, AR 72762
479/361-4624
info@nwacommunityfoundation.org
www.nwaccommunityfoundation.org

AR, LA, MS, TX
Foundation for the Mid-South
134 East Amite Street
Jackson, MS 39201
601/355-8167
Fax: 601/355-6499
www.fndmidsouth.org

California
Statewide
The Women's Foundation of California
340 Pine Street, Suite 302
San Francisco, CA 94104
415/837-1113
Fax: 415/837-1144
www.womensfoundca.org

L.A. County California Community
Foundation
445 South Figueroa Street, Suite 3400
Los Angeles, CA 90071-1638
213/413-4130
Fax: 213/622-2979
info@ccf-la.org
www.calfund.org

Alameda, Contra Costa, Marin,
Napa, San Francisco, San Mateo,
Santa Clara, Solano, and
Sonoma counties
Horizons Foundation
870 Market Street, Suite 728
San Francisco, CA 94102
415/398-2333
Fax: 415/398-4733
info@horizonsfoundation.org
www.horizonsfoundation.org

San Diego Foundation for Change
3758 30th Street
San Diego, CA 92104
619/692-0527
info@foundation4change.org
www.foundation4change.org

Colorado
Statewide
Chinook Fund
2418 West 32nd Avenue
Denver, CO 80211
303/455-6905
Fax: 303/477-1617
office@chinookfund.org
www.chinookfund.org

Colorado Springs Community Trust Fund
PO Box 1443
Colorado Springs, CO 80901
713/389-1251

The Summit Foundation
108 N. French Street
PO Box 4000
Breckenridge, CO 80424
Telephone: 970/453-5970
Fax: 970/453-1423
sumfound@summitfoundation.org
www.summitfoundation.org

Connecticut
The Community Foundation for
Greater New Haven
70 Audubon Street
New Haven, CT 06510
Telephone: 203/777-2386
Fax: 203-/787-6584
www.cfgnh.org

Hartford Foundation for Public Giving
10 Columbus Boulevard, 8th Fl.
Hartford, CT 06106
860/548-1888
Fax: 860/524-8346
hfpg@hfpg.org
www.hfpg.org

The Torrington Area Foundation for
Public Giving
32 City Hall Avenue
PO Box 1144
Torrington, CT 06790
860/626-1245
Fax: 860/489-7517
info@tafpg.org
www.tafpg.org

Delaware
Main Office
Delaware Community Foundation
PO Box 1636
Wilmington, DE 19899
302/571-8004
Fax: 302/571-1553
info@delcf.org
www.delcf.org

Southern Delaware Office
#36 The Circle
Georgetown, DE 19947
302/856-4393
Fax: 302/856-4367
info@delcf.org
www.delcf.org

District of Columbia
The Community Foundation for the
National Capital Region
1201 15th Street, NW
Suite 420
Washington, DC 20005
202/955-5890
Fax: 202/955-8084
www.cfncr.org

Florida
Community Foundation of Broward
1401 East Broward Boulevard, Suite 100
Fort Lauderdale, Florida 33301
954/761-9503
Fax 954/761-7102
info@cfbroward.org
www.cfbroward.org

Community Foundation of
Central Florida
1411 Edgewater Drive, Suite 203
Orlando, FL 32804
407/872-3050
Fax 407/425-2990
info@cfcflorida.org
www.cfcflorida.org

Pinellas County Community Foundation
5200 East Bay Drive, Suite 202
Clearwater, FL 33764
727/446-0058
Fax: 727/446-0948
info@pinellasccf.org
www.pinellasccf.org

Georgia
Community Foundation for
Greater Atlanta, Inc.
50 Hurt Plaza, Suite 449
Atlanta, GA 30303
404/688-5525
Fax: 404/688-3060
info@atlcf.orgwww.atlcf.org

Community Foundation of
Central Georgia
277 Martin Luther King Jr. Boulevard,
Suite 303
Macon, GA 31201-3489
478/750-9338
Toll Free: 866/750-9338
Fax: 478/38-9214
www.cfcga.org

The Savannah Foundation
7393 Hodgson Memorial Drive, Suite 204
Savannah, GA 31406
912/921-7700
Fax: 912/921-3230

Hawaii
Hawaii Community Foundation
Oahu
1164 Bishop Street, Suite 800
Honolulu, Hawaii 96813
808/537-6333
Toll Free: 888/731-3863
Fax: 808/521-6286
www.hawaiicommunityfoundation.org

Hawaii Island
65–1279 Kawaihae Road
Parker Square Suite 203
Kamuela, Hawaii 96743
808/885-2174
Toll Free: 888/731-3863
Fax: 808/885-1857

Kauai
4370 Kukui Grove Street, Suite 207
Lihue, Hawaii 96766
808/245-4585
Toll Free: 888/731-3863
Fax: 808/245-5189

Maui County
(includes Lanai and Molokai)
2241B Vineyard Street
Wailuku, Hawaii 96793
808/242-6184
Toll Free: 888/731-3863
Fax: 808/242-1505

Idaho
Statewide Idaho Community Foundation
210 West State Street
Boise, Idaho 83702
208/342-3535
Fax: 208/342-3577
Toll Free 800/657-5357
info@idcomfdn.org; grants@idcomfdn.org
www.idcomfdn.org

Teton County, ID; Teton County, WY
Community Foundation of Jackson Hole
255 E. Simpson Street
PO Box 574
Jackson, WY 83001
307/739-1026
Fax: 307/734-2841
info@cfjacksonhole.org
www.cfjacksonhole.org

Canyon County, excluding city of Nampa
Caldwell Community Foundation, Inc.
PO Box 1358
Caldwell, ID 83606-1358
208/459-0091

Eastern Washington and the
Idaho Panhandle
Foundation Northwest
Old City Hall
North 221 Wall Street, Suite 624
Spokane, WA 99201-0826
509/624-2606
Toll Free outside of Spokane: 888-267-5606
Fax: 509/624-2608
admin@foundationnw.org
www.foundationnw.org

Illinois
The Aurora Foundation
111 W. Downer Place, Stuie 312
Aurora, IL 60506-5136
630/896-7800
Contact: Sharon Stredde, C.E.O., Pres.,
and Secy.
info@aurorafdn.org
sstredde@aurorafdn.org
grant@aurorafdn.org
www.aurorafdn.org

The Chicago Community Trust
111 East Wacker Drive, Suite 1400
Chicago, IL 60601
312/616-8000
Fax: 312/616-7955
info@cct.org
www.cct.org

The Community Foundation of
Northern Illinois
946 North Second Street
Rockford, IL 61107
815/962-2110
Fax: 815/962-2116
www.cfnil.org

The Create Foundation
105 North Harvest Crest Court
Highland, IL. 62249
618/558-0054
www.createfoundation.org

Indiana
The Blue River Foundation, Inc.
54 W. Broadway, Suite 1
PO Box 808
Shelbyville, IN 46176
317/392-7955
Fax: 317/392-4545
www.blueriverfoundation.com

Central Indiana Community Foundation
(Main Office)
615 North Alabama Street, Suite 199
Indianapolis, IN 46204-1498
317/634-2423
Fax 317/684-0943
www.cicf.org

Heritage Fund of Bartholomew
County, Inc.
538 Franklin Street
PO Box 1547
Columbus, IN 47201
812/376-7772
Fax: 812/376-0051
www.heritagefundbc.com

Iowa
Community Foundation of
Greater Dubuque
Dubuque Building, Suite 195
700 Locust Street
Dubuque, Iosa 52001
563/588-2700
Fax: 563/583-6619
www.dbqfoundation.org/index.cfm

The Greater Cedar Rapids Community
Foundation
200 First Street S.W.
Cedar Rapids, IA 52404
319/366-2862
Fax: 319/366-2912
www.gcrcf.org

Siouxland Community Foundation
505 Fifth Street, Suite 412
Sioux City, IA 51101
712/293-3303
office@siouxlandcommunityfoundation.org
www.siouxlandcommunityfoundation.org

Iowa West Foundation
25 Main Place, Suite 550
Council Bluffs, IA 51503
712/309-3003
www.iowawestfoundation.org

Kansas
E. Kemper Carter and Anna Curry Carter
Community Memorial Trust
c/o UMB, N.A.
PO Box 419692
Kansas City, MO 64141-6692
816/860-7711

Greater Salina Community Foundation
113 North Seventh, Suite 201
PO Box 2876
Salina, KS 67402-2876
785/823-1800
communityfoundation@gscf.org
www.gscf.org

McPherson County Community
Foundation
206 South Main
McPherson, KS 67460
620/245-9070
1/800/245-9070
www.mcphersonfoundation.org

Wichita Community Foundation
200 W. Douglas, Suite 250
Wichita, KS 67202
316/264-4880
Fax: 316/264-7592
wcf@wichitacf.org
www.wichitacf.org

Kentucky
Appalachian counties in KY; TN; VA;
WV
Appalachian Community Fund
530 South Gay Street, Suite 700
Knoxville, TN 37902
865/523-5783
Fax: 865/523-1896
info@appalachiancommunityfund.org
www.appalachiancommunityfund.org/

Central and Eastern Kentucky
Blue Grass Community Foundation
250 W. Main Street, Suite 1220
Lexington, Kentucky 40507-1714
859/225-3343
Fax: 859/243-0770
info@bgcf.org
www.bgcf.org/

Eastern Kentucky, Southern Ohio and
Southwestern West Virginia
Foundation for the Tri-State Community,
Inc.
PO Box 2096
Ashland, KY 41105-2096
606/324-3888
Fax: 606/324-5961
www.tristatefoundation.org/

The Community Foundation of
Louisville, Inc.
Waterfront Plaza, Suite 1110
325 W. Main Street
Louisville, KY 40202-4251
502/585-4649
Fax: 502/587-7484
info@cflouisville.org
www.cflouisville.org

Louisiana
Community Foundation of Acadiana
PO Box 3892
Lafayette, LA 70502
337/266-2145
Fax 337/266-2162
www.cfacadiana.org/

Baton Rouge Area Foundation
402 N. Fourth Street
Baton Rouge, LA 70802
225/387-6126
TollFree: 877/387-6126
Fax 225/387-6153 or 225-408-8125
mail@braf.org
www.braf.org

Foundation for the Mid-South
134 East Amite Street
Jackson, MS 39201
601/355-8167
Fax: 601/355-6499
www.fndmidsouth.org

Greater New Orleans Foundation
K & B Plaza
1055 St. Charles Avenue, Suite 100
New Orleans, LA 70130
504/598-4663
Fax 504/598-4676
info@gnof.org
www.gnof.org

Maine
The Maine Community Foundation, Inc.
245 Main Street
Ellsworth, ME 04605
207/667-9735
Toll Free: 877/700-6800
Fax: 207/667-0447
info@mainecf.org

Portland mailing address:
1 Monument Way, Suite 200
PO Box 7380
Portland, ME 04101
207/761-2440
Fax: 207/773-8832
www.mainecf.org

Maryland
Community Foundation of Carroll
County, Inc.
255 Clifton Boulevard
Westminster, MD 21157
410/876-5505
Fax: 410/851-9031
info@carrollcommunityfoundation.org
www.carrollcommunityfoundation.org

Community Foundation of the Eastern
Shore, Inc.
1324 Belmont Avenue
Salisbury, MD 21804
410/742-9911
cfes@cfes.org
www.cfes.org

The Community Foundation of Frederick
County, MD, Inc.
312 E. Church Street
Frederick, MD 21701
301/695-7660
Contact: Elizabeth Y. Day, Pres.
Fax: 301/695-7775
info@cffredco.org
www.cffredco.org

Massachusetts
Berkshire Taconic Community Foundation
271 Main Street, Suite 3
Great Barrington, MA 01230
413/528-8039
Fax: 413/528-8158
info@berkshiretaconic.org
www.berkshiretaconic.org

Boston Foundation, Inc.
75 Arlington Street, 10th Floor
Boston, MA 02116
617/338-1700
Fax: 617/838-1604
info@tbf.orgwww.tbf.org

Cambridge Community Foundation
99 Bishop Allen Drive
Cambridge, MA 02139
617/576-9966
Fax: 617/876-8187
cambridgecf@igc.org

Greater Worcester Community
Foundation, Inc.
370 Main Street, Suite 650
Worcester, MA 01608-1738
508/755-0980
www.greaterworcester.org

Michigan
Community Foundation of the Upper
Peninsula
2500 7th Avenue South, Suite 103
Escanaba, MI 49829-1176
906/789-5972
Fax: 906/786-9124
cfup@chartermi.net
www.cfup.org

Community Foundation for
Southeastern Michigan
333 W. Fort Street, Suite 2010
Detroit, MI 48226
313/ 961-6675
Fax: 313-961-2886
cfsem@cfsem.org
www.cfsem.org

Kalamazoo Community Foundation
151 S. Rose Street, Suite 332
Kalamazoo, MI 49007
269/381-4416
Fax: 269/381-3146
info@kalfound.orgwww.kalfound.org

Saginaw Community Foundation
100 S. Jefferson Avenue, Suite 201
Saginaw, MI 48607
989/755-0545
Fax 989/755-6524
info@saginawfoundation.org
www.saginawfoundation.org

Minnesota
Minnesota Community Foundation/
The St. Paul Foundation
55 5th Street East, Suite 600
St. Paul, MN 55101-1797
651/224-5463
Toll Free : 800–875-6167
Fax: 651/224-9502
inbox@mncommunityfoundation.org
www.mncommunityfoundation.org

Rochester Area Foundation
2200 2nd Street Southwest, Suite 300
Rochester, MN 55902-4125
507/282-0203
Fax 507/282-4938
info@rochesterarea.org
www.rochesterarea.org

West Central Initiative
1000 Western Avenue
Fergus Falls, MN 56537
218/739-2239
Toll Free: 800/735-2239
Fax: 218/739-5381
grants@wcif.org
www.wcif.org

Mississippi
Community Foundation of East
Mississippi, Inc.
PO Box 865
Meridian, MS 39302
601/696-3035
www.cfem.org

The Greater Pine Belt Community
Foundation
1507 Hardy Street, Suite 208
Hattiesburg, MS 39401
www.hattiesburgfoundation.org
601/583-6180
Fax: 601/583-6188

Missouri
Community Foundation of the Ozarks
425 East Trafficway
Springfield, MO 65806
417/864-6199
Toll Free: 888/266-6815
Fax: 417/864-8344
www.cfozarks.org

Greater Kansas City Community
Foundation
1055 Broadway, Suite 130
Kansas City, MO 64105-1595
816/842-0944
Fax: 816-842-8079
info@gkccf.org
www.gkccf.org

Greater Saint Louis Community
Foundation
319 N. 4th Street, Suite 300
St. Louis, MO 63102-1906
314/588-8200
Fax: 314/588-8088
www.gstlcf.org

Truman Heartland Community
Foundation
Commerce Bank Building
300 N. Osage Street
Independence, MO 64050
816/836-8189
Fax: 816/836-8898
www.thcf.org

Montana
Montana Community Foundation
101 N. Last Chance Gulch, Suite 211
Helena, MT 59601
406/443-8313
Fax: 406/442-0482
mtcf@mt.netwww.mtcf.org

Nebraska
Kearney Area Community Foundation
2207 Central Avenue
PO Box 1694
Kearney, NE 68848
308/237-3114
Fax: 308-237-9845
cmtyfndn@kearney.net
www.kearneyfoundation.org

La Vista Community Foundation
8116 Park View Boulevard
La Vista, NE 68128-2198
402/331-4343
Fax: 402/331-4375
www.lavistacommunityfoundation.org

Mid-Nebraska Community
Foundation, Inc.
120 N. Dewey Street
North Platte, NE 69101
308/534-3315
Fax: 308/534-6117
mncf@hamilton.net
www.midnebraskafoundation.org

West Point Community Foundation
PO Box 65
West Point, NE 68788-0065

Nevada
Statewide
Nevada Community Foundation, Inc.
300 S. Fourth Street, Suite 1009
Las Vegas, NV 89101
702/892-2326
Fax: 702/892-8580
info@nevadacf.org
www.nevadacf.org

Community Foundation of
Western Nevada
1885 S. Arlington Avenue, Suite 103
Reno, NV 89509
775/333-5499
Fax 775/333-5487
info@cfwnv.orgwww.cfwnv.org

Lake Tahoe Community Trust
PO Box 9281
Incline Village, NV 89452
775/823-4810
Fax: 775/831-8892

Parasol Foundation, Inc.
948 Incline Way
Incline Village, NV 89451
775/298-0100
Fax: 775/ 298-0099
info@parasol.orgwww.parasol.org

New Hampshire
Statewide
The New Hampshire Charitable
Foundation
37 Pleasant Street
Concord, NH 03301-4005
603/225-6641
Fax: 603/225-1700
info@nhcf.org

NHCF-Piscataqua Region application
address: 446 Market Street
Portsmouth, NH 03801

NHCF-Upper Valley Region application
address:
16 Buck Road, Hanover, NH 03755-2700
www.nhcf.org

Dublin Community Foundation
PO Box 190
Dublin, NH 03444-0190

New Jersey
Community Foundation of New Jersey
35 Knox Hill Road
PO Box 338
Morristown, NJ 07963-0338
973/267-5533
Toll Free: 800-659-5533
Fax: 973/267-2903
info@cfnj.orgwww.cfnj.org

Princeton Area Community
Foundation, Inc.
15 Princess Road
Lawrenceville, NJ 08648
609/219-1800
Fax: 609/2199-1850
info@pacf.org
www.pacf.org

The Summit Area Public Foundation
PO Box 867
Summit, NJ 07902-0867
908/277-1422

The Westfield Foundation
PO Box 2295
Westfield, NJ 07091
908/233-9787
Email:foundation@westfieldnj.com
www.westfieldnj.com/wf/

New Mexico
Santa Fe Community Foundation
PO Box 1827
Santa Fe, NM 87504-1827
505/988-9715
Fax: 505/988-1829
www.santafecf.org

Carlsbad Foundation
116 S. Canyon Street
Carlsbad, NM 88220
505/887-1131

El Paso Community Foundation
PO Box 272
El Paso, TX 79943-0272
915/533-4020
Fax: 915/532-0716
info@epcf.org
www.epcf.org

West Texas and Southeast New Mexico
Permian Basin Area Foundation
200 North Lorraine, Suite 500
Midland, Texas 79701
432/617-3213
Fax: 432/617-0151
www.pbaf.org

New York
Adirondack Community Trust
2884 Saranac Avenue
Lake Placid, NY 12946
518/523-9904
Fax: 518/523-9905
info@generousact.org
www.generousact.com

Chautauqua Region Community
Foundation, Inc.
418 Spring Street
Jamestown, NY 14701
716/661-3390/3392
Fax: 716/488-0387
www.crcfonline.org

Long Island Community Foundation
Nassau Hall
1864 Muttontown Road
Syosset, NY 11791
516/348-0575
Fax: 516/348-0570
www.licf.org

The New York Community Trust
909 Third Avenue, 22nd Floor
New York, NY 10022
212/686-0010
Fax: 212/532-8528
info@nycommunitytrust.org
grants@nycommunitytrust.org
www.nycommunitytrust.org

North Carolina
Community Foundation of Greater
Greensboro
Foundation Place
330 S. Greene Street, Suite 100
Greensboro, NC 27401
336/379-9100
Fax: 336/378-0725
info@cfgg.org
www.cfgg.org

Community Foundation of Southeastern
North Carolina
Chandler's Wharf
225 South Water Street
Wilmington, NC 28401
910/251-3911
Fax: 910/251-7782
info@communityfoundationsenc.org
www.communityfoundationsenc.org

Cumberland Community Foundation
PO Box 2345
Fayetteville, NC 28302
910/483-4449
Fax: 901/483-2905
www.cumberlandcf.org

Triangle Community Foundation
324 Blackwell, Street, Suite 1220
Durham, NC 27701
919/474-8370
Fax: 919/941-9208
info@trianglecf.org
www.trianglecf.org

North Dakota
Community Foundation of Grand Forks,
East Grant Forks and Region
412 Demers Avenue
Grand Forks, ND 58201-4508
701/746-0668
Fax: 701/746-6454
sheilabruhn@netscape.net

Fargo-Moorhead Area Foundation
502 1st Avenue North, Suite 202
Fargo, ND 58102-4804
701/234-0756
office@areafoundation.org
www.areafoundation.org

North Dakota Community Foundation
309 North Mandan Street, Suite 2
PO Box 387
Bismarck, ND 58502-0387
701/222-8349
www.ndcf.net

Ohio
Akron Community Foundation
345 W. Cedar Street
Akron, OH 44307-2407
330/376-8522
acfmail@akroncommunityfdn.org
www.akroncommunityfdn.org

Bryan Area Foundation, Inc.
102 N. Main Street
PO Box 651
Bryan, OH 43506
419/633-1156
baf@williams-net.com
www.bryanareafoundation.org

The Greater Cincinnati Foundation
200 W. 4th Street
Cincinnati, OH 45202-2602
513/241-2880
Fax: 513/852-6886
info@greatercincinnatifdn.org
www.greatercincinnatifdn.org

The Youngstown Foundation
PO Box 1162
Youngstown, OH 44501
330/744-0320
Fax: 330/744-0344
info@youngstownfoundation.org
www.youngstownfoundation.org

Oklahoma
Enid Community Foundation
PO Box 263
Enid, OK 73702
580/234-3988
Fax: 580/234-3311
mary@enidcommunityfoundation.com
www.enidcommunityfoundation.com/

Oklahoma City Community Foundation
1000 North Broadway
Oklahoma City, OK 73102
405/235-5603
info@occf.org
www.occf.org/occf/index.php

Tulsa Community Foundation
7020 South Yale, Suite 600
Tulsa, OK 74136
918/494-8823
info@tulsacf.org
www.tulsacf.org

Oregon
Statewide
The Oregon Community Foundation
1221 S.W. Yamhill, Suite 100
Portland, OR 97205
503/227-6846
Fax: 503/274-7771
info@ocf1.org
www.ocf1.org

Four Way Community Foundation
PO Box 652
Grants Pass, OR 97528-0056
541/479-9775

The Salem Foundation
c/o Pioneer Trust Bank, N.A.
PO Box 2305
Salem, OR 97308
503/363-3136
Contact: Carol Herman
salemfoundation@pioneertrustbank.com

Pennsylvania
Berks County Community Foundation
501 Washington Street, Suite 801
PO Box 212
Reading, PA 19603-0212
610/685-2223
Fax: 610/685-2240
info@bccf.org
www.bccf.org

Centre County Community
Foundation, Inc.
PO Box 648
State College, PA 16804-0648
814/237-6229
Fax: 814/237-2624
info@centrecountycf.org
www.centrecountycf.org

The Erie Community Foundation
459 W. 6th Street
Erie, PA 16507
814/454-0843
www.cferie.org

York County Community Foundation
14 W. Market Street
York, PA 17401
717/848-3733
Fax: 717/854-7231
info@yorkfoundation.org
www.yccf.org

Puerto Rico
Puerto Rico Community Foundation, Inc.
PO Box 70362
San Juan, PR 00936-8362
787/721-1037
Fax: 787/721-1673
fcpr@fcpr.og
www.fcpr.org

Rhode Island
The Rhode Island Foundation
(also known as The Rhode Island
Community Foundation)
1 Union Station
Providence, RI 02903
401/274-4564
Fax: 401/331-8085
www.rifoundation.org

South Carolina
Central Carolina Community Foundation
2711 Middleburg Drive, Suite 213
Columbia, SC 29204
803/254-5601
Fax: 803/799-6663
info@yourfoundation.org
www.yourfoundation.org

Community Foundation of Greater
Greenville
27 Cleveland Street, Suite 101
Greenville, SC 29601
864/233-5925
Fax: 864/242–9292
info@cfgg.comwww.cfgg.com

Community Foundation of the
Lowcountry
4 Northridge Drive, Suite A
PO Box 23019
Hilton Head Island, SC 29925-3019
843/681-9100
Fax: 843/681-9101
foundation@cf-lowcountry.org
www.cf-lowcountry.org

Foothills Community Foundation
907 N. Main Street
Anderson, SC 29622
864/222-9096
Fax: 864/222-9727
www.foothillscommunityfoundation.org

South Dakota
Statewide
South Dakota Community Foundation
207 E. Capitol Avenue
PO Box 296
Pierre, SD 57501-0296
605/224-1025
Toll Free: 800/888-1842
Fax: 605-224-5364
www.sdcommunityfoundation.org

Sioux Falls Area Community Foundation
300 N. Phillips Avenue, Suite 102
Sioux Falls, SD 57104-6035
605/336-7055
Fax: 605/336-0038
www.sfacf.org

Watertown Community Foundation
211 East Kemp Avenue
PO Box 116
Watertown, SD 57201-0116
605/882-3731
Fax: 605/753-5731
foundation@lw.net
www.watertowncommunityfoundation.org

Tennessee
The Chattanooga Christian Community
Foundation
736 Market Street, Suite 700
Chattanooga, TN 37402
423/266-5257
Fax: 423/265-0949
www.cccfdn.org

Community Foundation of Greater
Memphis
1900 Union Avenue
Memphis, TN 38104
901/728-4600
Fax: 901/722-0010
www.cfgm.org/

Community Foundation of Middle
Tennessee, Inc.
3833 Cleghorn Avenue, No. 400
Nashville, TN 37215-2519
615/321-4939
Toll Free: 888/540-5200
Fax: 615/327-2746
mail@cfmt.org
www.cfmt.org

East Tennessee Foundation
625 Market Street, Suite 1400
Knoxville, TN 37902
865/524-1223
Toll Free: 877/524-1223
Fax: 865/637-6039
www.easttennesseefoundation.org

Texas
Amarillo Area Foundation, Inc.
801 S. Fillmore, Suite 700
Amarillo, TX 79101
806/376-4521
Fax: 806/873-3656
www.amarilloareafoundation.org

Community Foundation of the Texas Hill
Country
PO Box 291354
Kerrville, TX 78029
830/896-8811
Fax: 830/792-5956
www.communityfoundation.net

San Antonio Area Foundation
110 Broadway, Suite 230
San Antonio, TX 78205-1948
210/225-2243
info@saafdn.org
www.saafdn.org

Foundation for Southeast Texas, Inc.
700 North Street, Suite C
Beaumont, TX 77701
409/833-5775
Fax: 409/833-7885
www.cfsetx.org

Vermont
Vermont Community Foundation
3 Court Street
PO Box 30
Middlebury, VT 05753
802/388-3355
Fax: 802/388-3398
info@vermontcf.org
www.vermontcf.org

Virginia
Arlington Community Foundation
2525 Wilson Boulevard
Arlington, VA 22201
703/243-4785
Fax: 703/243-4796
www.arlcf.org

Greater Lynchburg Community Trust
101 Paulette Circle, Suite B
Lynchburg, VA 24502
434/845-6500
Fax: 434/845-6530
challglct@ntelos.net
www.lynchburgtrust.org

The Virginia Beach Foundation
PO Box 4629
Virginia Beach, VA 23454
757/422-5249
Fax: 757/442-1849
mainoffice@vabeachfoundation.org
www.vabeachfoundation.org

Washington
Blue Mountain Community Foundation
8 S. 2nd, Suite 618
PO Box 603
Walla Walla, WA 99362-0015
509/529-4371
Fax: 509/529-5284
bmcf@bluemountainfoundation.org
www.bluemountainfoundation.org

Kitsap Community Foundation
PO Box 3670
Silverdale, WA 98383
360/689-3622
kcf@kitsapfoundation.org
www.kitsapfoundation.org

The Greater Tacoma Community
Foundation
950 Pacific Avenue, Suite 1220
Tacoma, WA 98402
253/383-5622
Fax: 253/272-8099
www.tacomafoundation.org

West Virginia
The Community Foundation for the
Ohio Valley
PO Box 670
Wheeling, WV 26003
304/242-3144
Fax: 304/234-4753
director@cfov.orgwww.cfov.org

The Greater Kanawha Valley Foundation
1600 Huntington Square
900 Lee Street East
Charleston, WV 25301
304/346-3620
Toll Free: 800/467-5909
Fax: 304/346-3640
tgkvf@tgkvf.orgwww.tgkvf.org

Parkersburg Area Community
Foundation
PO Box 1762
Parkersburg, WV 26102-1762
304/428-4438
Toll Free: 866/428-4438
info@pacfwv.comwww.pacfwv.com

Wisconsin
The Evjue Foundation, Inc.
1901 Fish Hatchery Road
Madison, WI 53713
www.madison.com/captimes/evjue

Greater Kenosha Area Foundation, Inc.
600 52nd Street, Suite 110
Kenosha, WI 53140
262/654-2412
Fax: 262/654-2615
email@kenoshafoundation.org
www.kenoshafoundation.org

Oshkosh Area Community Foundation
230 Ohio Street, Suite 100
Oshkosh, WI 54902
920/426-3993
info@oshkoshareaf.org
www.oshkoshareacf.org

St. Croix Community Foundation
PO Box 39
516 Second Street, Suite 214
Hudson, WI 54016
715/386-9490
Fax: 386-1250
info@scvcf.org
www.scvcf.org

Wyoming
Community Foundation of
Jackson Hole
255 E. Simpson Street
PO Box 574
Jackson, WY 83001
307/739-1026
www.cfjacksonhole.org

Appendix 6: Websites

The following list of websites is not intended to be exhaustive; there are hundreds—no, thousands—of useful sites that offer information on foundation, corporate, and government grants. We've selected a number of sites that we use extensively (and others that we use less often but think are representative). For those of you who are not experienced in Internet research, at each site we describe the first couple of steps you can take to find the information you need.

Since we wrote the first edition of this book, much has changed on the Internet—especially the sophistication of those who use the web for research. This appendix may be less useful to you now than readers told us it was then. But we've updated the material anyway for those of you who still may not be all that comfortable doing grants research online and for those of you who will just use it to get there a little faster. If you are experienced at using the Internet, you undoubtedly can find the following sites and many others on your own, using a search engine such as Google or Ask, but we hope this list makes it easier for you too. You probably don't need the tips we're providing on how to navigate each site, but we figured that you wouldn't be annoyed with us if we gave you a few helpful hints.

If you look at three or four of the sites we've listed below, you'll see how very different they are in terms of how you search for grant information. Some sites make it easy for you, while others require a little patience. Sometimes the information is right up front. You click on clearly visible words such as "grants" or "funding opportunities" on the home page, and the list pops up. At other sites, the link is still on the home page, but you can miss it if you don't scroll all the way to the bottom. And be aware that the link to funding opportunities may say something very different from "grants" (an example is a government site in which grants are in a section called "Living"). Usually you have to click through two or more links in order to find what you're looking for. Sometimes the easiest thing to do is find a "site map" or "site index," but it may not be there or may not be helpful. Sometimes there's a search engine—a small box somewhere on the home page or on another page that says "search." Putting in the keyword "grants," or more than one keyword, such as "grants AND aging," often will bring up the funding opportunities for your topic. (At most state and local government sites, "aging" alone will give you a list of services available for the elderly, but won't say anything about grants to organizations working in the field.) If "grants" doesn't bring up any relevant information, sometimes other words or phrases, such as "requests for proposals" or "funding opportunities," will get you there.

Keep in mind that websites change regularly. Sometimes you will go back to one that was . . . clunky, and find it has become streamlined and easy to use. Sometimes you may revisit a site after a few weeks and get a message that it has been updated or has changed its address. Just click on the directions that lead to the new site.

As you can see, you sometimes need to be pretty tenacious in order to figure out how to get where you need to go—but it's worth the effort once you get there. Be patient.

Two last suggestions: First, if your state or locality has an e-grants system, sign up for it immediately. Because the categories for these systems are broad (e.g., youth, aging, health), you may get a lot more announcements than just those that are appropriate for your organization, but it's well worth sifting through them to have these announcements come directly to your desk. And even if an online grant function is available and easy to use, it still won't hurt to get in touch with specific state and local agencies of interest to your organization and ask to be placed on their mailing lists.

Federal Websites

The Federal Register: www.gpoaccess.gov/fr/advanced.html. When it comes to finding federal grant opportunities, the first step is to go to the source: the *Federal Register* online. Although the federal government has worked to make it easier to access grant information through other websites (especially Grants.gov, described below), and some agencies are using their own websites instead, the *Register* is still the official daily record of all meetings, notices, regulations, and other functions of the federal government.

Follow the directions we gave in Lesson 2, and use the *Federal Register*'s Helpful Hints link at the site itself if you have questions. One suggestion for using this site (and other comprehensive government sites) is that you create and keep a list of keywords and phrases that represent the population you serve and/or the programs you operate and want to operate, and search at least once a week on each of the items in your list. This will ensure that you identify federal sources in plenty of time to prepare a proposal, and usually you can download the application forms directly from the site. If you don't have time to search so often, try pooling resources with another organization in your geographic area or field of interest.

Grants.gov: ***http://grants.gov.*** Grants.gov is a centralized grant site for the federal government. The home page has a link to grant opportunities released during the previous week (organized by agency); a search feature to focus in on specific opportunities; a list of subscriptions you can sign up for to get direct notice of grant opportunities; a list of resources, such as foundation sites, state point of contacts lists, and links to other federal sites; and grant applications, among other helpful items. Although most agencies continue to use the *Register*, some agencies have begun to post their grant opportunities to Grants.gov instead, so definitely bookmark the site and check back often.

Catalog of Federal Domestic Assistance (CFDA): ***www.cfda.gov.*** As we discussed in Lesson 2, this is another useful source for federal grant and contract information. The *Catalog* online is searchable by a variety of categories and keywords. Click on "Search for Assistance Programs" on the home page to get to the search page, then click on "Find a Grant." This brings you to a list of categories (such as Education, Health, Housing, Disaster Planning), each of which has its own subcategories (for instance, dental education and training, elementary and secondary education, emergency health services), and each subcategory has a number of grant programs. As you click through, you can find exhaustive information: type of programs funded; past, current, and estimated future funding amounts; eligibility requirements; reporting requirements; and so forth. It also has an item you'll need for your federal grant application: the CFDA number, which identifies the program. Recent updates to this site have made it a very good starting resource to get the lay of the land and find out what types of funding are available in your program areas.

But remember that *all* federal programs are listed in this directory, including many that no longer receive funding in the federal budget. If you're interested in a particular grant program, scroll down to this very important item in the Catalog description: Obligations, under Financial Information. This tells you whether funds are obligated (committed in the federal budget for the current fiscal year), and if so, how much is available. If no funds are obligated, the program is either dormant or dead. If funds are obligated, you should pursue the opportunity further in the *Federal Register*, in Grants.gov, and/or at the agency's website.

Individual Federal Agency Websites. Remember that these sites are likely to change from time to time. Most have a great deal of information beyond the availability of grants and descriptions of previous grant recipients. Some of this information may be very useful to you for your needs assessment, or just to keep up on developments in your field. The sites differ in their degree of user friendliness and the ability to customize your searches. But log on regularly to those that are of interest to your organization to see what's new. If you're not sure which agency may have information you're looking for, try Grants.gov first.

The major federal grantmaking agencies are listed below. Each federal agency has many departments, each with its own website. We're giving you the web addresses for some of the department sites that are most relevant for grants to local governments and nonprofits, but it's impossible to list all the federal sites in a book this size. For many departments of major agencies (such as Health and Human Services), you will need to click through several menus from a main site. Some of the following websites are user friendly; others are not quite so easy to navigate.

- **Department of Agriculture: www.usda.gov.** This site is easy to search by keywords (at the top left of the home page), and contains an extensive

and sometimes surprising range of grant opportunities, including some
that are not from the Department of Agriculture. On the top menu bar
is a link to "Agencies & Offices" housed under the USDA. Several of
these have links to funding opportunities in their particular issue areas.

- **Department of Commerce: www.commerce.gov.** Grants and contracts
  tend to be geared primarily to businesses (including small businesses)
  and academic research. Click on "Grant Opportunities" on the right
  side of the home page under Commerce and You. This brings you to
  www.commerce.gov/grants.html, which lists grant programs run by the
  various offices and agencies under Commerce, such as National Institute of Standards and Technology and the National Oceanic and At-
  mospheric Administration.

- **Department of Education: www.ed.gov/index.jhtml.** On the left side
  of the home page is a keyword search panel; on the right side is a link to
  "Grants to Apply for" and "Grant Opportunities." This leads you to a
  wealth of information about seeking funding from the Department of
  Education, a guide to its programs, a forecast of funding opportunities
  for the coming year, how to submit an application and policies for submitting applications electronically, links to discretionary grant application packages, and a list of *Federal Register* notices announcing funding
  opportunities.

- **Department of Energy: www.energy.gov.** Type "grants" in the search box
  on the upper right and follow the link. This page offers information about
  the agencies within DOE that give grants, such as the Office of Science.

- **Environmental Protection Agency: www.epa.gov.** Halfway down the
  home page on the right there is a link to "Grants." This brings you to a
  page that links to current funding opportunities, how to apply for EPA
  grants, grant awards, policies and regulations, and more.

- **Department of Health and Human Services: www.hhs.gov.** On the
  top panel there is a link to "Grants and Funding." This brings you to a
  page that has information about grant funding from HHS agencies as
  well as scholarships, internships, and financial aid. HHS is a huge

agency, so it pays to take the time to look through the list of agencies
and identify the areas dedicated to grants on their web pages. Below are a
few of the larger HHS agencies and their grant sites:

- **Administration for Children and Families: http://www.acf.hhs
  .gov/grants/.** Lists funding opportunities as well as additional funding
  by offices, such as the Family and Youth Services Bureau, Office of
  Family Assistance, and the Office of Refugee Resettlement.

- **Centers for Disease Control and Prevention: www.cdc.gov/about/
  funding.htm.** This takes you to the page for CDC's Procurement and
  Grants Office. There's a box called Web Resources right next to the
  heading. You can click on "PGO Grant Information" in that box,
  then on "Funding Opportunity Announcements" to get to a table
  showing requests for applications (when available) from each of the
  CDC agencies. The site also offers information about the grants process, and there's an alphabetic index where you can click on the initial letter of a topic of particular interest to you.

- **Health Resources and Services Administration: http://www.hrsa
  .gov/grants/.** You can click on the various steps of the grant application process on the right-hand side. HRSA also publishes an annual
  Grant Preview, which lists the programs it will fund during the up-
  coming fiscal year, with estimated application and award dates.

- **National Institutes of Health: http://grants1.nih.gov/grants/oer
  .htm.** This is a robust page that lists funding opportunities, awarded
  grants, NIH forms and applications, and more.

- **Substance Abuse and Mental Health Administration: www.samhsa
  .gov/grants/index.aspx.** This page has grants organized by fiscal year
  and lays out anticipated funding for the year ahead.

- **Department of Homeland Security: http://www.dhs.gov/xopnbiz/
  grants/.** The page lists grants available from some of this department's
  major agencies, including homeland security, FEMA, U.S. Fire Administration, and the National Transportation Safety Board. A lot of homeland security funding is awarded via formulas to states and large urban

areas, so one of the most helpful sources of information here may be the state contact list on this page. Each state allocates its funding differently, but at least 80 percent of all funds must be regranted to localities, which may in turn grant some funding to nonprofit organizations or other agencies. Some limited funding opportunities are aimed at nonprofits (such as a "facility hardening" grant for some jurisdictions, under which nonprofits may apply for up to $100,000 for items such as lighting and/or fencing). There are also some training and research opportunities. You might start by researching the grants listed on the DHS site, and then call or e-mail your state contact. The state contact will be able to give you the name of your local contact so you can find out how your locality is spending its homeland security dollars.

- **Department of Housing and Urban Development: www.hud.gov.**
  Halfway down the menu on the left side of the site, under "Working with HUD," is a "Grants" link. This brings you to a page with information on grants for government and nonprofit organizations, individuals, and small businesses. Both the left-hand and right-hand menus are worth exploring. The page includes links to program descriptions, funds available, assistance to grant seekers ("Resources for Individuals"), lists of awards HUD has made are available, and a "What's Hot" section that talks about HUD's e-grants initiative. The page is also available in Spanish.

Note that HUD publishes what it calls a SuperNOFA once a year (NOFA stands for "notice of funding availability"). This combines a large number of programs into one grant announcement (a small number of programs remain outside the SuperNOFA). Nonprofit organizations that are interested in programs in the SuperNOFA need to get in touch with their local municipal housing agency, which is required to establish priorities and coordinate the application process.

- **Department of Interior: www.doi.gov.** Entering "grants" in the search function on the upper left results in links to funding programs supported by Interior. DOI offers a Spanish-language version of the site. Note that some of the departments and agencies within DOI also offer grants information. For example,

- **Fish and Wildlife Service: www.fws.gov/grants.** This agency has a good grants page that lists opportunity by eligible group (government agencies, conservation organizations, individuals, etc.), as well as by topic area.

- **Department of Justice: www.usdoj.gov/10grants/index.html.** This site gives you brief descriptions of the functions of its different offices and allows you to click on links to the websites of interest. Each of those sites offers grants information. Each site has a somewhat different search function, and sometimes you need to click through several screens, but all are relatively easy to use and allow you to click on particular grants; most also let you search by keyword. Some of these sites include:

- **Bureau of Justice Assistance: www.ojp.usdoj.gov/BJA/resource/index.html.**

  - **Bureau of Justice Statistics: www.ojp.usdoj.gov/bjs.** This site can be instrumental in gathering statistics for a needs assessment or other research-based sections of an application.

  - **COPS (Community Oriented Policing Services): www.cops.usdoj .gov/.**

  - **National Institute of Justice: http://www.ojp.usdoj.gov/nij/funding/welcome.htm.** NIJ is the research branch of DOJ and funds primarily research-focused grants.

  - **Office of Justice Programs: https://grants.ojp.usdoj.gov/#.** Lists current funding opportunities.

  - **Office of Juvenile Justice and Delinquency Prevention: http:// ojjdp.ncjrs.org/funding/funding.html.**

  - **Office for Victims of Crime: http://www.ojp.usdoj.gov/ovc/fund/ welcome.html.** Lists discretionary and formula grants, as well as other resources, such as additional funding opportunities.

- **Department of Labor: http://www.doleta.gov/grants/.** This site offers competitive grant and contract announcements, forms, and lists of grants awarded. It also includes information on the Workforce Investment Act (WIA) and other resources.

- **Institute of Museum and Library Services: www.imls.gov.** Link to grants page that lists grant programs, deadlines, applications, and grantee resources, including a good section on outcome-based evaluations.

- **National Archives and Records Administration: www.archives.gov.** Link at the bottom left corner to the grants page, which lists programmatic grants and other resources.

- **National Endowment for the Arts: www.nea.gov.** A prominent menu provides a link to a page that lets you click on one of three categories: "Apply for a Grant," "Manage Your Award," and "Recent Grants." Clicking on "Apply for a Grant" takes you to a page that lists categories of funding available; clicking on one of these categories takes you to the listing and descriptions of grants available.

- **National Endowment for the Humanities: www.neh.gov.** You can click on "Grant Management" in the center of the horizontal menu at the top of the page to get to a page that provides links to information about grants, how to apply, how to manage a grant, matching fund guidelines, and other relevant information and application forms.

- **National Science Foundation: www.nsf.gov.** A very prominent "Funding Opportunities" tab at the left of the home page takes you to a grants page for the research and education communities, which lists current grant opportunities and provides links to specific program areas. Each of the program areas also provides information on or links to funding. Alternatively, from the NSF home page, under "Looking for Funding?" go directly to the link "Find Funding Opportunities," which takes you to a page that lets you search by index, text, NSF organization, or program status. This page also offers links to guidance on proposal preparation and managing a grant award.

- **Small Business Administration: www.sba.gov/expanding/grants.html.** This is a federal grant resource site that has information about SBA grants and other federal agencies. It also has a list of some state resources.

- **Department of Transportation: www.dot.gov/ost/m60/grant**. (Website last updated in 2006.) Even with this centralized grant site, you still have to root through a lot of information to get to current grant opportunities. A better way may be accessing grant information through the individual agencies that comprise the DOT. You can find a list by clicking on "DOT Agencies" at the left of the DOT home page, www.dot.gov.

Emergency Funding

When we were doing research for the second edition, the headlines were full of natural disasters and we included some information on how you could apply for emergency funds. At the moment, the big emergencies are man-made. Nevertheless, whether you are a government or education agency or a not-for-profit, if you are involved in disaster relief, or see a need that you want to address, there are some areas to start with to seek funding. You also should go to state and local websites (some are listed in a later section) to find help or identify agencies that can give you additional information.

FEMA, www.fema.gov. The federal agency established to help individuals and organizations with disaster funding is the Federal Emergency Management Agency (FEMA). At the top left on FEMA's website, click on "Disaster Information" or go to www.disasterhelp.gov. You can find multiple resources available for different types of emergency responses to a catastrophic event. FEMA also provides a preparedness guide (*Are You Ready?*). It is primarily for individuals and families, but it may give you some pointers your organization can use in planning for a number of different types of disasters. If you work with individuals needing immediate help, you can click on "Apply for Assistance," either at disasterhelp.gov or back on FEMA's home page. This function takes you through the prescreening or application process online and offers other information about where to go for help.

State Emergency Management Offices. The state emergency management offices (SEMOs) are the agencies responsible for emergency planning and response. They also disburse FEMA or other disaster funding. They can be accessed through your state's homepage. Your jurisdiction probably also has a local or regional emergency management office that may assist in funding and have other resources available.

Federal Sites Where You May Find Information for Needs Assessments and Program Planning

Now that you know how to find federal grant opportunities, we should step back for a minute to talk about using the government agency websites (federal, state, and local) for other purposes than finding funding. There is a wealth of information on these pages that can help nonprofits and municipal agencies to develop and evaluate their programs, based on information from government research and program evaluations. Best practices in many fields often emerge from government demonstration projects. Take the time to browse all of the government sites of interest to you, to see what you can use in your programs as well as in your fundraising. Here are some other useful sites:

- For general information about the federal government, across all categories and agencies (including a site for grants by type of funding), try *http://www.usa.gov/*. Its home page has a link to a "Reference Center and General Government" under "Government Information by Topic," which you may want to explore. It also offers links to funding opportunities by category; click on "Benefits and Grants" also under the heading "Government Information by Topic" on the home page.
- *The U.S. Census Bureau: www.census.gov.* Although the Census Bureau is a part of the Department of Commerce, it deserves and has its own independent website. This site is the key to demographics and other useful statistics for your needs statement. A nice feature is the state and county "Quickfacts" right on the home page.
- A helpful site related to education is the National Center for Education Statistics, *www.nces.ed.gov.* This has lots of statistics, such as math and reading scores and school and crime statistics.

- After-school program information: ***www.afterschool.gov.*** This is an interagency site with research, statistics, funding (check out "How to Get Money" under "Running a Program" on the home page—a site searchable by the type of organization you are and the type of program you're interested in), and a lot more.

State and Local Websites

As noted in Lesson 2, the best place to start looking for state information is the Grantsmanship Center's link: ***www.tgci.com/funding/states.asp***. This takes you to a map of the United States that connects you to each official state site via one convenient location.

Following is a partial list of state and local websites (many of them found through the Grantsmanship Center site, and provided here as examples of the ways you may need to search online). Almost all are set up primarily to offer information about government services in each area. Most also provide some information about grant opportunities for local government agencies and not-for-profits. In some of them, you have to read through press releases to find any mention of grants. If your state is not here, find it at the Grantsmanship Center map site or through any search engine, then read through the search suggestions from some of the other sites here to see how to approach yours. Remember that you may have to try several routes. Be patient about searching before you decide that you can't find the information you're looking for online. Again, keep in mind that websites are constantly being updated, and more information is constantly being added, so if you search your state's website and don't find grants information, or if there isn't much there, or if it's hard to find easily, keep checking back. One day, you will be pleasantly surprised.

And to keep attuned to the broader political and social climate in which you're operating, become familiar with all the relevant information available on your state's website, not just grants information.

- ***Alaska: http://alaska.fws.gov/grants***. Highlights grants and partnerships from the U.S. Fish and Wildlife Service–Alaska region. Also check out http://www.fundsnetservices.com/searchresult.php?sbcat_id=51.

- *Arkansas: http://www.arkansas.gov.* This takes you to a searchable database of available funding opportunities by name and state agency.

- *California: www.state.ca.us.* Although there is a lot of useful information here, it doesn't offer specific material for the grant seeker. You probably should go directly to the source: Contact those state agencies that are most relevant to your organization, and ask to receive grant announcements. One way in which this site may help is that if you search on "grants" you find a list of press releases announcing grants from various state agencies. You might look through these for information about which agencies fund programs of interest to you.

- *City of Los Angeles: www.ci.la.ca.us.* Los Angeles lists its grant opportunities through the Los Angeles Business Assistance Virtual Network (www.labavn.org). There is a searchable database titled "RFP Search" that allows you to search by agency, date, program type, etc. There is a disclaimer on the site that the information is only as up-to-date as that of the individual agencies, so it is a good idea to check out specific agencies you are interested in working with as well.

- *Florida: www.myflorida.com.* There is no central grants page, but if you type "grants" into the search function, you get links to several agencies, including arts, education, cultural affairs, and health and human services. Your best bet is probably to seek out the agencies you are interested in and contact them directly to ensure you are on their mailing list.

- *Illinois: www.illinois.gov/living/grants.cfm.* This has a comprehensive listing of available state and federal grants, as well as other resources.

- *Iowa: www.iowagrants.org.* This links you to Iowa's Grant Enterprise Management System. This system is designed to provide information on finding and applying for grants. It also maintains a list of competitive grant applications. It shows federal and foundation grant applications that Iowa state agencies are applying for. This is helpful because these funds are often then granted by the state to local government and nonprofit agencies. The site also shows the status of the applications (funded, denied, applied for, intend to apply). It also gives the contact person in the state government.

Iowa is also working on a common web-based grant application and review process that state and local government agencies will use when awarding grants. It also lists grant training opportunities given by the state, such as seeking, writing or managing grants. There is a tutorial that is helpful—even if you are not seeking grants in Iowa—including explaining what a DUNS number is, research data sources of information on developing a proposal, a glossary, and more.

- *Kansas: http://www.governor.ks.gov/.* The Kansas Governor's Federal & Other Grants Program is responsible for the administration of grants that fund organizations that enhance the criminal justice system, improve public safety, and support crime victim services and drug and violence-prevention programs. Grant funds are awarded to state and local units of government and to nonprofit organizations throughout the state. The Federal Grants Program also staffs the Kansas Criminal Justice Coordinating Council, which is responsible for oversight of six federal grants. The program is also responsible for the administration of the National Governors Association grant for workforce development. The Federal & Other Grants Program also offers training opportunities. (Note: the website address changes with the appointment of new governors. Another pertinent website is https://www.accesskansas.org/ssrv-ksgrants/contact.do).

- *Louisiana: http://www.louisiana.gov/.* This brings you to the Louisiana home page, where you will find a search function on the upper right. Searching for "grants" brings you to a page that lists a number of categories; clicking on any of these gets you to additional information, but not all of them contain grants information. Try "grants" and another keyword or phrase such as "grants, nonprofit" or "grants, human services."

- *Maine: www.maine.gov.* Typing "grants" into the search function at the upper right brings up information from many of Maine's state agencies.

- *Maryland: www.gov.state.md.us/grants.html.* The Governor's Grants Office coordinates state agencies in identifying and winning competitive federal grants; assists local governments and community-based organizations in identifying federal grant opportunities and state or foundation grants; provides grant-writer training and technical assistance; and more. For state funding, click on the icon for "Redbook" at the left to get to the Catalog of State Assistance Programs, then click on "Check here to conduct a search . . . by subject."

- *Minnesota: www.state.mn.us.* There's no central grants page, but you can find a lot of information though the search engine, or by exploring the headings at the top of the page (education, health and safety, natural resources, and so forth). Each of these pages has a grants link.

- *Montana: www.montana.gov/doa/gsd/osbs/default.asp.* This is a page set up for bids and proposals. Search by topic area or state agency of interest. For example, a search of health-related services brought up six opportunities, although some of the deadlines had already passed.

- *New Hampshire: www.nh.gov.* Click on "Business" at the left, then on "Doing business with New Hampshire," then "Sell to state or federal government," then "Selling to state government." Finally, you'll find "Current bids and proposals," and when you click here you come to a list of requests for proposals and requests for bids. This site really does appear to be for businesses rather than nonprofits. But check it out from time to time.

- *New Jersey: http://www.nj.gov.* Lists information on available state grants by topic area. Clicking on an item of interest brings up additional information.

- *New York: www.nysegov.com.* There is a link to "Funding Programs" and one for "Grants." Both links bring you to current funding opportunities in individual agency websites and to other information, forms, and so on.

- *City of New York: nyc.gov/html/selltonyc/html/rfps.html.* This provides a list of RFPs the city is currently seeking to fund. However, whenever we visited this site, we noticed that it did not include some funding opportunities we knew were available at the time, so we suggest that you familiarize yourself with the *City Record*, http://a856-internet .nyc.gov/nycvendoronline/home.html, a hard copy and online daily newspaper that is akin to the *Federal Register*. Among other notices, the *Record* lists the city's contracting opportunities. (Note that the city calls its grants "contracts.") Many city agencies do list their contracting opportunities on their own web pages, so it is a good idea to check them out regularly and ask to be put on their mailing lists.

- *Pennsylvania: www.state.pa.us.* Searching the site brings up mainly educational grants.

- *Philadelphia: www.phila.gov.* At the right of the home page is a list of Quick Hits. Clicking on "Request for Proposals" brings you to a list of RFPs from different agencies. Don't try to use the search function.

- *Texas: www.texas.gov.* We didn't find a specific grants page, but searching by topic brings up grant opportunities in individual agencies.

- *Washington: http://access.wa.gov/.* Searching for grants at the home page brings up opportunities and information about grant programs.

- *Washington, D.C.: http://opgd.dc.gov/opgd/site/default.asp.* The Mayor's Office of Partnerships and Grants Development (OPGD) seeks to establish partnerships between public and private for-profit and nonprofit organizations to help them obtain financial support and technical assistance from public and private sources. This site lists grant opportunities at the district and federal levels, as well as from private sources, and has information about nonprofit and faith-based support services.

- *Wyoming: www-wsl.state.wy.us/sis/grants/index.html.* This is a catalog of Wyoming state grants, and also boasts a Wyoming foundation directory.

Foundation Research

The Foundation Center: www.foundationcenter.org. As we said in Lesson 2, we were disappointed to find that much that once was free at the Foundation Center website now is by subscription or for sale. Still, this is the first place to begin your research on foundations and corporate giving in any area of the country. The site provides links to individual foundations' websites, offers news about foundations and giving trends, links to research materials, links to foundations' 990 tax forms, and more.

For example, click on "Find Funders" at the top of the home page, then on "Foundation Finder." This allows you to search for a specific funder and link to each foundation's website. You can do the same to find the tax returns for a foundation of interest.

- *fconline.fdncenter.org.* The Foundation Directory Online has a basic annual subscription of $19.95 a month or $195 a year. It allows you to search by a number of foundation characteristics, including foundation name, foundation city, geographic area in which it makes grants, type of funding available, foundation priorities, trustees and officers, and more.

The University of Wisconsin Grants Information Center, a cooperating collection of the Foundation Center Library Network: www.library.wisc.edu/ libraries/Memorial/grantshp.htm. This site has everything from funder databases and technical advice to listings of workshops and seminars in Wisconsin; from how to start a foundation to where to find 990s. It has links to federal funding information. It also has several subscription services, including a link to foundation grants for individuals, one to funding for graduate students, and one to scholarships for overseas study. Some sites are available only to university users or to Wisconsin individuals and organizations, and some of the resources that are listed are only available on CD-ROM, diskette, or hard copy.

The Grantsmanship Center: www.tgci.com. The Grantsmanship Center, based in California, offers a fine range of technical assistance to nonprofits, most now requiring purchase or fees. Information available at the website includes schedules of workshops and seminars, publications, and other resources. One of these resources is a searchable site containing abstracts of winning federal grant proposals and offering CDs for sale that contain the top-scoring proposals by topic. These are pricey, but maybe less costly than a trip to Washington, D.C., or Atlanta, or some other location where you can examine the winning proposals at no charge. Some subordinate sites include:

- *www.tgcigrantproposals.com.* This is the location that offers summaries of winning proposals online and tips about how to win grants.
- *http://www.tgci.com/funding.shtml.* This lists community foundations by state, similar to the listing we've provided in Appendix 5. At this page, every community foundation that has a site is listed; otherwise, other contact information is given.
- *www.tgci.com/intl/index.asp.* This site lets you find corporate and foundation giving in Canada, Central and South America and the Caribbean, Europe, the Middle East, Africa, Asia, Australia, New Zealand, and the Pacific Islands.

Fundsnet Services: http:/www.fundsnetservices.com. This site lists fundraising resources by topic (arts, children, computers and technology, etc.) and includes foundation, government, and corporate funders, along with organizations that provide in-kind resources such as computers. It has sections on international funding funders in Canada, the United Kingdom, and Australia. It also includes grant-writing resources and a list of community foundations.

- *www.fundsnetservices.com/corp02.htm* lists topics you can click on specifically to find corporations that give for that purpose ("youth and families" only brought up 34 listings). It also allows you to click on a letter of the alphabet that brings up corporations under that letter, with a brief description of each corporation's giving priority and a link to the corporation's website.

GrantSmart: www.grantsmart.org. You used to be able to find the tax reports of foundations and nonprofit organizations here, but the site has been taken over by another organization and appears not to have been updated recently.

Regional Forum of Grantmakers: http://www.givingforum.org/s_forum. This is a membership site for foundations, but there is information that may be of interest to grant seekers, including giving trends and links to tools that regional associations make available for grant seekers.

Websites for Individual Grant Seekers

Here are just a few websites that may be of interest to individual grant seekers:

- *http://gtionline.fdncenter.org. Grants and scholarships for individuals.* This site requires a subscription that costs $9.95 a month, but is probably well worth it for anyone looking for grants, scholarships, and fellowships, including students, artists, writers, researchers, and others.

- *www.lib.msu.edu/harris23/grants/3subject.htm.* This compilation of websites includes funding opportunities for individuals, including financial aid or scholarships for students. You can search by academic level, population group, or educational subject. Clicking on "music" brought up 72 funds and funding programs for music education and related projects and links to databases and books on this subject. Examples of the websites listed include Aaron Copland Fund for Music Performing Ensembles Program, Chopin Foundation of the United States, and the National Federation of Music Clubs Competitions and Awards.

- *www.hhmi.org/grants/individuals.* The Howard Hughes Medical Institute (HHMI) grants support promising biomedical research scientists working outside the United States, medical and dental students seeking research training, and leading research scientists who are developing new approaches to undergraduate science education. "HHMI no longer offers predoctoral and postdoctoral fellowships for research training."

- *http://grants.library.wisc.edu/individuals/individuals.html.* The University of Wisconsin-Madison's grants information collection has a section for individuals.
- *www.chesapeake.va.us/services/depart/finearts/grants.shtml.* The Chesapeake Virginia Fine Arts Commission provides arts education grants to individuals and also project and challenge grants to nonprofit cultural and fine arts organizations and city agencies.
- *www.florida-arts.org/grants/forindividuals.htm.* The Florida Division of Cultural Affairs funds The Individual Artist Fellowship Program to recognize the creation of new artworks by individuals of exceptional talent and demonstrated ability. Fellowship awards support the general artistic and career advancement of the individual artist.

Appendix 7: Answers to Pop Quizzes

Lesson 1: Who Am I (and What in the World Do I Want to Do?)

Multiple Choice

1. a (Small grassroots organizations should "think small" while they are small.)
2. b (The 501(c)(3) proves to funders that you're a tax-exempt organization.)
3. a (The key is "not-for-profits of all kinds"; not specific types of not-for-profits.)
4. d (Hey—if you don't know who you are, funders won't either.)

Essay Questions

(Example for a grassroots organization) The Elm Street Garden Association is a grassroots organization whose mission is to plant flowers along the length of Elm Street every spring. The association needs money for seeds and plants, and to replace some very old gardening tools this coming spring.

(Example for a larger not-for-profit organization) The Rosemont Teen Center is a 501(c)(3) not-for-profit organization with a twelve-person board comprising of community residents and a professional staff of one full-time teen center director and a part-time staff of four youth workers. The center serves 120 teenagers in athletics and arts programs each year and needs money to hire a part-time teacher to start a drama program.

(Example for a government agency) The Rosemont Department of Health (DOH), an agency in a city of 55,000, addresses all the health and mental health needs of Rosemont's residents. DOH plans to start an asthma initiative for young children living on the north side of the city.

Lesson 2: Wait a Second—What Is a Grant . . . And Where Do I Get One?

Multiple Choice

1. d (So read the fine print in those requests for proposals.)
2. d (You'll find a foundation of the right size and shape for you if you look hard enough.)
3. c (It's always good not only to do your homework but also to show grantmakers that you've done it.)
4. c (So make sure you check out the *Federal Register* often.)
5. c (Getting a track record is an important first step in grant seeking— and starting small makes sense.)

Essay Questions

(Grassroots organization) The Elm Street Garden Association needs approximately $120 to purchase seeds, plants, and gardening equipment. This is an other-than-personnel-services (OTPS) budget item; staffing is done by volunteers. The likely funders for this project are the merchants located at the east end of Elm Street.

(Larger nonprofit) The Rosemont Teen Center's drama teacher will work for approximately four hours each week, for 40 weeks, at $20/hour; the center needs

$3,200 for personnel services (PS). The most likely funders for this project are the Rosemont Community Trust, the Johnson Foundation for the Arts, and Mrs. Ann Johnson, director of the community theater company (who may provide a drama teacher in kind).

(City agency) The Rosemont Department of Health (DOH) needs $100,000 to conduct a needs assessment, provide education about asthma prevention and treatment to families and caregivers, and to treat children with asthma at day care centers and preschools. Approximately $75,000 will be used to pay part-time salaries of physicians and nurses to provide training and care; a consultant from the Rosemont Community College will conduct the needs assessment and evaluate the project ($10,000). The remaining $15,000 will be spent for printing and supplies; resource guides to be given to families; transportation expenses for staff to visit preschools and day care centers; and games and toys for children who participate in the program. The most likely funders for this project will be the state health department and the U.S. Department of Health and Human Services. The Rosemont Health Foundation may provide some funding for the resource guides, and the Broome Street Toy Shop will provide some of the toys.

Lesson 3: Making (Dollars and) Sense of Grant-Application Packages

True or False?

1. True (No matter what application packages look like, they all contain certain basic pieces of information. Some contain much, much, much more of this stuff than others.)

2. False (You can call and ask questions about the application package; different funders have different policies, but most will all answer at least some general questions.)

3. False (You are expected to answer every question or cover every topic in the grant application. If you don't understand how a question

pertains to you or your organization, you can call and ask—but it is possible that the funding source isn't right for you!)

4. False (Sure, this is America, but it's up to the grantmaker to decide whether you are an eligible applicant. So you'd better check eligibility requirements before you apply.)

5. False (It makes no sense to submit an application that asks for more money than the grantmaker indicates—it means you have ignored the guidelines or not followed directions. If the funder decides to give you more money later—well, that's another story.)

Lesson 4: Getting Ready to Write a Grant Proposal

True or False?

1. False (Be prepared to show proof of your not-for-profit status, the names and affiliations of your board members, and other materials the funder might want to see.)

2. False (Grants for individuals follow many of the same steps that grants for not-for-profits and government agencies follow. All grants require homework, and all proposals must be clear responses to certain questions.)

3. False (Not-for-profit organizations are eligible for—and win—a slew of government grants, so check out that eligibility section.)

4. False (National Endowment for the Arts is an example of a government grant for individuals. In fact, foundation funding for individuals can be much scarcer and harder to get.)

5. False (School districts should apply for the myriad grants available that will actually help them teach the three Rs, as well as science, technology, art, music . . . not to mention assist in reducing violence, substance abuse, teen pregnancy, and so forth.)

6. False (Individuals can sometimes get a grant without a 501(c)(3). Mostly, though, individuals do need to affiliate with an existing not-for-profit to be eligible for a grant.)

Essay Question

The three best ways to prepare yourself for a proposal in advance of a funding announcement are to:

- Develop and maintain solid boilerplate material, including the organization's mission, programs you run, budget, staffing, funding sources/grants, evaluations that have been conducted, and publicity documents.
- Develop and maintain collaborations within your sector (health care, youth, aging, transportation) and across other sectors (schools, other government agencies, clergy, businesses, and universities).
- (Government agency or not-for-profit) Develop and maintain up-to-the-minute files consisting of census data, needs assessments, and other statistics that you can pull out the minute a funding announcement is made.
- (Individual) Keep your portfolio of work, reviews, and other relevant materials up-to-date.

Lesson 5: Foundations of Proposal Writing

True or False?

1. False (Developing and writing a grant proposal is in no way as straightforward as filling out an application for a credit card. In no way!)
2. False (Okay, maybe it takes a little luck to win a grant . . . very little. Mainly, winning a grant takes hard work, lots of homework, good programs, great leadership, fiscal responsibility . . . well, you get the picture.)
3. False (Being greedy has no part in the grants process. Ever.)
4. False (Grant applications never say a word about abbreviations—it's one of those "intangibles"—but you shouldn't use them in your proposals.)

5. True (Most grant applications leave all decisions about hiring grant-funded staff up to you. But you must explain the qualifications of staff in your proposal.)

Lesson 6: Writing (Proposals) with Style: A Few Basic Rules

True or False?

1. False (Maybe the PC police are out of style, but sensitive language isn't.)
2. False (You can never be too organized.)
3. False (Let the facts speak for themselves.)
4. False (Save your poetry for an anthology.)
5. False (But make sure to let the funder know why it is an effective reading program.)
6. False (Be selective!)

Short Answer

1. Rule 4: Exaggeration. (If the Meridian Mews Center is known all over the world, there had better be some proof!)
2. Rule 12: Common knowledge; Rule 5: Grammar. (Everyone in the neighborhood respects . . .)
3. Rule 10: Passive voice; Rule 6: Spelling. (Meridian Mews Center's program . . .)
4. Rule 9: Adjectives; Rule 4: Exaggeration.
5. Rule 5: Grammar. (. . . neighborhood schools and churches for its activities.)
6. Rule 5: Grammar. (. . . their grades and their behavior . . .)
7. Rule 11: Acronyms. (HHS, DOJ, and DOE)
8. Rule 2: Write as you should speak ("awesome" is teen talk)
9. Rule 3: Insensitive terminology and slang. (Geezer; old folks; kids)
10. Rule 9: Adjectives; Rule 4: Exaggeration (cutting-edge; innovative)

Lesson 7: Writing with Style: Tackling the Blank Page

Editing Exercise

Item	Broken Rule No.	Correction
Paragraph 1		
My	10	The Meridian Mews Center provides. . . .
cutting-edge	4	Computer, English as a Second Language, etc. programs
kids	3	Children!
our	10	The Center's address . . .; The North Meridian Mews neighborhood . . .
smack in the heart	2	This sounds like the result of a gunshot. In the center of Metropolis is better.
Paragraph 2		
Unfortunately	8	Delete—it may be unfortunate, but let the reader decide.
handicaps	3	"Disabilities" should be used instead of handicaps."
tragic health problems	4	Delete "tragic"—it may be an exaggeration and it is a value judgment.
bunch	3	Slang—how many parents make a *bunch* of parents?
was	5	Grammatical error—"were" is correct.
kids	3	Children!
hot water	3	Adults might say this aloud, but they aren't likely to *write* it.
cops	3	Police
Paragraph 3		
kids	3	Did we say this before? CHILDREN!
Our	10	The Meridian Mews Center's programs . . .
kids	3	Never mind . . .

Item	Broken Rule No.	Correction
Paragraph 3 (*continued*)		
We	10	The Meridian Mews Center received . . .
Metropolis is very into basketball	2	Metropolis may be very into basketball, but it's better to say that Metropolis residents support professional, college, and hight school basketball teams.
Paragraph 4		
Our	10	Meridian Mews Center's Board . . .
Paragraph 5		
We	10	Meridian Mews Center receives grants . . .
DCW; ED	11	Department of Child Welfare; Education Department
a few foundations	3	This is imprecise. Is it three foundations? More? Fewer?
Paragraph 6		
has been around	2	Sounds like a lyric from a Beach Boys song. "Jane Manning has been the executive director at the Meridian Mews Center since it was created" is better.
a couple of years ago	2	Is that two years . . . or about two years . . . or a year and three months? Why not say the precise year instead?
kids	3	Hmmm
us	10	The staff . . .
We	10	The Meridian Mews Center . . .
on board	3	Social workers who work at the Center . . .
We	10	The Center . . .
their	5	Wrong one—it should be "there."

Proposal-Organizing (Short-Answer) Exercise

Outline Sections Statement Number(s)

  A. Need for the project: 1, 12, 14, 16

  B. Goals and objectives of the proposed project: 4, 6, 11, 19

  C. Project description and activities: 3, 5, 9, 11, 18

  D. Target population: 7, 22

  E. Project staffing: 17, 33

  F. Partnerships: 3, 5, 9, 11, 18

  G. Evaluation plan: 21, 25

  H. Budget information: 15, 20

  I. Sustainability of the project: 24

  J. Organization's capacity to implement the proposed project: 2, 8, 10, 13

Statements

Put the numbers of the following sentences into the correct section in the proposal outline above:

1. Although there are tutoring and recreational programs for very young children and sports and job training activities for older teenagers, boys between the ages of 13 and 16 have few structured activities after school and on weekends. (Need for the project)

2. The center's 12-member board of directors includes executives of local businesses, faculty of universities and schools, representatives of churches and hospitals, as well as two parent members. The chairman is William Jones, the chief operating officer of the Municipal Life Insurance Company of Indiana. (Organization's capacity)

3. Basketball coaches from Meridian University will teach basketball skills, teamwork, and rules of good sportsmanship to 25 boys, age 13 to 16. (Project description)

4. The basketball project will improve the boys' physical and social skills, enhance their self-esteem, improve their awareness of options for themselves, and help them control their behavior. (Goals and objectives)

5. Throughout the program, staff will work to communicate the positive impact on sports achievement of good nutrition and other healthy habits and the negative impact of substance use. (Project description)

6. By the end of the first year of the program, 80 percent of the 25 boys in the basketball project will demonstrate a significant decrease in acting-out behavior in school. (Goals and objectives)

7. The boys who will be recruited for the project live in the North Meridian Mews neighborhood of downtown Metropolis, Indiana, which has a disproportionately low income and a population that is approximately 50 percent African American, 30 percent Hispanic, and 20 percent white. (Target population)

8. Since it was founded, the center has provided services for approximately 3,000 children, teenagers, and their families, with more than 500 people participating in program activities each year. (Organization capacity)

9. Project participants will receive lessons on "dressing for success" and will participate in individual and group counseling. (Project description)

10. Executive director Jane Manning has held that position since the center was founded. A former teacher, principal, and school superintendent, she is a leader in the field of education and has been featured in news articles (for instance, in 2009, the Metropolis Star described her "generosity to the children and her enthusiasm for her work"). (Organization capacity)

11. By the end of the first month of the project, the staff of the Meridian Mews Center will recruit and hire a project director and staff for the basketball project. (Project description)

12. There are swimming programs at the YMCA, but they attract children who are younger than the ones who will participate in the basketball project. (Need)

13. The center's "all-purpose room" is large enough for all 25 boys who are in the program to participate in group activities. (Organization capacity)

14. No other local youth programs in this community have attempted to tackle the problems confronting 13-to 16-year-old boys with a history of behavior problems. (Need)

15. Facilities and resources will be donated by organizations and businesses in the community at no cost to the project. (Budget)

16. John Jones, in a study conducted in the summer of 2005, found that teenagers from North Meridian Mews were terrorizing the malls and shopping centers of the north side of Metropolis. When he interviewed the boys, almost all of the 15 teenagers he interviewed complained that they "didn't have anything else to do." (Need)

17. Experienced basketball coaches, a physical education professor, and a psychologist will participate in the basketball project activities. (Staffing)

18. Team competition will culminate in an award ceremony at which members of the winning team will receive gift certificates from a local business, Ace Sports Supplies. (Project description)

19. The overall goal of the basketball project is to increase the likelihood that the teenagers who participate in the activities will stay in school longer and become productive members of the North Meridian Mews community. (Goals and objectives)

20. The Meridian Mews Center will contribute the time of the executive director, social worker, bookkeeper, and secretary to the basketball project at no cost to the project. (Budget narrative)

21. School guidance reports and teacher evaluations will be used to measure this outcome. (Evaluation)

22. The proposed basketball project targets 25 teenage boys, between the ages of 13 and 16, with severe behavior problems and a history of acting out in school. (Target population)

23. The project director will be a licensed social worker with a minimum of three years' experience directing programs. (Staffing)

24. The Meridian Mews Center is committed to supporting the basketball project in the second year, through additional foundation grants, support from local businesses, and other approaches (see letter of commitment from the board chairman in the appendix) (Sustainability)

25. To measure whether acting-out behavior in school has been reduced for the participants of the basketball project, project staff will develop a short questionnaire that can easily be completed by the coaches, recreation specialists, teachers, and guidance counselors who work with the boys. (Evaluation)

Project Summary (Short-Answer) Exercise

1. Project Summary 1 breaks every rule in the book over and over again. Project Summary 2 follows the rules faithfully.

2. Project Summary 1 doesn't explain the program concisely; Summary 2 does.

3. Why wouldn't a funder give money to Summary 2? And why would a funder give money to Summary 1?

Lesson 8: Identifying and Documenting the Need: What Problem Will a Grant Fix?

Multiple Choice

1. d (Along with a quality program, the bottom line to winning grants is your documented "compelling need." But many funders also look for continuity of leadership.)

2. d (As good as your intuition may be, it just doesn't work as data in a grant proposal.)

3. d (Documenting need can take many forms.)

4. d (There is no rule of thumb about how many footnotes to include.)

Lesson 9: Goals and Objectives:
What Do You Hope to Achieve If You Get the Money?

Multiple Choice

1. b ("The literature" suggests that rewards are usually better than punishments, right?)

2. b (Intergenerational programs are creative; bringing more televisions into a senior center probably would increase the seniors' sense of isolation.)

3. c (Both community involvement and police presence make neighborhoods safer.)

Realistic/Unrealistic

1. Unrealistic (The program only lasts for one year; a three-year objective is outside the control of the organization that's running it.)

2. Realistic (It's a one-year program and expecting improved attitudes by the end of the year is reasonable; we hope you also expect that participants will get jobs.)

3. Realistic (Since the program is for one year, a one-year objective makes perfect sense; because participants' motivation to get a job is high, the 85 percent attendance figure is probably realistic.)

Lesson 10: Developing and Presenting a Winning Program

True or False?

1. False (Activities are the most important part of the grant proposal—they make the program you are describing believable.)

2. False (There is no such thing as too much detail—which doesn't mean repetition—if it makes your program come alive.)

3. True (In fact, use the grantmakers own language whenever possible to ensure that you both are on the same page.)

4. False (Funders expect to see exactly as many activities in the proposal as you expect to conduct—and the more the merrier.)

5. False (Write in specifics, not in generalities . . . and don't expect to change your mind. This is a grant, for cryin' out loud!)

6. True (Specific activities should be linked to each and every measurable objective in your proposal. You're conducting the activities to achieve your objectives.)

7. False (First comes your compelling need, then your objectives, and finally the activities to achieve these objectives.)

8. Timelines are anything but baloney—they show that the grant program is doable, real, and accountable.)

9. False (The proposal should never be vague; if the person writing it doesn't know what's going on, funders will be anything but sympathetic.)

10. True (If at all possible, you should do some grant-related work even before you find out if you've won the money.)

Lesson 11: Finding Partners and Building Coalitions (The MOUs That Roared)

True or False?

1. False (Collaboration is very hard. We're all essentially team players . . . as long as we can be team captain.)

2. False (It can't always be about the money. Collaboration is about solving problems.)

3. False (If collaboration isn't required, think about trying it anyway—it's often a better option for getting things done than going it alone.)

4. False (Let's face it. No one likes to collaborate with anyone, whether they're in the same sector or not.)

Short Answer

1. The best way to actually prove that you collaborated with other groups on a grant proposal is to include a memorandum of understanding, let-

ters of commitment, and/or sign-in sheets for collaborative program development meetings in your application.

2. Some different sectors of the community that might collaborate on a winning grant include large and middle-sized not-for-profit organizations and clergy, small grassroots organizations, faith-based organizations, businesses, school districts, municipal government agencies, hospitals/health care providers, colleges, and even foundations.

3. Some synonyms for "collaboration" are partnering, cooperating, coalition building, team building.

Lesson 12: The Evaluation Plan: How Can You Be Sure If Your Program Worked?

True or False?

1. False (Evaluation is necessary for grant-funded programs even if they are tiny. In fact, all programs should be evaluated whether they are grant-funded or not. The evaluation does not have to be elaborate; it just needs to be a systematic way of assessing your program's performance.)

2. True (Often called formative evaluation, this type of evaluation allows you to make changes throughout.)

3. False (If you wait until a large multiyear grant program is over to conduct the evaluation, it's far too late to make any changes along the way.)

4. False (If an outside evaluator is required by the funder, consider working with a university or consultant who will help in the preparation of the proposal and get paid to conduct the evaluation only if the grant is funded.)

5. False (Evaluations can use simple before-and-after questions and surveys as well as more complex measures.)

6. False (A program evaluation looks at all kinds of data, from personal interviews and observations to standardized, reliable measures.)

7. False (Whether an evaluation plan is required by the grantmaker or not, it should be included. Otherwise how will you know if you achieved your objectives?)

8. True (Too many grant writers start thinking about the evaluation plan just as they are about to submit their proposals. Evaluation methods should be linked to your objectives: How will you know if you achieved them?)

9. False (Small demonstration projects need rigorous evaluations to determine if they are worth replicating in other places.)

10. False (Frankly, there often is no need to work with an outside evaluator; your staff should know very well what data would provide the information you need to be sure it's working as you designed it.)

Essay Question

1. Three important things you can learn from an evaluation are whether the program worked the way you hoped it would; whether there were any surprise results that will help you design programs in the future; and which elements of the program were successful and which weren't.

Lesson 13: The Budget: How Much Will It Cost . . . and Is the Cost Reasonable?

True or False?

1. False (Don't include the new copier you're desperate for unless you can show why the housing program you're applying for needs a copier to achieve the objectives you've set out. Our guess is that the copier probably has no place in the grant proposal.)

2. False (If the funder says you can't include laptop computers in your budget, don't. Try to find another grantmaker who may pay for them.)

Short Answer

1. If you are teaching reading as an in-kind contribution, it means that your organization has (or you have) donated your time to the project. The way this is reflected in the budget is to indicate the percentage of

your time you spend on the project—say 25 percent of your job is now spent on this program. If your yearly salary is $50,000, you're "donating" a quarter of it to the grant-funded program. Your in-kind contribution is $12,500. This, along with other contributions by the applicant, can be reflected in a column called "In-Kind."

2. PS (Personnel Services) describes personnel (staffing) costs and OTPS (Other Than Personnel Services) lists everything that does not relate to personnel that you include in the grant's budget.

3. Examples of OTPS costs include equipment that you may be buying or leasing, consultants that you may need to bring on board, and supplies that you need to purchase.

Lesson 14: Sustainability: How Will You Continue the Program Once the Grant Funds Have Run Out (and You'd Better Not Say, "I Won't!")

Essay Questions

1. To sustain the literacy program for immigrants at the Rosemont Center, the center staff will apply to the state's department for youth and families when it issues a request for proposals for literacy programs next year. Rosemont's development director has begun identifying other foundations that support literacy programs like Rosemont's. The executive director and program staff believe that the local community college will be willing to provide some services in kind once the program has begun.

2. The Edgewood Senior Center might apply for a foundation grant for an intergenerational arts program even if we aren't sure we can sustain it because it is so important to find ways to relieve the depression and isolation our seniors are experiencing. When the city sees how successful the program is, it may provide unexpected resources that will keep the program running.

Short Answer

1. Some other words for sustainability are "likelihood of institutionalizing" the program. That's a fancy way of saying making it a permanent part of your organization.

Lesson 15: Capacity: Proving That You Can Get the Job Done

True or False?

1. True (An organization's leadership says a great deal about the strength of the organization.)

2. True (Only an organization that maintains strong financial controls will win the confidence of a government funder—or any other funder.)

3. False (Every grantmaker cares about your board if you're a nonprofit organization.)

4. False (But you want to include as much history, program, and staff information as possible to highlight your organization's capacity to run effective programs.)

5. True (Government agencies should mention the size of their budgets, the grants and other funding they receive, and their history of fiscal responsibility. But brag? We don't like bragging.)

Essay Question

1. Here's an example of some things you might describe in detail to convince the grantmaker that you're the right choice for a grant for a literacy program:

   - The quality, background, and experience of leadership and key staff, and their success in running strong literacy programs (talk about the outcomes of those programs).
   - The quality of your facilities and resources. If you have special classrooms and equipment that will enhance the program, say so here.

- The positive evaluations that other funders have given to your programs.
- Any awards that your organization and staff have received.

Lesson 16: Front and Back: The Cover Letter, the Abstract, the Table of Contents, and the Appendix

True or False?

1. False (The overall cost of the project should appear in the abstract, along with the amount you are requesting.)
2. False (A table of contents should be included whether the application mentions it or not, unless the proposal is very short or, for some reason, a grantmaker says, "No table of contents.")
3. False (The average length of a comprehensive abstract is under two pages.)
4. False (Letters of support from elected officials should be placed in the appendix.)
5. False (If you are permitted to have attachments and the funder doesn't stipulate specific items, certainly include information about your board.)
6. False (An abstract should be short and to the point. Don't use as many words as you need to. Use as few as you can to clearly describe the program.)
7. True (But sometimes government grants don't even let you include an appendix and, lately, they have required a certain number of pages when they do allow one. You have to be creative in deciding what to attach.)
8. False (Not all grantmakers want or will accept attachments or appendix material. When in doubt, ask.)
9. True

Essay Question

1. See Appendix 4 for a sample cover letter.

Lesson 17: The Site Visit—Playing Host

Essay Question

1. The first thing we will do when a funder calls to say he or she would like to visit is to arrange a time when activities of interest to the funder are available and so are all the key staff members and partners who will be involved with the program. The next thing is to review the proposal to be sure everyone who will meet with the funder is up to speed on the program plan, budget, staffing, and all other aspects about which the funder may have questions. Finally, we will have available all the information the funder might want, like a list of other funders, our agency budget if we haven't sent it before, and other relevant documents.

Lesson 18: So Now You Know—What's Next?

True or False?

1. False (Sometimes you should apply for a grant after you've been rejected—ouch, there's that word again—and sometimes you shouldn't. There are many factors involved in your decision.)

2. False (If a foundation turns you down for a grant, definitely ask why . . . but very nicely, of course.)

3. False (There's nothing in the law that forbids you to receive scores on federal grant proposals. It's up to the individual agencies, and most do give you the information.)

4. False (While the same reviewer probably won't read your grant if you submit it again, the comments may have been right on the money—so why not take them to heart to improve your next proposal?)

5. False (It's not pushy to ask grantmakers to suggest other foundations that might be appropriate for your proposal. But don't get pushy if they can't help you!)

ACKNOWLEDGMENTS

How often have you heard people say, "I know so much about such-and-such a topic I should write a book—it would probably be a best-seller"? Yet most of these potential authors either never get around to writing the book or can't find anyone to publish it if they do manage to get all their accumulated wisdom down on paper.

Neither of us ever had thought of writing a book. It was Christina Lyndrup Farrell who suggested—very convincingly—that we should get busy and start writing . . . and it was Howie Schuman who helped us (that's an understatement) figure out how to navigate the world of publishing. Without them, there would be no *The Only Grant-Writing Book You'll Ever Need*.

Many people gave us helpful advice as we prepared all three editions. Barbara Bryan, formerly president of the New York Regional Association of Grantmakers that is now Philanthropy New York, and Lisa Philp, managing director and head of Philanthropic Services for the Private Bank at JPMorgan, brainstormed all aspects of grantsmanship with us and spoke candidly about the issues and trends in the ever-changing world of philanthropy.

Eileen Auld, Citi Global Consumer Group's state director of community relations for New York, continues to be a role model for grantmakers, a real team player, and a generous friend.

We are indebted to the following grantmakers and proposal writers who spoke about the grants process with candor, compassion, and eloquence: Jocelyn Ancheta, Alison Wheeler Bauer, Joan Brody, Gordon J. Campbell, Cathy Cha, Denise Clayton, Sybil Del Gaudio, Kanyere Eaton, Peter Eldridge, Christina Farrell, Marilyn Gelber, Lorenzo Harrison, Erica Hunt, June Kress, Tamra Lhota,

Kristen Mahoney, Paula J. Olsiewski, Catherine Giron Pino, Anita Rogers, Karen Rosa, Elmy Savoie, Chris Shearer, Jane Taylor, MaryAnn Tierney, Robert Uyeki, and Patty Wineapple. We have omitted the names of a few individuals who preferred to remain anonymous, but want them to know how grateful we are. And almost everyone we spoke to generously recommended friends and colleagues for yet another, slightly different point of view.

The Washington, D.C., Regional Association of Grantmakers very kindly gave us permission to publish the common grant application form that it developed and produced. This is one of several Regional Association of Grantmaker common application forms that we think are valuable models for structuring any proposal.

Mark Litzler is a talented, witty, and generous cartoonist—and we hope to actually meet him in person one of these days.

Alix Sleight and Kay Mariea of the Perseus Books Group never lost their cool and were amazingly patient when we hit snags.

Our warmest thanks to Judy Bernstein, and Jocelyn Szczepaniak-Gillece for their help and support. Dahlia Lagos provided much-valued assistance for the third edition.

Nancy Needle helped us in ways too numerous to mention on all three editions. She gets her own paragraph as proof of our appreciation.

And finally, we want to thank our family and friends (the ones not mentioned elsewhere!) who are always encouraging and supportive—especially Mark Rosenfeld, the whole, happily expanded Barish family, Emily Karsh, Lauri Karsh, Sylvia Fuhrman, Leni Fuhrman, Charlie DeFanti, Brian Berk, Ray Wright, Bill Dionne, Susan Levine, Rachel Simmons, Judith Applebaum, Judy Morrison, Linda and George Lamb, and Diane Koenig.

ABOUT THE AUTHORS

Ellen Karsh, now writing and consulting full time, was director of the New York City Mayor's Office of Grants Administration for more than seven years under both Mayor Giuliani and Mayor Bloomberg, and developed and wrote grants for the New York City Department of Education for five years before coming to the Mayor's Office. She has a doctorate in special education from Columbia University and taught for years in the New York City public schools and in area colleges and universities. She has won tens of millions of dollars for the City of New York by writing grant proposals to government agencies and private foundations. In addition to developing and writing grant proposals, she has taught program development and grant writing to thousands of people representing not-for-profits, schools and colleges, and government agencies throughout New York City, using materials and resources that she developed over the years. While working in the Mayor's Office, she was the only public sector member of the City Connect Committee of the New York Regional Association of Grantmakers, comprising foundations and corporations interested in collaborating (among themselves and with government leaders) to address issues of interest to both the philanthropic community and government. Karsh has written articles that have appeared in *Newsweek*, the *New York Times*, and other publications.

Arlen Sue Fox has many years of experience in program planning and evaluation, writing, and editing (including editing social science textbooks for a major publisher). Her background includes 10 years as the director of research, planning, and evaluation for the New York City Commission on Human Rights and 12 years as a consultant to nonprofit organizations, from small grassroots groups to national organizations including AARP and The Lighthouse. She spent three years as the coordinator of the City Connect Federal Grantsmanship Network, a foundation-initiated project designed to help nonprofit organizations improve their ability to obtain federal funding. She provided technical assistance and training on the federal grant process to dozens of nonprofit organizations. As part of this project, she wrote *Preparing Federal Proposals: An Introduction* and managed the development of an automated grants information system that alerts enrolled nonprofit organizations to relevant federal and state funding opportunities. Fox has written—and has taught her clients to write—proposals that have brought them tens of millions of dollars for their programs. Currently she is the associate executive director for development at Sunnyside Community Services, a settlement house that provides services for more than 18,000 children, teenagers, families, and well and frail older adults in Queens.

Mark Litzler is a nationally published cartoonist whose work appears in the *Wall Street Journal, Barron's Financial Weekly, Harvard Business Review, Saturday Evening Post*, and *Chronicle of Higher Education*, among other newspapers and journals. He has drawn a weekly panel feature for a number of American *City Business Journal* papers. His cartoons have been featured in the business pages of the *Kansas City Star*. He has contributed to numerous college texts as the primary illustrator. In the real world, Litzler is executive director of the Saint Luke's Hospital Foundation, responsible for managing assets of $125 million and raising $15 million annually. Litzler's entire career has focused on fundraising and endowment development in higher education and health care.

INDEX